Nancy
109 Ch nqu
, Ct

GOD'S

MASTER PLAN

FOR

YOUR LIFE

PUTNAM PRAISE
Published by G. P. Putnam's Sons
a member of the Penguin Group (USA) Inc.
New York

GOD'S
MASTER PLAN
FOR
YOUR LIFE

Ten Keys to Fulfilling
Your Destiny

GLORIA COPELAND

PUTNAM
PRAISE

Published by
G. P. PUTNAM'S SONS
Publishers Since 1838
a member of the Penguin Group
Penguin Group (USA) Inc., 375 Hudson Street, New York, New York 10014, USA • Penguin Group
(Canada), 90 Eglinton Avenue East, Suite 700, Toronto, Ontario M4P 2Y3, Canada (a division of
Pearson Canada Inc.) • Penguin Books Ltd, 80 Strand, London WC2R 0RL, England • Penguin Ireland,
25 St Stephen's Green, Dublin 2, Ireland (a division of Penguin Books Ltd) • Penguin Group (Australia),
250 Camberwell Road, Camberwell, Victoria 3124, Australia (a division of Pearson Australia
Group Pty Ltd) • Penguin Books India Pvt Ltd, 11 Community Centre, Panchsheel Park,
New Delhi–110 017, India • Penguin Group (NZ), 67 Apollo Drive, Rosedale, North Shore 0632,
New Zealand (a division of Pearson New Zealand Ltd) • Penguin Books (South Africa) (Pty) Ltd,
24 Sturdee Avenue, Rosebank, Johannesburg 2196, South Africa

Penguin Books Ltd, Registered Offices:
80 Strand, London WC2R 0RL, England

Unless otherwise noted, Scripture quotations are taken from the New King James Version®. Copyright ©
1982 by Thomas Nelson, Inc. Used by permission. All rights reserved.
Scripture quotations marked "AMP" are taken from the Amplified® Bible, copyright © 1954, 1958, 1962,
1964, 1965, 1987 by The Lockman Foundation. Used by permission. (www.Lockman.org)
Scripture quotations marked "NLT" are taken from the *Holy Bible*, New Living Translation, copyright ©
1996. Used by permission of Tyndale House Publishers, Inc., Wheaton, Illinois 60189. All rights
reserved.
Scripture quotations marked "NIV" are taken from THE HOLY BIBLE, NEW INTERNATIONAL
VERSION®, NIV®. Copyright © 1973, 1978, 1984 by International Bible Society®. Used by
permission.
Scripture quotations marked "TLB" are taken from *The Living Bible*, copyright © 1971. Used by permission of Tyndale House Publishers, Inc., Wheaton, Illinois 60189. All rights reserved.

Library of Congress Cataloging-in-Publication Data

Copeland, Gloria.
God's master plan for your life : Ten keys to fulfilling your destiny / [Gloria Copeland].
p.   cm.
ISBN-13: 978-0-399-15473-7
1. Christian life.   I. Title.
BV4501.3.C6695   2008   2008006581
248.4—dc22

Printed in the United States of America
1   3   5   7   9   10   8   6   4   2

BOOK DESIGN BY AMANDA DEWEY

While the author has made every effort to provide accurate telephone numbers and Internet addresses at the
time of publication, neither the publisher nor the author assumes any responsibility for errors, or for
changes that occur after publication. Further, the publisher does not have any control over and does not assume any responsibility for author or third-party websites or their content.

I'd like to acknowledge and thank Gina Lynnes, who transforms into print the messages I teach.

Additionally, I want to express my gratitude to Leah Lee and Delaine Neece, who have also been a tremendous blessing in this endeavor.

Thank you, too, for taking the time to allow me to share the Word with you.

God is good.

Love in Him,
Gloria

I dedicate this book to my husband, Kenneth, who faithfully supports me in everything I do.

Thank you, Kenneth, for continually teaching me great truths from God's Word and for walking out the Master Plan with me.

I love you with all my heart. You are my special blessing.

All my love,
Gloria

CONTENTS

GOD'S MASTER PLAN FOR YOUR LIFE

One

GOD ALWAYS HAS A PLAN

—⟋⟍—

God always has a plan.

The Lord first spoke these words to my heart years ago when Ken and I were preaching in San Juan, Puerto Rico. I don't remember what challenge we were facing at the time, but the words still ring loud and clear in me today.

God always has a plan.

His plan isn't just some haphazard scheme thrown together at the last minute, either. His plan is a Master Plan—a plan uniquely designed for every person in every situation on the face of the earth.

The Bible is absolutely full—from beginning to end—of such divine plans. In Genesis, we see the plan God had for Adam and Eve when He put them in the Garden of Eden. What a wonderful plan that was! God surrounded them with every conceivable blessing and then gave them dominion over the earth and all that was in it.

God's original plan for Adam and Eve didn't include sickness, pain, or lack of any kind. They were divinely designed to live in continual victory and abundance. To connect with that plan, all Adam and Eve had to do was obey the one commandment God gave them. They simply had to refrain from eating from the tree of the knowledge of good and evil.

Sadly, Adam and Eve fell prey to Satan, disobeyed that one directive, and disconnected from God's original plan.

But their disobedience didn't catch God by surprise. He knew what they were going to do before they did it. And He was ready. He had already prepared His Master Plan. He announced it to Satan the very day Adam and Eve sinned. Speaking of Jesus, God warned the devil about the "seed" of the woman who would one day come and crush his head (Genesis 3:15, NLT).

That's a classic example of the way God operates. No matter how crazy and confusing things may seem, no matter how hard the devil works to mess them up, God always has a way to set things right. He always has a plan.

He had a plan for Abraham when He told him to leave the land of his fathers and go to a country he'd never seen before. He had a plan to make that seventy-five-year-old man and his barren wife the father and mother of many nations. Abraham connected with that plan and, just as God promised, his son Isaac was born.

That, in itself, was miraculous. But God's Master Plan for Abraham didn't stop there. God also promised Abraham that his descendents would inherit the land of Canaan, a prosperous land that flowed with milk and honey. He said they could live in it and call it their own.

As usual, the devil attempted to steal that promise and Abraham's descendents found themselves in Egyptian slavery for several hundred years. Eventually, they cried out to God for help. When they did, once again, God revealed His plan.

He sent a deliverer named Moses to confront Pharaoh and produce signs and wonders so powerful, they brought the mighty nation of Egypt to its knees. He split the Red Sea, led the Israelites to the other side on dry ground, and buried the enemy army that pursued them in a watery grave.

Now that's what I call a plan!

Once the Israelites were out of Egypt, all they had to do to successfully reach the Promised Land was follow Moses and obey God's instructions. But they didn't do it. Like Adam and Eve, they disconnected from God's Master Plan and decided to do things their own way. As a result, they found themselves stuck in the wilderness.

Forty years went by and it looked like the whole nation would die off and disappear in the desert, never to be heard from again. But two men named Joshua and Caleb refused to let that happen. They stayed connected to the Master Plan, believing year after year that despite the rebellious Israelites surrounding them, God would one day fulfill His promise to them.

They were right! When they were about eighty years old, God spoke to Joshua and said, "Arise, go over this Jordan, you and all this people, to the land which I am giving to them—the children of Israel" (Joshua 1:2).

Despite the delay and all the wilderness wanderings, the descendents of Abraham inherited the land of Canaan, just as Abraham believed they would . . . because God always works His plan.

NOT JUST ACCIDENTS OF NATURE

What does that have to do with us today? A great deal. The New Testament tells us everything that happened to the children of Israel "happened to them as examples, and they were written for our admonition, upon whom the ends of the ages have come" (1 Corinthians 10:11).

That's why I was so delighted while reading a Jewish commentary some time ago. The author said that God has a Master Plan for the Israelites and that man has the ability to connect with it. Praise God! The Israelites are our example. So if God had a Master Plan for them, He has a Master Plan for us.

He has a Master Plan for me.

He has a Master Plan for you.

He has a Master Plan for everyone who will accept Jesus Christ as Lord and Savior. John 3:16 says, "For God so loved the world that He gave His only begotten Son, that whoever believes in Him should not perish but have everlasting life."

We aren't just accidents of nature God had pity on and decided to save. We aren't just wilderness wanderers destined to stumble through life trying to do the best we can. Romans 8:29 says, "For whom He foreknew, He also predestined to be conformed to the image of His Son, that He might be the firstborn among many brethren." He made preparations for us before we ever took our first breath on the earth.

God didn't wait until you and I were born to begin figuring out what to do with us. According to the Bible, God designed a Master Plan for us long before that. He fashioned it before the foundation of the world when, in His great love, He looked into the future and chose us (actually picked us out for Himself!) as His own (Ephesians 1:4, AMP).

God considers every one of us special. In Ephesians 2:10 He actually calls us His *workmanship*. The Greek word for workmanship, *poema* (from which we get our English word *poem),* is translated "masterpiece" in the *New Living Translation.*

The Amplified Bible says it this way:

For we are God's [own] handiwork (His workmanship), recreated in Christ Jesus, [born anew] that we
may do those good works which God predestined
(planned beforehand) for us [taking paths which He
prepared ahead of time], that we should walk in them
[living the good life which He prearranged and made
ready for us to live].

A MASTERPIECE WITH A MASTER PLAN

For we are God's masterpiece. He has created us
anew in Christ Jesus, so that we can do the good things
he planned for us long ago.

(Ephesians 2:10, NLT-96)

Think about that. If you have asked Jesus to take charge of your
life, you are a "born again" child of God, or as this verse says, "created . . . anew in Christ Jesus." You are God's masterpiece—a masterpiece with a Master Plan!

If you haven't connected very well with God's plan yet, you may
feel more like a mess than a masterpiece right now. You may be
tempted to think that the divine blueprint for your life—if it ever
existed—has long ago been lost or forgotten. You may even be so far
off God's prearranged path, you don't think you can ever find your
way back. Or perhaps you have never made the decision to make
Jesus the Lord of your life.

If so, I know exactly how you feel. I felt the same way in 1962,
just before I connected with God's Master Plan for my life.

Ken and I were recently married and already desperately broke and deeply in debt. We didn't start out that way. (Well, that's not quite true. Ken had a boatload of debt when I married him, but, even so, we had high hopes in the beginning.) As newlyweds, we became part of a new business we fully expected would make us rich. So certain were we that the money would soon come rolling in, we'd even signed a lease-purchase agreement on a house, and moved in. I quit my job and, along with Ken, went to work in this promising new venture.

The venture's promise, however, didn't exactly pan out. Within two weeks, the company went broke, leaving us without an income and lots of unpaid bills, with people threatening to sue us.

Day after day, while Ken went looking for a job, I sat alone in the house we had once hoped to buy, knowing we couldn't even afford to pay the lease. We had no furniture except a rollaway bed we rented for seven and a half dollars a month, a folding lawn chair my mother had given me, a small black-and-white television set, and a wrought-iron coffee table that Ken made in high school. The decor, you might say, was *contemporary poverty*.

We didn't have a refrigerator, but it was winter, so we put food that needed cooling in a box on the porch. We didn't have a stove either, so I cooked in an electric coffeepot.

I had no car, so I spent my days in the empty house with little more to do than watch the distorted picture on our nineteen-inch television. It had a picture about two inches tall. *The Beverly Hillbillies* was a new television show back in those days and gave us an opportunity to laugh. We needed a laugh!

Ken and I weren't born again, but his mother had been praying for him for years. On his birthday, she had given him a *New English Bible*. That was the only book I remember having in the house. I picked it up one day, and on the inside cover I found these words written by Ken's mother, Vinita:

Ken Precious,
  *Happy Birthday today. Seek ye first the kingdom of God
and* His righteousness, *and all these things shall be added unto
you. Matthew 6:33*
    With all of our love,
    Mother and Daddy

Those words sparked my curiosity, so I quickly began thumbing through the pages, trying to find Matthew 6. I wanted to know what else was in that chapter.

Although I wasn't born again (I'd never even heard of such a thing!), I'd always tried to do the "right" thing. My parents rarely attended church when I was growing up, but sometimes I'd attend with a friend. Over the years, I often resolved to become a regular churchgoer, but my resolve always failed because the church I attended didn't have much to offer.

In spite of those experiences, however, I still had a reverence for God, and I definitely believed in the Bible. So when I found Matthew 6, I read with amazement the words that would forever change my life:

> "No servant can be a slave to two masters; for either he will hate the first and love the second, or he will be devoted to the first and think nothing of the second. You cannot serve God and money. Therefore I bid you put away anxious thoughts about food and drink to keep you alive, and clothes to cover your body. Surely life is more than food, the body more than clothes. Look at the birds of the air; they do not sow and reap and store in barns, yet your heavenly Father feeds them. You are worth more than the birds! Is there a man of you who

by anxious thought can add a foot to his height? And why be anxious about clothes? Consider how the lilies grow in the fields; they do not work, they do not spin, and yet, I tell you, even Solomon in all his splendour was not attired like one of these. But if that is how God clothes the grass in the fields, which is there to-day, and tomorrow is thrown on the stove, will he not all the more clothe you? How little faith you have! No, do not ask anxiously, 'What are we to eat? What are we to drink? What shall we wear?' All these are things for the heathen to run after, not for you, because your heavenly Father knows that you need them all. Set your mind on God's kingdom and his justice before everything else, and all the rest will come to you as well. So do not be anxious about tomorrow; tomorrow will look after itself. Each day has troubles enough of its own" (Matthew 6:24–34, NEB).

As I sat alone in my unfurnished house looking at those verses, they seemed to speak directly to me. There I was, a young wife with no money, seemingly no hope, and no future. I had every reason in the world to be worried and anxious. But here, the Bible—*the Bible!*—was telling me to stop being anxious or worried about my life and my financial condition.

It was telling me God cared about the birds. That may not seem like a very deep revelation to you, but it meant a lot to me back then. It had never occurred to me that God cared about the birds. *Certainly, if He cares about the birds,* I thought, *He cares about me!*

That was great news. No one had ever told me that God cared about me. I knew I was supposed to care about Him, but they never mentioned He was interested in me. I would have been comforted by that fact alone. But, according to this passage, God not only cared for me, He had promised that if I'd seek Him first, He would add all other things to me.

The very idea was shocking—wonderful, but shocking—and I was thrilled by it. After all, I didn't have a job. I didn't have a refrigerator. I didn't have a stove. I cooked potatoes in a coffeepot. I definitely needed some *things* added to my life.

And the Bible itself had promised I could have them!

Immediately, I responded. Without fully understanding what I was doing, I prayed very simply, "Lord, take my life and do something with it."

KEN'S PREPOSTEROUS IDEA

I believe I was born again that day, though I didn't realize it until sometime later. Just like the Bible says, I became a new creation. Suddenly, I wasn't the same girl I had been in grade school. I wasn't the same person I had been in high school or college. I was re-created in Christ Jesus—changed on the inside into the likeness and image of God. The sin nature within me was driven out and God's own righteousness was put into me. I didn't even realize the words the Apostle Paul wrote in 2 Corinthians 5 had become a reality within me:

> Therefore, if anyone is in Christ, he is a new creation; old things have passed away; behold, all things have become new. . . . For He made Him who knew no sin to be sin for us, that we might become the righteousness of God in Him (2 Corinthians 5:17, 21).

I'll admit, I didn't look very righteous on the outside at first, but the early signs of what God had done in my heart were definitely there. I immediately wanted to start going to church, for example, and I was eager to read more of the Bible.

Ken, however, wasn't too interested in such things. He'd been resisting God for years. Unlike me, he'd grown up in church. He had heard the plan of salvation. He'd tried once to connect with the plan of God as a young man, but someone in church had offended him and turned him away. As a result, he'd been bitter and rebellious ever since.

I began seeking God through His Word—the Bible—and dared to believe that He was going to do just what Matthew 6 said He would do.

Of course, He did. Within two weeks, Ken and I had moved out of that empty house and into a fully furnished apartment. Ken had a job and things were looking up.

One night, I was cooking dinner—*on a real stove instead of in a coffeepot*—in the kitchen of our little, but new, apartment, when Ken walked in with a stunning question: "What would you think if I started doing some talks about God?"

Frankly, I thought that was the most preposterous idea I'd ever heard. Ken didn't even want to go to church! Why on earth would he want to give talks about God?

I soon learned the reason. Just moments earlier, Ken had been sitting in the living room, taking his shoes off when, seemingly out of the blue, the Lord spoke to him. *If you don't get this family in line with Me, you're going to a devil's hell!*

Ken knew exactly what that meant, and he'd been to enough church services to know it was true. So he gave his life to the Lord then and there.

For the first time in our lives, Ken and I began to connect to God's Master Plan on purpose.

IT'S NEVER TOO LATE

If you've received Jesus Christ as the Lord of your life, you've already made that initial connection with God's plan for you. You're already on your way.

If you haven't, you may be wondering if all this really applies to you. You may be wondering if God even knows who you are. If so, I can assure you that He does.

He not only knows you, He loves you so much that He designed the plan of redemption so that you can have eternal and abundant life. He has a storehouse of blessings prepared for you. He has a plan for your life that is greater and more satisfying than anything you could ever dream up on your own.

If you will simply trust Him and put your life in His hands, you'll be able to boldly believe and declare over your own life the words of Psalm 138:8: "The Lord will work out his plans for my life—for your faithful love, O Lord, endures forever" (NLT-96).

"But, Gloria," you may say, "I've rebelled against God time and time again. Are you sure I'm still eligible for His plans?"

Certainly, you're eligible. The Bible says that "God so loved the world, that he gave his only begotten Son, that whosoever believeth in him should not perish, but have everlasting life" (John 3:16, KJV).

Are you a *whosoever*? (I know you are because I've never met anyone who wasn't.) If you're a whosoever and you're willing to believe in Jesus, you qualify for God's plan of redemption. You qualify to be born again and start over in life.

The instant you receive God's gift of redemption, you will be delivered out of the sin and darkness that passed to all mankind through the sin of Adam and Eve, and you'll become God's very own child, a joint heir with Jesus.

None of us could ever earn that kind of relationship with God. We could never merit it in our own strength by doing good works or being religious. But when we put our faith in Jesus and make Him our Savior and Lord, God by His grace—His favor, His blessing— simply gives us right-standing with Him as a free gift. From that moment on, instead of attempting to futilely work our way into God's favor and trying to earn access to His Master Plan, we can rejoice by faith:

> Giving thanks to the Father, Who has qualified and made us fit to share the portion which is the inheritance of the saints (God's holy people) in the Light. [The Father] has delivered and drawn us to Himself out of the control and the dominion of darkness and has transferred us into the kingdom of the Son of His love (Colossians 1:12–13, AMP).

Once you're born again, you're not the same person you used to be. You're remade in the image of God. Instead of being limited to your own natural talents and abilities, you suddenly have the resources of Jesus Himself available to you. The Holy Spirit of God comes to dwell in you to lead you into *the good life* that God has *prearranged and made ready* for you. I don't know about you, but I like the good life. That's the kind of life I want to live!

"But I've wasted a lot of time," you may say. "I'm getting older. Maybe it's too late for me to connect with God's plan for my life. Maybe I've missed my window of opportunity."

It's never too late. No matter how old you are or what mistakes you've made, God has a Master Plan ready for you. He will wipe out the past. He will wipe out the sin. He will wipe out the failures that lie behind you. He will give you a clean slate.

Perhaps you were born again years ago but you strayed away from God. Perhaps you've messed things up terribly. If so, don't despair. You can repent and start over with God. He promises us that "if we confess our sins, He is faithful and just to forgive us our sins and to cleanse us from all unrighteousness" (1 John 1:9).

If you'll repent right now and start obeying God, He can reconnect you with His Master Plan. It doesn't matter what you've done or where you are, He is able to do it.

Ken and I have seen God do that in people's lives again and again. There are times when we've been out somewhere, eating dinner at a restaurant or shopping, and someone will come up to us and say, "A few years ago, I was in prison. My life was a wreck. But I heard you preach about Jesus on television. I read your books and found out I could get right with God. Now I'm born again. I'm free. My life is good!"

Some people find it hard to believe that God would have a good plan for someone bad enough to be sent to prison. They might think such people don't deserve to enjoy a good life.

In a way, they're right. In fact, *none* of us deserves the good life God has planned for us. Before we were born again, we were *all* sinners! We had all fallen short of the glory of God. All we really deserved was the wages we'd earned with our sin; and the Bible tells us clearly what those wages are. It says, "The wages of sin is death" (Romans 6:23).

> But God, who is rich in mercy, because of His great
> love with which He loved us, even when we were dead

in trespasses, made us alive together with Christ (by grace you have been saved), and raised us up together, and made us sit together in the heavenly places in Christ Jesus, that in the ages to come He might show the exceeding riches of His grace in His kindness toward us in Christ Jesus. For by grace you have been saved through faith, and that not of yourselves; it is the gift of God, not of works, lest anyone should boast. For we are His workmanship, created in Christ Jesus for good works, which God prepared beforehand that we should walk in them (Ephesians 2:4–10).

Thank God, Jesus came to pay the price for our sin so we don't have to get what we deserve. He came so that by simple faith in Him we could get what *He* deserves. He came so that God could show the exceeding riches of His kindness to us—not just in this life but in the ages to come.

TAKE THE SECOND STEP

So don't let the devil tell you that it's too late for you, or that you don't deserve God's blessings. No matter what your history or where you are in life, if you still have breath in your body, you can connect with God's Master Plan. You just have to take the first step and receive Jesus as your Lord and Savior. Repent of sin and be cleansed. You can be born over a new creature in Christ Jesus. You can start a new life today.

When you do that, you'll step in to the good life God has prepared for you.

"The thief comes only in order to steal and kill and destroy. I came that they may have and enjoy life, and have it in abundance (to the full, till it overflows)" (John 10:10, AMP).

Life till it overflows is wonderful! So don't stop with the first step. Keep going, taking step after step, continually growing and connecting with God so that you can have and enjoy the fullness of His plan and do all He has called you to do.

The second step you'll want to take right away (if you haven't already) is to receive the "Baptism in the Holy Spirit."[1] I can tell you, not only from the Word but from personal experience, how important that is.

One day we went to a church service with Ken's mother and dad, where people were invited to come forward for prayer and be filled with the Holy Spirit. Ken was so hungry for God by that point, he didn't want to miss out on anything, so he looked at his mother and said, "Is that something a man ought to have?"

"You ought to have it," she said.

Ken and I both received the Holy Spirit that night and took another very important step forward in God's Master Plan for our lives. It is so much easier to fulfill your Master Plan after you receive the power of the Holy Spirit, and have the Teacher Himself living in fullness within you. The Holy Spirit will continually direct you, speak to you, lead you, and give you His wisdom every day. God's instructions become clearer as you learn to respond to the mighty power of His Spirit.

If you have not yet received the Baptism in the Holy Spirit, why not do it right now? In the back of this book, you'll find a section that will tell you what the Bible says about it and help answer some of the questions you might have. You don't have to be in church, like Ken and I were, to receive. You don't even have to have some-

---

1. See Acts 1:8, Acts 2:1–21, Luke 24:49. See also Chapter 8.

one else pray for you (although that is certainly scriptural if you desire it). Just ask in faith and you will receive. (See Matthew 19:13; Mark 16:15–18; Luke 4:40 and 13:13.)

GET READY FOR THE RIDE OF YOUR LIFE

Once you take those two steps and begin to connect with God's Master Plan, you'd better fasten your seat belt, because if you stick with His plan, you're about to have the ride of your life! You're about to have your horizons expanded and to go further and climb higher than you ever dreamed you could.

Why? Because God's plans for you are far better than the plans you've made for yourself. "'For My thoughts are not your thoughts, nor are your ways My ways,' says the Lord. 'For as the heavens are higher than the earth, so are My ways higher than your ways, and My thoughts than your thoughts'" (Isaiah 55:8–9).

I can tell you from my own experience just how true that is. When I look back on the plans I had for my life before I was born again—plans I thought were lofty and glorious—I can see now how pitiful they were compared to the plans God has for me. I didn't have a clue back then the amazing things God had in store for me.

Ken, on the other hand, did have a clue. But that's all he had— just a clue. When he gave his life to the Lord that day in the living room of our apartment, all he wanted to do was give talks about God. Well, he's done that . . . and a whole lot more.

We've both done and experienced things that were beyond anything we could have asked or thought about back in 1962. We have a life that's more wonderful and blessed than anything we could have imagined. All because we dared to connect to God and His Master Plan.

Of course, we didn't always connect perfectly to that plan. We made our share of mistakes. But when we stumbled, we repented and God helped us get back up and begin moving forward again.

That's what we've been doing for more than forty years now, and we've learned some helpful things along the way. We know a lot more now about how to stay connected to God's plan than we did when we began. That's why I'm writing this book. I want to share with you what we've learned, both from our successes and from our mistakes. I want you to benefit from our experiences and from the truths we've found in God's Word, so you can more easily discover and enjoy the fullness of the Master Plan God has for you.

Years ago, Rufus Moseley, a very wise man of God, wrote, "Everything is done for them [the children of God] that can be done, and nothing but receiving and responding is expected of them."[2]

Even as you read these words, God has your Master Plan ready. He's available to help you with it. As far as He's concerned, all systems are go. He is ready now for you to receive and respond.

The next step is up to you.

KEY ONE

Accept Jesus as your Lord and Savior.

KEY TWO

Receive the Baptism in the Holy Spirit.

---

2. J. Rufus Moseley, *Perfect Everything,* Revised Edition (Saint Paul: Macalester Park Publishing Co., 1988), p. 39.

Two

GOD'S SHINING PATH

—⚍—

Initially, most people are excited when they realize God has a Master Plan for their lives. Their hearts leap at the thought of discovering their divine calling and destiny. Eager to pursue their God-ordained purpose, they lace up their spiritual running shoes and get ready to go for it.

Sadly, however, many of those people stumble and fall before they even get started. They trip over the same obstacle that has stopped countless others from wholeheartedly following God's Master Plan.

They are stopped cold by fear.

What are they afraid of?

Any number of things. They're afraid God's plan will be too hard, that it will cost them more than it will pay. They're afraid His plan won't be any fun, or that it will leave them unfulfilled, dissatisfied, and deprived of the pleasures of life. They're afraid God will ask more from them than they have the strength to give.

But, according to the Bible, nothing could be further from the truth. It tells us again and again that God is good, and that His plans for us are glorious. It assures us He will give us the desires of our hearts and, when the going gets tough, He'll substitute His strength for our weakness.

- Psalm 31 says, "Oh, how great is Your goodness, which You have laid up for those who fear You, which You have prepared for those who trust in You in the presence of the sons of men!" (verse 19).
- Psalm 145 says, "The Lord is good to all, and His tender mercies are over all His works" (verse 9).
- Psalm 34 says, "I sought the Lord, and He heard me, and delivered me from all my fears . . . Oh, taste and see that the Lord is good; blessed is the man who trusts in Him! . . . There is no want to those who fear Him. The young lions lack and suffer hunger; but those who seek the Lord shall not lack any good thing" (verses 4, 8–10).
- Psalm 37 says, "Delight yourself also in the Lord, and He shall give you the desires of your heart" (verse 4).

Just those Scripture passages alone make you wonder where on earth anyone could get the idea that God might not really have their best interests at heart. Whatever made us think His Master Plan might disappoint us?

The lies the devil has been selling, like false religious teachings (and other means), have convinced people that God can't really be trusted. He's given us the idea that God is a fierce tyrant just waiting for an opportunity to knock us in the head for doing something wrong.

Of course, if we really thought about that, we'd realize right away it couldn't be true. We've all given God ample opportunities to knock us out. We've sinned and messed up so many times that none of us would have survived to this point if God had that kind of attitude.

No, thank God, the Bible assures us He doesn't think that way. He has the attitude of a loving father. When we do something wrong, He doesn't want to knock us in the head. He wants us to run to Him and repent so He can forgive us and help us get back on track again.

I've done a lot of studying and teaching about the goodness of God and found that many people are totally shocked when they realize how good God actually is. For years, they've believed all the pain and heartache they've experienced in life has come from Him. Some have been religiously taught that God sends those hurts and hardships to teach them something. Some think God could help them if He wanted to, but He just doesn't care. Others have been hurt and disappointed so many times, they've come to the conclusion God is simply against them, that He truly *is* knocking them in the head.

But the fact is, God is not the source of pain and suffering in the world. He's not our problem.

Satan, the enemy of God, is the problem. He is the one who has bad plans for people. He is the one who is trying to steal from them and destroy them at every turn. God is endeavoring to bless us and give us abundant life. Jesus Himself told us that in John 10:10: "The thief comes only in order to steal and kill and destroy. I came that [you] may have and enjoy life, and have it in abundance (to the full, till it overflows)" (AMP).

Jesus said if we would just connect with His plan by loving God with all our heart, soul, mind, and strength, and love our neighbor as ourselves, we would live and "enjoy active, blessed, endless life in the kingdom of God" (Luke 10:28, AMP). He didn't tell us that God would do bad things to His obedient children in order to teach them something. On the contrary, Jesus said:

> Or what man is there among you who, if his son asks for bread, will give him a stone? Or if he asks for a fish, will he give him a serpent? If you then, being evil, know how to give good gifts to your children, how much more will your Father who is in heaven give good things to those who ask Him! (Matthew 7:9–11).

The Apostle Paul later echoed those truths when he wrote, "Command those who are rich in this present age not to be haughty, nor to trust in uncertain riches but in the living God, who gives us richly all things to enjoy." (1 Timothy 6:17).

Clearly, God isn't the One trying to make us miserable. He isn't the One hounding us with sickness, lack, and destruction. The Bible flatly contradicts such thinking. It assures us that because we're His children and He is a loving Father, God wants us to enjoy life. He wants to give us good gifts. As 3 John 2 says, He wants us to *"prosper and be in health, even as [thy] soul prospereth"* (KJV).

DON'T BUY THE SAME OLD LIE

The devil, however, has been lying to God's people about Him since the world began. He's been talking them out of God's Master

Plan by telling them that God can't be fully trusted, that He wants to rob them of the best life has to offer.

Ever since the Garden of Eden, the devil has been slithering around telling people God isn't really good, after all. He's been saying, "If you'll just follow me, I'll show you a better way. I'll free you from the bondage of God's commands so you can truly live the good life."

That's tantamount to what he told Adam and Eve.

Amazingly enough, they believed it. That, in itself, is a marvel. After all, God had already demonstrated His goodness to them in every conceivable way. He had created a world for them where everything was good. He'd put them in a beautiful place where their every need was abundantly supplied. Their food grew on trees. They didn't have to sow or reap. They didn't even have to cook or wash dishes. Adam had a perfect wife. Eve had a perfect husband. There was no pain, sickness, or grief in their lives. God had given them full fellowship with Him and complete dominion on the earth. His Master Plan for them was to enjoy His blessings, be fruitful, multiply, and reign as kings over this planet.

Talk about a great plan! What else could anyone want?

But they let the devil deceive them out of it. They listened to him when he told them the one command God had given them was meant to deprive instead of bless them. They believed God was trying to keep them from blessings by telling them not to eat from the tree of the knowledge of good and evil.

They let the devil convince them he had a better plan.

Before the day was out, Adam and Eve found out what his "better plan" included: spiritual death and separation from God, the darkness of sin, and the curse that comes with it. If Adam and Eve had chosen God's path, they would have never experienced sickness, sadness, or death. There would have been no murder, homelessness, or lack in their family, as they later experienced.

But they made the wrong choice. They stepped off God's shining path onto the devil's—a slippery slope that always leads to sorrow and death.

That's the difference between God's path and the devil's. The devil's path often looks good initially. Sin does offer passing pleasures (Hebrews 11:25). But the longer you stay on that path, the darker your life becomes.

The path to God's Master Plan is just the opposite. Initially it may seem less inviting. It may require you to make some choices that seem difficult. But the longer you stay on God's path, the better and brighter your life will be and the more of His blessings you will enjoy.

As Proverbs 4:18 (KJV) says, "The path of the just is as the shining light, that shineth more and more unto the perfect day."

GOD'S RULES FOR OUR GOOD

To see a demonstration of how the devil's way grows progressively darker and God's way shines progressively brighter, all we have to do is look back at our example—the Old Testament people of Israel. The book of Genesis tells us that when they first began living in Egypt, the Israelites were simply strangers in a strange land. Because Joseph, who was one of their own, had a position of power and favor with the government, they were relatively safe. They were a little uncomfortable in their new surroundings, and no doubt, a little out of place, but their lives weren't too bad. They were allowed to prosper and increase.

After Joseph died, however, things began to go downhill. The longer they stayed in that ungodly nation, the more miserable their lives became. Their lot grew worse and worse as the years passed. Eventually, they were no longer just strangers, they were slaves forced to make bricks for Pharaoh's building projects.

Things went from bad to worse when the Egyptian government began to view them as a threat and tried to thin their numbers by killing all the male Hebrew babies. By that time, the Israelites were living in abject poverty with no say over their own lives. When Moses was raised up to deliver them, their slavery had become so harsh that they were required to make bricks without even being given the straw they needed to do it.

What a clear and dramatic picture of the ever-increasing oppression people experience under the devil's hand!

As we've already seen, God had a better plan for Israel. He had a shining path that would lead them out of Egypt, out of poverty and the bondage of slavery. In the beginning, that path didn't look very bright. It began in the wilderness. The wilderness may not have been paradise, but it was better than Egypt. At least the Israelites were safe and had sufficient provision there and they were free from the task-master's whip.

Had they had stayed on God's shining path, their lives would have grown brighter and brighter from there. They would have arrived fairly quickly in the Promised Land where they could be free, prosperous, healthy, and blessed in every way. Once there, God planned to keep increasing them, gradually giving them victory over their enemies and blessing them more and more.

God never gave up on that plan. Despite centuries of hardheartedness and rebellion during which the Israelites departed from His plan for them, the Lord continued to declare through the mouths of His prophets, that if they would only obey Him, He would bless them and do them good. Even in the days of Jeremiah, centuries after their exodus from Egypt, when the disobedient Jewish nation was taken captive and Jerusalem had been destroyed by the Babylonians, God looked forward to the day when they would turn wholeheartedly back to Him. He said:

> Behold, [in the future restored Jerusalem] I will lay upon it health and healing, and I will cure them and will reveal to them the abundance of peace (prosperity, security, stability) and truth. And I will cause the captivity of Judah and the captivity of Israel to be reversed and will rebuild them as they were at first. And I will cleanse them from all the guilt and iniquity by which they have sinned against Me, and I will forgive all their guilt and iniquities by which they have sinned and rebelled against Me. And [Jerusalem] shall be to Me a name of joy, a praise and a glory before all the nations of the earth that hear of all the good I do for it, and they shall fear and tremble because of all the good and all the peace, prosperity, security, and stability I provide for it. Thus says the Lord: Yet again there shall be heard in this place of which you say, It is a desolate waste, without man and without beast—even in the cities of Judah and in the streets of Jerusalem that are desolate, without man and without inhabitant and without beast—[there shall be heard again] the voice of joy and the voice of gladness, the voice of the bridegroom and the voice of the bride, the voices of those who sing as they bring sacrifices of thanksgiving into the house of the Lord, Give praise and thanks to the Lord of hosts, for the Lord is good; for His mercy and kindness and steadfast

love endure forever! For I will cause the captivity of the
land to be reversed and return to be as it was at first, says
the Lord (Jeremiah 33:6–11, AMP).

Think of it! God's plan was to bless His people so richly that the
nations of the world would tremble when they heard of all the good
He did for them. That wasn't just God's plan for His First Covenant
people. It's His plan for us, too. He always has a shining path and a
glorious Master Plan for His people. The words He spoke in Jeremiah 29:11 are eternally true: "'For I know the plans I have for you,'
declares the Lord, 'plans to prosper you and not to harm you, plans
to give you hope and a future'" (NIV).

You would think the Israelites would have jumped at the opportunity to experience the hope and future God promised them. You
would think they would have eagerly embraced His Master Plan. But
instead, they repeatedly rejected it. When we read the First Covenant
accounts of the Israelites, we find them turning away from God's
plans again and again.

Thus says the Lord, your Redeemer, the Holy One of
Israel: I am the Lord your God, Who teaches you to
profit, Who leads you in the way that you should go.
Oh, that you had hearkened to My commandments!
Then your peace and prosperity would have been like
a flowing river, and your righteousness [the holiness
and purity of the nation] like the [abundant] waves of
the sea (Isaiah 48:17–18, AMP).

Tragically, despite all God's warnings and urgent pleas, the Israelites habitually drew back from God's good plans for them. And they did it for the same reason people often do it today. They were afraid that if they followed God's path, they were going to miss out on something.

They didn't believe He was truly good.

When they encountered difficulties in the wilderness, for example, they immediately assumed God was holding out on them. They were continually afraid He was going to neglect them and let them die of thirst or starve to death. They didn't believe He would supply their needs.

When God gave them commandments and laws to live by, they assumed (as we often do) that He did it to burden them with rules and make their lives harder. But they were mistaken. God was giving them the requirements for victorious living in a world order of sin and death.

Every commandment and law God gave to the Israelites was designed to protect them and enable them to live in victory. The regulations He gave them about cleanliness and diet, the instructions He gave them about washing and preparing their food, were meant to protect them from germs and bacteria and keep them healthy. Those regulations were so far ahead of their time, it wasn't until thousands of years later that the rest of the world caught up with the Jews and realized that washing properly can stop the spread of disease.

The financial laws God gave the Israelites were intended to help them handle their money so they could prosper and be blessed. The agricultural rules He gave them showed them how to cultivate their land so their crops would produce abundant harvests without depleting the soil. He gave them rules for dealing with everything from leprosy to mildew and every one of those rules was for their good.

The Lord endeavored to communicate that to them, over and over, because He loved them and wanted to bless them. In Deuteronomy 28, He told them if they would only obey Him and connect with His Master Plan, they'd be the most blessed people on earth. If you want to get an idea of just how good God's plan for the Israelites actually was, take a moment to read and consider what He said to them just before they went into the Promised Land:

"Now it shall come to pass, if you diligently obey the voice of the Lord your God, to observe carefully all His commandments which I command you today, that the Lord your God will set you high above all nations of the earth. And all these blessings shall come upon you and overtake you, because you obey the voice of the Lord your God: Blessed shall you be in the city, and blessed shall you be in the country. Blessed shall be the fruit of your body, the produce of your ground and the increase of your herds, the increase of your cattle and the offspring of your flocks. Blessed shall be your basket and your kneading bowl. Blessed shall you be when you come in, and blessed shall you be when you go out. The Lord will cause your enemies who rise against you to be defeated before your face; they shall come out against you one way and flee before you seven ways. The Lord will command the blessing on you in your storehouses and in all to which you set your hand, and He will bless you in the land which the Lord your God is giving you. The Lord will establish you as a holy people to Himself, just as He has sworn to you, if you keep the commandments of the Lord your God and walk in His ways. Then all peoples of the earth shall see that you are called by the name of the Lord, and they shall be afraid of you. And the Lord will grant you plenty of goods, in the fruit of your body, in the increase of your livestock, and in the produce of your ground, in the land of which the Lord swore to your fathers to give you. The Lord will open to you His good treasure, the heavens, to give the rain to your land in its season, and to bless all the work of your hand. You shall lend to many nations, but you shall not borrow. And the Lord will make you the head and not the tail; you shall be above only, and not be beneath, if you heed the commandments of the Lord . . ." (Deuteronomy 28:1–13).

There's no question about it, these verses epitomize what we call "the good life." All of us want what God promised to give them.

"Sure we do," you might say, "but that was God's Master Plan for the Israelites. The plan He has for me can't possibly be that good."

Yes, it can be. In fact, God's plan for you is even better.

The New Testament says so. It says that you, as a believer, have inherited all the blessings listed in Deuteronomy 28 because through Jesus "the blessing of Abraham" has come on the Gentiles (Galatians 3:13–14). It says that in Christ you have been "blessed . . . with every spiritual blessing in the heavenly places" (Ephesians 1:3). What's more, Hebrews 8:6 compares the covenant God made with the Israelites through the Law of Moses to the one we, as believers, have today. It says: "But now He [Jesus] has obtained a more excellent ministry, inasmuch as He is also Mediator of a better covenant, which was established on better promises."

Isn't that amazing? According to the Bible, those of us who have received Jesus as Lord and been born again have an even better covenant with God than the Israelites did. What God has for us surpasses anything anyone has seen or imagined. As 1 Corinthians 2:9–10 says: "'Eye has not seen, nor ear heard, nor have entered into the heart of man the things which God has prepared for those who love Him.' But God has revealed them to us through His Spirit. For the Spirit searches all things, yes, the deep things of God."

Think about that! God has such wonderful things in store for you, He has such a marvelous Master Plan for you that it's beyond anything your natural eye has ever seen or your ear has ever heard. It's so supernatural, the Holy Spirit Himself has to reveal it to you. That's why you must be born again and baptized in the Holy Spirit before you can even begin to grasp the depth of it.

When you do begin to see that plan, I guarantee you'll be saying what Psalm 31:19 (AMP) says. You'll be praising God and shouting, "Oh, how great is Your goodness, which You have laid up for those who fear, revere, and worship You, goodness which You have wrought for those who trust and take refuge in You before the sons of men!"

GET READY FOR SOME SURPRISES ALONG THE WAY

God's shining path—glorious as it may be—is anything but predictable. There are always surprises along the way. Some of the things God has planned for you may even shock you at first. They may be entirely different from what you had in mind for your life. I'm living proof of that.

The last thing I ever thought I'd be was a Bible teacher. I had other ideas for my life. When I was in high school, I set my sights on a job that would allow me to travel and make a little money in the process. Compared to what I do now, that job looks so pitiful and low it seems almost silly. But I was excited about it back then. I hadn't been anywhere. I hadn't done anything much. So it looked big to me.

I didn't plan on marrying for a while, either. I wanted to be on my own, and when I did marry, I certainly didn't want to marry a preacher. I always said that was one thing I'd *never* do.

In a way, I kept that promise because Ken appeared to be anything but a preacher when I married him. He didn't look like a preacher, he didn't talk like a preacher, and he didn't act like a preacher. Professionally, he was a pilot. Socially, he was a comedian and the life of every party. So the preacher part of him was well disguised.

Still, it was a miracle that we ever got together. I'm convinced that the only reason it happened was because it was a part of God's Master Plan for our lives.

Although neither of us was born again, God knew us, and what we could be in Him. He knew we were going to respond to Him down the road. He knew the end from the beginning (as only He can), so in His mercy and grace He was maneuvering us into place even before we committed our lives to Him.

Actually, Ken and I would never have met had my father not insisted on it. He met Ken at a party one Saturday night, was impressed with him, and wanted to introduce me to him. As a college girl, I couldn't have cared less about meeting my dad's friends. But he insisted, so Sunday morning we went to meet Ken at the insurance company penthouse where he was staying with his father.

When Ken opened the door, it looked to me like a light was shining behind him. At the time, I assumed it was natural light coming from a window. But years later, when I went back to that place, I realized there was no window there. The light I had seen must have been a supernatural light.

While the others chatted inside, Ken and I went out on the balcony that overlooked the city and talked for a while. It was amazing how comfortable I felt with him. Later, when we took him to the airport, we were walking side by side and I just patted him on the back like I'd known him forever. (At the time, I wondered why I did that, since we had just met.)Then he went home to Texas and I went back to college.

About six weeks later, I was home from college one weekend. Though I had not heard anything from Ken since we'd met weeks earlier, I *knew* he was going to call me that weekend! My parents were going out of town and invited me to go along, but something—now I realize it was the Spirit of God—told me not to go because that guy I had met weeks before was going to call.

So I stayed home and, sure enough, he called. We had our first date and when we got home that night, he walked me to the porch and then did something that totally stunned me. He asked, "Will you marry me?"

Dear heavens! He hadn't even kissed me. I was so shaken by his abrupt proposal that before I even thought about it, I said, "OK." Then I went into the house and closed the door. (We still laugh at that abrupt proposal and acceptance.)

After I went to bed that night, the reality of what I'd done began to dawn on me. I lay awake for hours thinking, *Why did I say that? I don't want to get married. I hardly know this guy. I've only been with him a few hours. What was I thinking?*

As I finally drifted off to sleep, I shrugged the whole thing off. *Oh well,* I thought, *I'll get out of it later.*

More than forty-five years have come and gone since then, and I'm not out of it yet. I'm in deeper than ever . . . and I wouldn't have it any other way.

GOD MAY HAVE A BETTER IDEA

Perhaps today you're like I was when I first connected with God's Master Plan. Maybe you have some ideas of your own that you hope will be included in God's plan for you. That's okay . . . but be ready for some surprises because God may just have a better idea.

Marrying Ken wasn't in my plan, but it was in God's Master Plan for me. Preaching the gospel wasn't on the path I had mapped out for myself, but it was on the shining path God had prepared for me. Those things came as a surprise, but they've turned out to be wonderful blessings.

The life God had planned for me is more than I could have ever dreamed of as a nineteen-year-old college sophomore from Arkansas. That little career I had my eye on back then would have been a total bore compared to what God had in mind. Looking back at it now, I realize it would have left me tired, empty, and unfulfilled.

God knew that. He certainly understood me better than I understood myself. In retrospect, I can see just how true these words from Psalm 139 have proven to be in my life:

> O Lord, you have examined my heart and know everything about me. You know when I sit down or stand up. You know my every thought when far away. You chart the path ahead of me and tell me where to stop and rest. Every moment you know where I am. You know what I am going to say even before I say it, Lord. You both precede and follow me. You place your hand of blessing on my head. . . . You saw me before I was born. Every day of my life was recorded in your book. Every moment was laid out before a sin-

gle day had passed. How precious are your thoughts about me, O God! They are innumerable! Search me, O God, and know my heart; test me and know my thoughts. Point out anything in me that offends you, and lead me along the path of everlasting life (verses 1–5, 16–17, 23–24, NLT-96).

I'm so glad today that I chose to follow God's path those many years ago. I'm so grateful God taught me to pray like the psalmist did, asking Him to point out the thoughts and attitudes I had that were offensive to Him, and looking to Him to lead me in His way. God knew better than I did what would truly satisfy me and make me happy. And He is so good—so very good!—that in His kindness, He started maneuvering me in the right direction, even before I knew to ask Him.

Now, after years of following God's shining path for me, I can't even imagine a better life than the one He has given me. I can't think of anything I'd rather do than what I am doing right now. I wouldn't trade places with anyone else on earth. I am as thrilled with my life as I could possibly be.

I've literally seen the promise God gave in Psalm 25:12–13 come true in my life. It says: "Where is the man who fears the Lord? God will teach him how to choose the best. He shall live within God's circle of blessing, and his children shall inherit the earth" (TLB).

I live in the circle of God's blessing . . . and that circle just keeps getting better every day!

I'm not saying that just so you will be happy for me. I'm saying it because I want you to know that if you'll follow God's shining path, you too can live within God's circle of blessing. You will live a life that's divinely designed to fulfill your heart's desires. You will be more satisfied than you ever dreamed you could be.

If you'll stay on God's path, you'll always be increasing. You'll never be bored. Life will never be dull. There will always be fresh challenges, always new and higher hills to climb.

I want you to know that so the devil won't be able to sell you his lies, or succeed in scaring you away from God's shining path by telling you the same kind of thing he told Adam and Eve—that God isn't really good, that He will deprive you of your heart's desires, or that His plan for you will leave you poor, dull, and dissatisfied.

I want the truth about God's goodness to take root in your heart so the devil will never be able to lure you away with promises of worldly pleasure or money. He won't ever be able to convince you he has a better plan for you than God has.

Tragically, millions of people do fall for that deception. Some of them (not many, but some) get the glamorous lifestyles or the big money they hoped for. But even if they do, they're never happy. Some of the most miserable people in the world are entertainers, actors, or athletes who have all the money they need to buy anything they want. Often, they use that money to pursue sinful habits and lifestyles that cause them to die early without living out the full number of their days. What they thought would be a blessing, without God, turns out to be a curse. Many die young, and others end up living sad and unsatisfying lives.

Their lives bear out the serious truth of Proverbs 19:16 which says, "He who keeps the commandment [of the Lord] keeps his own life, but he who despises His ways shall die" (AMP).

Even born-again believers who draw back from God's plan because of fear, finish life in disappointment. They never get the opportunity to do what they were divinely designed to do. Ultimately, the desires of their hearts go unfulfilled and they're unsatisfied. They spend their whole lives feeling like something is missing.

That's always the way it is when people fail to connect with God's

Master Plan. No matter how successful they might appear, no matter how many of their own plans they carry out, things won't ever be quite right. They'll always be struggling.

People who find and follow God's shining path for their lives, on the other hand, have just the opposite experience. They discover that God's path—the path of righteousness—is a wonderful, delightful place to live. They experience the fulfillment of what the prophet Isaiah wrote:

> And the effect of righteousness will be peace [internal and external], and the result of righteousness will be quietness and confident trust forever. My people shall dwell in a peaceable habitation, in safe dwellings, and in quiet resting-places. . . . The Lord is exalted, for He dwells on high; He will fill Zion with justice and righteousness (moral and spiritual rectitude in every area and relation). And there shall be stability in your times, an abundance of salvation, wisdom, and knowledge; the reverent fear and worship of the Lord is your treasure and His (Isaiah 32:17–18, 33:5–6, AMP).

Those who choose God's shining path find that God blesses them with good things, and then gives them the wisdom to handle those things, so they continue to be a blessing. He also takes the bad things in their lives the devil intended for evil and turns them around for good. As Romans 8:28 says, ". . . all things work together for good to those who love God, to those who are the called according to His purpose."

Over the years, thousands of people have written Ken and me to share their testimonies and tell us how God delivered them from sickness, trouble, poverty, and distress, and filled their lives with His goodness. I've read many of their letters and I can tell you, they are happy people.

They've discovered the same thing I have—that when you do what God calls you to do and connect with His Master Plan, you're satisfied. The plan of God is where true peace is. His plan is where true joy is. God's shining path is the place of freedom.

IT TAKES COURAGE

I don't know where you are on God's shining path today. You may be taking your first few steps. You may have strayed away from that path and you want to return. You may have walked that shining path for years. Wherever you are, I can assure you it will take courage to keep going because along God's path there are surprises. There are twists and turns, mountains and valleys that will challenge your faith.

To meet those challenges, you must dare to believe God truly is as good as the Bible says He is. You must understand that you can trust Him absolutely and that everything He tells you to do is for your good. You have to trust God and what He says to you in His written Word and in your heart.

You must turn your back on the lies of the devil and believe what Psalm 145:8–9 says about God:

- *That He is gracious.* He is disposed to show favors and likes to do good things for you.
- *That He is full of compassion.* He is absolutely overflowing with love for you. He cares deeply about everything that concerns you and has promised never to leave nor forsake you. Because He loves you as a father, He wants you to succeed and be blessed even more than you do.

- *That He is slow to anger and great in mercy.* When you disobey Him or make a mistake, He's not quick to punish you or make you pay. He just asks you to repent and confess your sin so that He can forgive it and help you get back inside His circle of blessing. Even if you've been a repeat offender and you're afraid you've worn out God's patience, He'll still receive you with open arms when you turn to Him. As Lamentations 3:22–25 says, "Through the Lord's mercies we are not consumed, because His compassions fail not. They are new every morning; great is Your faithfulness. 'The Lord is my portion,' says my soul, 'Therefore I hope in Him!' The Lord is good to those who wait for Him, to the soul who seeks Him."

- *That the Lord is good to all and His tender mercies are over all His works.* He doesn't have a great plan for one person and a lousy plan for another. He doesn't love one of His children more than another. He has a glorious plan for every one of us because He loves us equally and He is good to all! His plans for each person will be different because we're all unique. But you can be sure His plan for you will be just as good for you as mine is for me.

How could His plan for you be anything less? It's been perfectly designed by the Master.

KEY THREE

—⟋⟍⟍—

Trust God's path and believe
He has good plans for you

Three

SEEK AND YOU WILL FIND

—⁓—

Once you begin to grasp how amazingly good God's shining path actually is, you'll have one burning question.

How do I find that path?

You won't be content to wander here and there, wherever circumstances might lead. You'll not be satisfied just getting up every morning, going to work, coming home, watching television, and going to bed. You'll want to take definite steps toward your destiny. You'll want to be sure you're living according to God's Master Plan.

If you're anything like I was when I began my relationship with God, at first, you may feel overwhelmed by the challenge. You may look back at the mistakes you've made and the wrong turns you've taken and wonder how you'll ever figure out exactly what God wants you to do.

If that's what you're thinking, I have good news for you. You don't have to be a spiritual genius to find God's shining path. You don't have to be an expert theologian or even an especially experienced Christian.

I can assure you of that, not only because the Bible says so, but also because I've proven it myself. I was totally clueless when I first gave my life to the Lord. I had no idea what God thought about things. I'd never learned much about the Bible. No one had ever taught me the powerful truths of the Word. I knew nothing about spiritual things. But God was able to help me anyway because He has made provision for people in that condition. His wisdom actually calls out to them. The Bible says:

> Does not wisdom cry out, and understanding lift up her voice? She takes her stand on the top of the high hill, beside the way, where the paths meet. She cries out by the gates, at the entry of the city, at the entrance of the doors: "To you, O men, I call, and my voice is to the sons of men. O you simple ones, understand prudence, and you fools, be of an understanding heart. Listen, for I will speak of excellent things, and from the opening of my lips will come right things. . . . I love those who love me, and those who seek me diligently will find me" (Proverbs 8:1–6, 17).

According to that passage, no matter who we are or where we might be in life, God is speaking His wisdom to us. He's making it available to everyone.

If we want this wisdom, however, we can't just wait for it to find us. We can't just sit around expecting God to look us up. He will do some maneuvering for us. He will help us. But ultimately, if we want to get the wisdom we need to find God's shining path for our lives, we'll have to do what this passage says. We'll have to seek God's wisdom diligently. To connect fully with God's Master Plan, we'll have to go after Him with our whole hearts.

The Bible makes that abundantly clear. It tells us again and again that the blessings and wisdom of God are reserved for people who avidly seek Him. It says:

- "Blessed are those who keep His testimonies, who seek Him with the whole heart!" (Psalm 119:2)
- "Seek the Lord and His strength; seek his face evermore!" (1 Chronicles 16:11)
- "He who earnestly seeks after and craves righteousness, mercy, and loving-kindness will find life in addition to righteousness (uprightness and rights standing with God) and honor" (Proverbs 21:21, AMP).
- "Seek the Lord while He may be found, call upon Him while He is near" (Isaiah 55:6).
- "'When you pray, I will listen. If you look for me in earnest, you will find me when you seek me. I will be found by you,' says the Lord. 'I will end your captivity and restore your fortunes. I will gather you out of the nations where I sent you and bring you home again to your own land'" (Jeremiah 29:12–14, NLT-96).
- "Seek first the kingdom of God and His righteousness, and all these things shall be added to you" (Matthew 6:33).

SAVE YOURSELF THE TROUBLE

There is nothing more important than going after God with your whole heart. It's the answer to everything. The more you seek Him, the more blessed you'll be, not only in spiritual things, but also in natural things. Seeking God will keep you healthy. It will enable you to prosper financially and bring peace to your home, healing to your body, and joy to your life.

If you get distracted and stop seeking God, on the other hand, your life will slowly but surely start to fall apart. You'll experience in a measure what Moses told the Israelites would happen if they stopped seeking God. "The Lord will scatter you among the peoples," he said,

> And you will be left few in number among the nations to which the Lord will drive you. There you will serve gods, the work of men's hands, wood and stone, which neither see nor hear nor eat nor smell. But if from there you will seek (inquire for and require as necessity) the Lord your God, you will find Him if you [truly] seek Him with all your heart [and mind] and soul and life (Deuteronomy 4:27–29, AMP).

Although we, as believers, may not literally be scattered among the nations and serve idols of stone, when we stop actively seeking God, we do lose sight of our Master Plan. Instead of being focused and moving ahead toward our glorious destiny, our lives become scattered and unproductive. We start finding ourselves enslaved by the natural circumstances and elements of the world, serving them instead of serving the Lord.

If we ever end up in that condition, God extends to us the same remedy He extended to the Israelites. He promises that if we'll begin seeking Him first, things will turn around. They'll begin to go well with us again.

One reason things go well with us when we're seeking God is because He helps us avoid a lot of dumb mistakes and saves us a great deal of trouble. And when we do happen to get into trouble, seeking God will get us out of it.

A person who proved that in a big way was Jehoshaphat, one of the Old Testament kings of Judah. During his reign, three enemy armies joined forces against him and endeavored to destroy his nation. Naturally speaking, there was no hope of victory. The multitudes that were marching against them were clearly more than Judah could handle. Jehoshaphat himself acknowledged, "We have no might to stand against this great company that is coming against us. We do not know what to do . . ." (2 Chronicles 20:12, AMP). Rather than yielding to despair and giving up, however, Jehoshaphat did the one thing that could save them: "[He] set himself [determinedly, as his vital need] to seek the Lord; he proclaimed a fast in all Judah. And Judah gathered together to ask help from the Lord; even out of all the cities of Judah they came to seek the Lord [yearning for Him with all their desire]" (2 Chronicles 20:3–4, AMP).

Just as He promised, God responded powerfully to those seekers. He caused the enemy armies to turn on and utterly destroy each other. Judah's army didn't even have to fight.

> And when Judah came to the watchtower of the wilderness, they looked at the multitude, and behold, they were dead bodies fallen to the earth, and none had escaped! When Jehoshaphat and his people came to take the spoil, they found among them much cattle, goods, garments, and precious things which they took for themselves, more than they could carry away, so much they were three days in gathering the spoil. On the fourth day they assembled in the Valley of Beracah. There they blessed the Lord. So the name of the

place is still called the Valley of Beracah [blessing]. Then they returned, every man of Judah and Jerusalem, Jehoshaphat leading them, to Jerusalem with joy, for the Lord had made them to rejoice over their enemies (2 Chronicles 20:24–27, AMP).

That story proves God is well able to turn the worst trouble into a blessing for those who seek Him. Yet many people—even good, Bible-believing Christians—claim they don't have time to seek God. I've noticed over the years, however, that most of those people do find time when they get sick to go to the doctor. They find time to go to the lawyer's office about the legal mess they've gotten themselves into. They find time to go to the bank and get a debt-consolidation loan when they get in financial trouble.

Seeking God first could have saved them all that time and trouble. If they had spent more time getting to know Him and learning what He has to say about their lives, they could have avoided the hospital and the lawyer's office. They wouldn't have had to go to the bank for help with their debts. Had they sought God first—not second, or third, or tenth—He would have given them wisdom along with everything else they needed.

It's not always easy to seek God. It takes extra time. It takes commitment. But the blessings that come as a result of seeking Him make life so much easier in the long run. It's easy to live in the blessings. When we seek God and find out how to live in His higher ways, we rise above many of the struggles and difficulties that plague people who live in the lowlands of natural, human wisdom.

Everything in life just works better when we do what Psalm 105:4 says: "Search for the Lord and for his strength; continually seek him" (NLT-96). The Israelites who obeyed that command in the Old Testament were surrounded with special favor and protection. "[God] allowed no man to do them wrong; in fact, He reproved kings for their sakes, saying, Touch not My anointed, and do My prophets no harm" (Psalm 105:14–15, AMP).

He will do the same for believers who seek Him today!

"But, Gloria," someone may say, "I've already sought God. I'm saved and have been going to church every Sunday for years."

That's great, but don't stop there. There is always more of God to find. He has many more blessings and plans in store for you (Jeremiah 29:11, NIV). Even if you're a seasoned Christian who has known the Lord for years, you can be sure He has some plans for you that you've not yet discovered. So keep on seeking and obeying because that's the secret to fulfilling your destiny and finishing all the good works God has planned for you to do. Determine to go after God with all your heart and say as the psalmist:

> One thing have I asked of the Lord, that will I seek, inquire for, and [insistently] require: that I may dwell in the house of the Lord [in His presence] all the days of my life, to behold and gaze upon the beauty [the sweet attractiveness and the delightful loveliness] of the Lord and to meditate, consider, and inquire in His temple. For in the day of trouble He will hide me in His shelter; in the secret place of His tent will He hide me; He will set me high upon a rock. And now shall my head be lifted up above my enemies round about me; in His tent I will offer sacrifices and shouting of joy; I will sing, yes, I will sing praises to the Lord. Hear, O Lord, when I cry aloud; have mercy and be gracious to me and answer me! You have said, Seek My face [inquire for and require My presence as your vital need]. My heart says to You, Your face (Your

presence), Lord, will I seek, inquire for, and require [of necessity and on the authority of Your Word] (Psalm 27:4–8, AMP).

I sought (inquired of) the Lord and required Him [of necessity and on the authority of His Word], and He heard me, and delivered me from all my fears. . . . O fear the Lord, you His saints [revere and worship Him]! For there is no want to those who truly revere and worship Him with godly fear. The young lions lack food and suffer hunger, but they who seek (inquire of and require) the Lord [by right of their need and on the authority of His Word], none of them shall lack any beneficial thing (Psalm 34:4, 9–10, AMP).

YOU CAN'T LIVE WITHOUT IT

According to *The Amplified Bible,* when God says, "Seek My face," He means *inquire for and require My presence as your vital need.* A vital need is something we can't live without. People who think they can live without seeking God are greatly mistaken. Without God, they're just existing. They're totally missing out on real, abundant life.

Once we, as believers, fully understand this, we'll get serious about seeking God. Once we realize it takes the wisdom and knowledge of God for us to live a truly blessed life, we'll find time to search out that wisdom, no matter how busy we are.

We'll get up early in the morning to spend time with the Lord or we'll go to bed a little later and seek Him at night. We'll even turn off the television. (Think of that!) We'll do whatever we have to do.

Obviously, it's going to take some effort. We can't just be casual

Christians and find the fullness of God's wisdom and plan for our lives. We can't just show up at church once a week, sing some songs, and listen to a sermon. Going to church is good, and any measure of seeking God will bring us a certain amount of blessing. But if we want to live in power and victory, if we want to operate in the gifts of the Spirit and see miracles in our lives, seeking God must be our No. 1 priority.

That's true whether you're the president of the United States, waiting tables, or scrubbing floors. To be a success, you must make a lifestyle of going after God for yourself. You must be determined to get to know Him personally and find out what He has to say. Be willing to seek . . . and seek . . . and seek.

Exactly what does it mean to *seek* something? According to the dictionary, it means "to try to find, to search for, to look for, to explore, to ask, inquire for, to learn, discern, try to acquire, aim at, and pursue." That definition, by itself, gives us a lot to think about. But the Hebrew definition for the word *seek* adds another dimension.

I discovered that definition when I was reading a book by a Jewish rabbi who became interested in what the Old Testament said about the Messiah. He went to various Jewish scholars and teachers and asked them about the subject, but they wouldn't talk to him about it. Finally, after he became a rabbi himself, he decided he would do his own scriptural study on the Messiah.

He discovered many scriptures that instruct God's people to *seek* or *search* for Him. I learned from him that in Hebrew, the word *seek* actually means "to research." So the rabbi decided to do exactly that. He studied the Bible and researched every Old Testament scripture he could find about the Messiah.

Do you know what happened? That rabbi researched the Messiah . . . and found Him. He ended up receiving Jesus as Messiah and was born again.

Even though you and I are already believers, we can do the same thing the rabbi did. We can research God and get to know Him better. The more of Him we seek, the more of Him we'll find.

Where do we do our research? First and foremost, we go to the Bible. When you see the word *seek,* think "research."

I think the word *research* best describes what it takes to walk with God. It helps you to get hold of what *seek* really means. It is the best word for what it takes to live victoriously in the earth. That is what Ken and I have done for more than forty years. We research God. The more we research, the more victory we find.

Rabbi Zwirn said:

> "Research (*doresh*) Yehovah and his strength; seek his face eternally" (1 Chronicles 16:11). If I am to entrust myself to God, I must be aware of what it means. And if I learn for myself of his strength, his power, his might, then I can confidently relax in his care.
>
> "Research (*doresh*) Yehovah if you are to find him. Call upon him, for he is always near" (Isaiah 55:6). How wonderful to know that he is available, and that when we seek (research) for him in his Word, that we will find him, "for he is always near."
>
> "Those who know thy name will trust thee, for thou hast not forsaken them who research (*doresh*) thee, Yehovah" (Psalm 9:11) [Psalm 9:10, KJV]. How does one come to know his name? By study, by research.
>
> "I researched (*doresh*) Yehovah and he answered me, and from all my confusions he saved me" (Psalm 34:5) [Psalm 34:4, KJV]. What a promise! When I sought him through his Word, he readily responded to my urgent needs! *Baruch ha Shem!* Praise his Name!"

"Those who research (*doresh*) Yehovah will never lack the goodness of life" (Psalm 34:11) [Psalm 34:10 KJV] How can anyone say that our great God is not interested in the most intimate details of our lives? Or that he is not concerned about such "mundane" things as our food, clothing, and shelter?

"When the meek saw they became glad. Those who will research (*doresh*) Yehovah, their (dead) hearts will be made alive" (Psalm 69:33) [Psalm 69:32, KJV].

Again, in addition to our physical well-being, God is interested in our emotional well-being. He wants us to be glad, happy and vibrant with his joy and his peace. All this and more he promises to all his children, when we see, research, study, and *know* him through his Word. I never cease to be amazed as I look at these references and the scores of others like them. God evidently expects us seek him with all of our powers. When we do, we have his Word that we will "find" him and "know" him. Of course, the connotation in this finding and knowing is that we will then offer ourselves to him in total obedience . . . "And ye shall seek me, and find me, when ye shall search (*doresh*) for me with all your heart. And I will be found of you, saith Yehovah" (Jeremiah 29:13–14).[3]

Matthew 6:31–33 (AMP) says:

---

3. Isidor Zwirn and Bob Owen, *The Rabbi From Burbank* (Fort Worth: Kenneth Copeland Publications, 2003) pp. 54–55, 108.

> Therefore do not worry and be anxious, saying, What
> are we going to have to eat? Or, What are we going to
> have to drink? Or, What are we going to have to wear?
> For the Gentiles (heathen) wish for and crave and dili-
> gently seek all these things, and your heavenly Father
> knows well that you need them all. But seek (aim at
> and strive after) first of all His kingdom and His righ-
> teousness (His way of doing and being right), and
> then all these things taken together will be given you
> besides.

There's nothing in your life more essential than knowing what
the Bible says because it's the revelation of God to you. God speaks
and shows Himself to you primarily through His written Word. It's
the key to connecting with God's will for your life. It's the place
you'll find your Master Plan.

The Bible doesn't have your name specifically written in it. It
doesn't spell out what vocation you should choose. It doesn't tell you
whom you should marry and how many children you should have.
But, even so, if you'll do what it says, step by step, the plan God
has for your life will begin to unfold in your heart and before your
very eyes.

A ROUGH AND DANGEROUS ROAD

That's exactly what happened to Ken and me. It took awhile for
it to happen because we didn't understand the power of God's Word
for the first few years we were saved. As a result, even though we were
born again and baptized in the Holy Spirit, we had difficulty finding
our way.

Actually, that's not quite true. We found our way just fine. That was the problem. We were going our own way instead of following the path God had prepared for us. And I can tell you firsthand, that road is rough. It's fraught with hardship and danger. We did see some of God's blessing in our lives. He helped us out of the dire straits we were in before we got born again. He gave us a decent place to live and an income. But we were still hopelessly in debt.

Ken felt like he was called to preach, but he didn't want to do it. So, instead of preaching, he would sing at church meetings sometimes and do a few things along that line. That would have been fine except it wasn't what the Lord wanted *us* to do.

He was leading us to move to Tulsa, Oklahoma, so Ken could go to Oral Roberts University. Ken, especially, felt strongly about that. But we wouldn't do it because we couldn't figure out how we could afford it. We were in debt and had no money. We hadn't had enough exposure to the Word of God to realize we could believe Him to provide the money, so we just stayed where we were—outside God's perfect will.

That's a dangerous place to be because the devil can get some access to you there. We found that out late one night driving down the highway, when a drunk driver pulled out into an intersection and slammed into us for seemingly no reason at all. Our son, John, just a baby at the time, and our daughter, Kellie, who was about three years old, were with us. It was a potentially deadly crash.

Probably due to Ken's mother's prayers *(Parents, never quit praying for your children!)*, God intervened and protected us. John had some broken ribs, but we all came through it without serious injury.

That wreck was a turning point in our lives. We immediately decided to go to the seminar at ORU that Ken's parents wanted us to attend. Ken's mother knew he was called to preach and was believing for him to answer that call. She probably hoped God would move on him at that seminar.

Before the wreck, I hadn't been especially interested in the seminar, but afterward, I strongly sensed what we had to do, and was willing and eager to do it. Ken felt the same way.

We'd been broke and behind on our bills for almost five years because nothing had worked for us financially. We'd get one job and find we were unable to do it. We'd get another one, do it, and the company wouldn't pay us. It didn't matter how hard we tried, nothing worked. We'd had enough of that kind of living. The car wreck had gotten our attention. It convinced us we didn't want to walk our own road anymore. We wanted to be on God's path. So we said, "Let's go!"

During that seminar, Ken had a vision from the Lord and fully accepted God's call to preach. God spoke to him and confirmed we were to move to Tulsa and he was to attend ORU. We still didn't have the money to do it but, at that point, we didn't care. We had discovered that living outside God's will was a dangerous place to be!

Because we hadn't been taught much of the Word yet, Ken was still struggling with the whole idea. He couldn't figure out how he could feed his family if we moved to Tulsa and he went to school. "Gloria, if we do that, we'll starve!" he said.

"We're starving now!" I answered. (I exaggerated but made my point.)

He agreed and that was that. From then on, we didn't try to figure out how everything was going to work. We just said, "We're going to do what God wants us to do. We're going to ORU."

It's amazing how things start working once you find God's plan. The only possibility of cash we had at that time was the eight-hundred-dollar equity we had in our little house. To get the money to move, we put a FOR SALE sign in the yard, and before the end of the day we had two offers.

Just that quick, we packed our little dab of stuff, loaded the kids into the car, and headed to Tulsa.

"It looks like, to me, things worked out," someone might say. "You ended up in the right place, even though you didn't know much of God's Word."

Yes, by the grace of God, we did. But we certainly did it the hard way—by trial and error—and the devil almost killed us in the process. Believe me, that's not the best way to find God's shining path. The best way to do it is by studying, believing, and obeying the Word of God.

Ken and I discovered that after we arrived in Tulsa. We started going to Bible seminars taught by Kenneth E. Hagin and found out how to act on God's Word and to live by faith. That's when our lives really began to change.

As we studied the Word and heard it preached by anointed ministers of God, we learned what to do when the trials of life came against us. We learned what to do when there seemed to be no way out—no money to pay the bills and other seemingly impossible situations. We found out we could obey the Bible: find promises of God, believe them, stand strong in our faith in them, and they would come to pass.

Until then, our hearts had been right but our heads and actions had been wrong. Our spirits were born again, but our minds and circumstances had largely stayed the same. God led us to Oral Roberts and Kenneth E. Hagin, both powerful and anointed men of God. As we heard the Word, our thinking began to change. And as our thinking began to line up with the Word, our circumstances began to change too.

WHO DETERMINES YOUR MEASURE OF SUCCESS?

If you research God's Word, believe it, and obey it, it will totally revolutionize your life from the inside out. It will take you from poverty to prosperity, from sickness to health. It will take you from failure to success in every area of life. That is how powerful God's Word is.

That's not just what I say, that's what God Himself has said in the Bible again and again. One of the people He said it to was the Israelite leader Joshua. Remember him? He was the man we referred to before who refused to let years of wilderness wandering make him give up God's promise. He's the man who, at eighty years old, connected with God's Master Plan, led the Israelites into the Promised Land and defeated every enemy.

If you've read the whole story, you know that Joshua had a difficult job. He had to get a whole nation back on God's shining path after they'd been off it forty years. He had to lead people who were famous for rebelling. They had a history of getting angry and blaming their leaders when things went wrong.

Even the great prophet and leader Moses couldn't keep them on track. So imagine how Joshua must have felt when God said to him, "Moses My servant is dead. Now therefore, arise, go over this Jordan, you and all this people, to the land which I am giving to them" (Joshua 1:2).

To Joshua, the task must have seemed almost impossible. The divine path he'd been given was littered with seemingly insurmountable obstacles. Not only was he supposed to get this group of former

grumblers all going in the right direction, he was also supposed to
lead them into battle. He was supposed to conquer enemy armies
with people who had never been trained and equipped to fight.
They'd grown up in the desert eating manna every day. They never
even had to hunt for food. How were they ever going to overcome
the Canaanites, Hittites, Amorites, and all the other *ites* that God
Himself had acknowledged were mightier than they were? (See Deuteronomy 7:1.) How was Joshua going to take this situation that had
been a forty-year fiasco and turn it into a success?

No doubt, that was the foremost question on Joshua's mind, and
God immediately answered it. He said:

> Be strong (confident) and of good courage, for you
> shall cause this people to inherit the land which I swore
> to their fathers to give them. Only you be strong and
> very courageous, that you may do according to all the
> law which Moses My servant commanded you. Turn
> not from it to the right hand or to the left, that you
> may prosper wherever you go. This Book of the Law
> shall not depart out of your mouth, but you shall med-
> itate on it day and night, that you may observe and do
> according to all that is written in it. For then you shall
> make your way prosperous, and then you shall deal
> wisely and have good success (Joshua 1:6–8, AMP).

The Book of the Law God referred to in those verses was the only
written Word available at the time. It was the Israelites' only "Bible."
God had personally given the Law to Moses. So, essentially God was
saying to Joshua, "Meditate on my Word day and night. Study it.
Observe it until you can act on it. Then you'll make your way prosperous and you'll be successful."

Notice, God didn't say He would make Joshua's way prosperous. He said Joshua would make his own way prosperous by researching and obeying the Word.

The same thing is true today. God doesn't determine how successful we are. We do. We determine the measure of blessing and prosperity we have by deciding what we're going to do with the Word of God.

God is always ready to bless us. He is always ready to help us find His shining path. He's made a way for us to find that path by putting His wisdom down in black and white on the pages of the Bible so that we can plainly read it.

Right now that wisdom is crying out to us. But we must respond and begin seeking it. The more we do that, the more we'll prosper and enjoy life. The more we research God and meditate on His wisdom through His written Word, the more we'll be like Joshua and have good success.

IT DOESN'T COME EASY

You don't have to go through what Ken and I did. You don't have to wait for a car wreck and financial failure to get your attention. You shouldn't wait until circumstances slap you down, or an illness forces you to sit still, to spend some time in the Word.

You know how important the Word is, so you can make the right choice now. You know it's the supernatural secret to your success, so you can decide today to make seeking God through His Word the first priority in your life.

God won't force you to do it. He has given you a free will. You have the privilege of choosing every day whether you're going to seek God or just live a natural life. He won't make you study your Bible.

He won't push you into a church that preaches the Word. He won't even make you do what He says. He'll lay it out there for you, but ultimately the choice is yours.

In some ways, you and I are in much the same situation the Israelites were when they went into the Promised Land. God has spread His blessings out before us. He has, through the plan of redemption, paid the price for us to have abundant life in our spirits, in our souls, and in our bodies. He's given us His Word to teach us how to lay hold of those blessings.

But at the same time, the devil has spread out *his* table before us. He pressures us with the cares and business of daily life, trying to convince us to spend our time pursuing natural things and to put them first in our lives.

Today, God is saying to each of us what He said in Deuteronomy 30. He is giving us the same sobering choice He gave to the Israelites when He said:

> "For this commandment which I command you today is not too mysterious for you, nor is it far off. It is not in heaven, that you should say, 'Who will ascend into heaven for us and bring it to us, that we may hear it and do it?' Nor is it beyond the sea, that you should say, 'Who will go over the sea for us and bring it to us, that we may hear it and do it?' But the word is very near you, in your mouth and in your heart, that you may do it. See, I have set before you today life and good, death and evil, in that I command you today to love the Lord your God, to walk in His ways, and to keep His commandments, His statutes, and His judgments, that you may live and multiply; and the Lord your God will bless you in the land which you go to

possess. But if your heart turns away so that you do not hear, and are drawn away, and worship other gods and serve them, I announce to you today that you shall surely perish; you shall not prolong your days in the land which you cross over the Jordan to go in and possess. I call heaven and earth as witnesses today against you, that I have set before you life and death, blessing and cursing; therefore choose life, that both you and your descendants may live; that you may love the Lord your God, that you may obey His voice, and that you may cling to Him, for He is your life and the length of your days; and that you may dwell in the land which the Lord swore to your fathers, to Abraham, Isaac, and Jacob, to give them" (Deuteronomy 30:11–20).

It's our choice what we do with God's Word. We can research it. We can put it first place in our lives . . . and prosper. Or we can leave it sitting on the nightstand unopened . . . and perish. Initially, it takes more time and effort to make the right choice. But in the long run, it's well worth it because the Bible promises us that investing our energies in the Word of God will extend our lives and add to us years of a life worth living.[4] If we're wise, we'll choose to do what Proverbs 4:20–23 says to do:

> My son, give attention to my words; incline your ear
> to my sayings. Do not let them depart from your eyes;
> keep them in the midst of your heart; for they are life

---

4. Proverbs 3:1–2 (AMP): "My son, forget not my law or teaching, but let your heart keep my commandments; for length of days and years of a life [worth living] and tranquility [inward and outward and continuing through old age till death], these shall they add to you."

to those who find them, and health to all their flesh.
Keep your heart with all diligence, for out of it spring
the issues of life.

Clearly, that seems to be the obvious choice. Attending to God's
Word brings us life, and life is what we all want. But filling our eyes
and ears with the Word isn't the easiest thing to do. It's easier just to
go with the flow of the world. It's easier just to let our ears be filled
with all the empty, unbelieving, foul talk around us and to allow our
eyes to look at the wrong things. These days, all we have to do is turn
on the television and we'll be confronted with depravity even unbe-
lievers wouldn't have tolerated fifty years ago. If we don't choose to
change the channel quickly, our eyes will be looking at immorality
and our ears will be filled with cursing.

Don't let that happen. Exert the effort to make the right choice.
Choose to seek God by spending time in His Word and doing what
His Word says to do. Start taking steps that will lead you onto His
shining path and into His Master Plan for your life. Begin to pray
the kind of prayer David prayed in Psalm 63:

O God, You are my God, earnestly will I seek You; my
inner self thirsts for You, my flesh longs and is faint
for You, in a dry and weary land where no water is. So
I have looked upon You in the sanctuary to see Your
power and Your glory. Because Your loving-kindness
is better than life, my lips shall praise You. So will I
bless You while I live; I will lift up my hands in Your
name. My whole being shall be satisfied as with mar-
row and fatness; and my mouth shall praise You with
joyful lips when I remember You upon my bed and
meditate on You in the night watches. For You have

been my help, and in the shadow of Your wings will I rejoice. My whole being follows hard after You and clings closely to You; Your right hand upholds me (Psalm 63:1–8, AMP).

God wants to do for you what He did for David. He wants to put you on the path where His blessings lie. He wants you to enjoy the good things He has planned for you. But the choice is yours, and if you haven't already made that choice, now is the time to do it. Now is the time to become, above all, a seeker of God.

If you'll do it—if you'll go after Him and His Word with all your heart—you'll not only find Him, you'll find everything else you need as well. You'll open the door to the treasure house of heaven. You'll find your Master Plan.

Four

UNLOCKING THE POWER
OF THE WORD

—⚏—

Some people are skeptical when I tell them they can connect with God's Master Plan for their lives through the written Word of God—and frankly, I don't blame them. They have good reason to be.

They may have read the Bible for years (or known others who have done so) out of a sense of religious duty. They may have read it because their mother, or their pastor, or their Sunday school teacher said, "That's just what good Christians do." But they can honestly say their knowledge of the Bible has done little to change their lives. It has not helped them find God's shining path.

They haven't realized that for the Bible to come alive for them, they must draw near to its Author. They must have fellowship with Him and trust Him to reveal—not just to their minds, but to their hearts—the powerful secrets of His Word.

As born-again children of Almighty God, we have the ability to simply believe and obey what God says in the Scriptures. We can draw near to the Lord every day and let Him personally teach us the truths of His Word. We can ask God to illuminate His Word to us and help us connect with His Master Plan for our lives.

"Do you really think God would do that for me?" you might ask.

Certainly He will. That's why He sent the Holy Spirit to live in you. He is there to be your Helper, to lead, guide, and teach you everything you need to know. Jesus made that very clear when He said:

> "The Helper, the Holy Spirit, whom the Father will send in My name, He will teach you all things, and bring to your remembrance all things that I said to you. . . . He will guide you into all truth; for He will not speak on His own authority, but whatever He hears He will speak; and He will tell you things to come. He will glorify Me, for He will take of what is Mine and declare it to you" (John 14:26, 16:13–14).

No matter what difficulties you might be facing, or how perplexing your problems may seem, the Holy Spirit is always ready, willing, and able to guide you through the Word and help you find the answers you need. If you are a Spirit-filled believer, He can teach and empower you to conquer every challenge. In every circumstance, He can show you the right way to go. But you must open the door and activate His ministry.

How do you do that?

By faith. Simply believe the Holy Spirit will do for you exactly what Jesus said He would do and expect Him to speak to you as you draw near to God in prayer and in the Word.

Psalm 25 assures us if we'll do that, if we'll trust God to teach and guide us, He will always do it for us. It says:

> Who *is* the man that fears the LORD? Him shall He teach in the way He chooses. He himself shall dwell in prosperity, And his descendants shall inherit the earth. The secret of the LORD *is* with those who fear Him, And He will show them His covenant. My eyes *are* ever toward the LORD, For He shall pluck my feet out of the net (Psalm 25:12–15).

The Living Bible translates verses 12–13 a little differently. It says, "Where is the man who fears the Lord? God will teach him how to choose the best. He shall live within God's circle of blessing, and his children shall inherit the earth."

Are you a person who fears or reverently respects God? If you don't honor Him enough to obey Him, you're not. If you're willfully doing things you know aren't right, you're not. But if you are sincerely trying to obey Him, walking in all the light you have and searching for more light, you qualify as a God-fearing person. And the Bible promises God will teach you how to choose what's best.

Every time you're faced with a choice, not just about your spiritual life, but about your job, your family, your health, or your finances, the Lord will help you make the right decision—the one that will connect you to the Master Plan. The Holy Spirit will illuminate the Word of God to you and help you apply it to specific situations so you make the choices that will open the door to more of His blessings in your life. All you have to do is expect Him to . . . and He will.

I learned that years ago. That's why, when I read my Bible and pray, I don't just do it by rote or as a religious exercise. I do it, expecting to hear from God, with an attitude of expectancy that says, "Lord, show me Your shining path today. Lead me by Your Spirit." As I study the Word and pray, I expect to receive revelation about His will for my life.

I don't just expect revelation every once in a while. I follow the example of the Apostle Paul who wrote to the Ephesians: "[I am] . . . *constantly,* asking God, the glorious Father of our Lord Jesus Christ, to give you spiritual wisdom and understanding, so that you might grow in your knowledge of God" (Ephesians 1:16–17, NLT-96). I figure if Paul needed to ask constantly for wisdom, I do too. I know if I have God's wisdom and follow it, everything in my life will be blessed.

MAKE AN APPOINTMENT WITH THE LORD

I don't just run to God when I get into trouble. I have a standing appointment with Him. I spend time in prayer every morning. Throughout the past forty years, I've learned that I need a daily dose of the Word of God, so I rarely let a day go by without putting the Word in my ears and before my eyes. I believe those two daily assignments are the way I maintain my strength and victory. That's the way I stay strong and keep unbelief out of my life.

As soon as I get up, I meet God in prayer and in the Word. He is always there, ready to listen and to talk to me. He never says, "I'm too busy right now. I have the Pope on the other line. I'll have to get back to you later."

No, He always has time for me because He's not only my Lord and my God, He's my covenant Friend. I've discovered for myself what Psalm 25:14 says is true: "Friendship with God is reserved for those who reverence him. With them alone he shares the secrets of his promises" (Psalm 25:14, TLB).

"But, Gloria," someone might say, "you've been seeking God for forty years now. Aren't you ready to slow down a little? Aren't you getting tired of it?"

Oh, no! I spend more time in the Word now than I ever have. I am hungrier for God than I've ever been in my life. My favorite part of the day is the time I spend reading my Bible, letting the Holy Spirit teach me what the Scriptures mean and giving me fresh revelations. I'm happiest first thing in the morning when I'm in my study or on the porch fellowshipping with God and studying the Bible.

Ken and I are both that way. We put our time with God first in our lives, even after all these years. As a result, we're more prosperous and blessed than we've ever been. We're still increasing, going from faith to faith and from glory to glory.

We've learned we can't ever afford to just coast along spiritually, resting in the momentum of the past. If we did that, we'd stop making progress and before long we'd be going backward. We'd start losing ground.

I determined in 1977 I'd never let that happen to me. Ken and I had been in the ministry about ten years at that time, and God had abundantly blessed us. We'd grown much more comfortable than we were when we first began learning the power of the Word. Our needs were met. We had a nice place to live, good cars to drive, and nice clothes to wear. We weren't broke and our debts were paid.

As a result, I'd started to relax a little. I wasn't in sin or rebellion, but I wasn't as zealous about the Word of God as I'd been a few years earlier. I'd allowed other interests to crowd out some of the time and attention I'd once given to God.

But that year I heard a prophecy by Kenneth E. Hagin that changed my attitude. It spoke of days to come when *men upon this earth shall walk and talk and act like God.* It referred to believers who would live in the power of God and become an army of light on the earth. Kenneth E. Hagin said:

> Many of those here tonight are part of that army. You can be one if you so desire. Purpose in your heart that you will not be lazy, that you will not draw back, hold back or sit down. But purpose in your heart that you will rise up and march forward, and become on fire.

When I heard those words, I examined myself spiritually and realized my desire for the Word wasn't as strong as it had once been. I didn't make excuses for it. I didn't try to justify myself. I just heeded the Holy Spirit's prompting and honestly assessed my spiritual condition.

I will be forever glad I did. If I hadn't, I don't know where I'd be today. I'd still be a Christian, I'm sure, but I wouldn't be on fire for the Lord like I am now, because to be on fire, you must stay zealous about the Word. You must continually put God first in your life.

In response to the Holy Spirit's warning that day, I made some decisions that changed my life. I decided I wanted to be in the spiritual army Kenneth E. Hagin prophesied about. I wanted to rise up and become on fire like I was at first.

JUST ONE HOUR OUT OF TWENTY-FOUR

So how did I reignite my faith? Just as I do with everything else in my life, I sought God's counsel. "Lord, what can I do?" I asked. "How can I stir myself up again?"

I didn't realize it then, but I believe now that much of my future depended on getting the answer to that question. I needed God's wisdom at that moment if I were to stay on God's shining path and fulfill His Master Plan. Of course, He gave me the wisdom I needed, just as He'll give it to you, if you ask for it, because the Bible says: "If any of you lack wisdom, let him ask of God, that giveth to all men liberally, and upbraideth not; and it shall be given him" (James 1:5, KJV).

When I asked the Lord how to rise up and become on fire again, He impressed upon me to begin reading one of John G. Lake's sermons every day. (Later, we published those sermons in a book, but at that time they were just loose, mimeographed copies.) John G. Lake was a powerful man of God who carried a divine spirit of dominion. The more I read his sermons, the more I began to catch the same spirit. Before long, I was conscious of God's power in a new and mighty way, and my fiery zeal for the Word was blazing brightly again.

A few years later, in 1982, Kenneth Hagin delivered another prophecy that added even more fuel to the fire:

> Don't take up all your time with natural things. Some of those things are legitimate and it's all right to take a certain period of time there, but see to it that you give heed unto your spirit. Give your spirit opportunity to feed upon the Word of God, and give your spirit opportunity to commune with the Father above. Build yourself up on your most holy faith by praying in the spirit. It doesn't take a lot of time, just an hour or two out of twenty-four. Just pay a tithe of your time unto me, saith the Lord, and all will be well with you. Your life will be changed. It will be empowered and you will be a mighty force for God.

I sensed God was talking to me when I heard that, so I considered whether I should spend one hour or two every day praying. Being the chickenhearted person that I was at the time, I decided on an hour. He gave me a choice, so I took the least amount of time. But at least I did become bold enough to commit to an hour.

After that, I started getting up early every morning to pray for an hour. (The Bible does say that those who seek God "early" will find Him, and that's how I like to do it. I like to spend time with the Lord before I spend time with anyone else. It makes me a nicer person.) My primary motivation when I first started came from my son, John. He was a wild teenager at the time, and my biggest problem in life was the fact that he wasn't doing what he was supposed to be doing. So when Kenneth E. Hagin, by the Holy Spirit, said praying an hour or two a day would cause all to be well with my family, I received it. I decided I would do it, expecting that all would be well with John.

When I first started, it was winter and because of the cold I really had to battle with my body to get up that hour earlier. I'd be sleepy, the bed would be warm, and my body would say, *Don't get up! It's too cold and dark outside. Sleep just a little while longer.* Initially, sometimes I'd give in, but I just kept at it until getting up early to pray became a way of life for me.

That was in 1982. In the years since, I haven't slept as much but I've enjoyed life more. And I can tell you, all is well with me. My son grew up to be a fine man of God. He's a strong believer, a good father, and oversees the ministry for us. So I got what I initially believed for . . . and a whole lot more.

It's been twenty-six years since I first made that commitment, and I've consistently prayed an hour a day ever since. I probably haven't missed more than a handful of days in all those years. That means I've prayed almost 9,490 hours just on that one assignment. God only knows the tremendous influence that has had on my life.

It wouldn't be an exaggeration to say I believe that one decision did more to help me connect to the Master Plan for my life than any other thing I've done as a Spirit-filled believer. It was a simple decision, but it wasn't an easy one to make. I don't mind telling you, I thought about it for a while before I made up my mind to do it because I don't like to commit to something and then back out. I prefer to count the cost in advance and make sure I'm fully willing to do whatever it takes to see my commitments through. (God, of course, has given me the grace to do it. He would love to do the same for you.)

Had I known then what I know now, however, I would have made that decision in a heartbeat. Looking back, I can see it transformed my whole personality. Spending that hour with God every day changed the course of my life.

The same thing is true of the decision I made back in 1977 to stir up my zeal for the Lord by reading the John G. Lake sermons. I wasn't preaching back then. Ken was the only preacher in our family, and I thought that was just fine. I had absolutely no aspirations to minister at the pulpit. Even though that has proven to be a major part of God's Master Plan for me, I had no inkling of it at the time.

What would have happened had I not obeyed those promptings of the Holy Spirit? What if I had never obeyed God to make those commitments to stir up my hunger for the Word and spend time every day in prayer?

Most likely, I would never have done what I'm doing now. The prayers, the study time, had everything to do with preparing me to minister. God might not have assigned me to preach because I would have been unprepared. I would have missed a major portion of the Master's Plan for my life. Determine right now that you'll never let that happen to you. Make up your mind you'll always expect such promptings from the Holy Spirit, and that you'll never ignore them when they come. Even if it seems costly at the time, always do what

God puts in your heart to do. Your whole future may depend on it. Remember, God is always endeavoring to make His plan a reality in your life.

IN THE LONG RUN, IT DOESN'T COST, IT PAYS

Actually, when God directs you to do something that looks like it's going to cost you dearly, it always pays off richly in the end. Ken and I know that well. When we first began seeking God and obeying His Word, God directed us to do something that was practically unthinkable to us back then. He told us to get out of debt . . . and stay out.

I'll never forget the first time He spoke to us about it. We were living in a shabby rental house in Tulsa and just barely getting by. But we were both spending lots of time in the Word because we knew we could not make it without God's supernatural help. Ken and I believed that God would make a way if we would just take His Word literally and do whatever He told us to do. So every day we searched the Bible, expecting God to correct and instruct us.

When He did, His instructions came as a shock. I was reading Romans 13:8 in *The Amplified Bible* at the time. It says very plainly, "Keep out of debt and owe no man anything, except to love one another."

Keep out of debt? I thought. *How would we ever do that?* We still had a mountain of debt from our past trailing behing us, and considering our meager income at the time, I had no idea how we would pay it all off. I wondered if Ken read this verse. He had never mentioned it to me, so I assumed he hadn't noticed it. Frankly, I didn't really want to draw his attention to it, but I decided I should. I got up my courage and handed him my *Amplified Bible,* pointing out Romans

13:8. When he read it, we both agreed God was speaking to us through that verse, telling us to stop borrowing money permanently.

Initially, that revelation was a blow to us. The devil immediately started telling us that we'd never have a decent house if we didn't borrow money. We thought about the ministry we believed God had called us to and it seemed if we obeyed this verse, that ministry would be over before it started.

How would we ever buy the ministry equipment we needed without borrowing? How could we pay for office space and buy vehicles we'd need to travel around the country—and the world— preaching the gospel? Ken was already praying for an airplane. Our dreams were doomed if we had to pay for all that in cash. We could hardly pay our grocery bill in cash.

But, after some discussion, we decided there was only one thing to do. We'd already made a commitment to God to obey His Word, no matter what it cost us, so we resolved we'd never borrow money again.

Of course, we didn't know then what we know now. Now we know that everything God tells us to do is for our good. In the long run, His way is always higher than man's way. Although it seems difficult at first, ultimately, it will bring the greatest blessing.

We experienced the fulfillment of that blessing eleven months later when we paid our debts off in full. What had seemed impossible just months before had become a reality. We were actually debt free. And, thank God, we are debt free today, more than forty years later.

We haven't lacked anything, either. God has enabled us to buy houses and cars, property, build ministry buildings, buy millions of dollars' worth of equipment, and even airplanes. We have stayed on national television twenty-nine years, preached the gospel around the world, and broadcast the *Believer's Voice of Victory* internationally. When we need or want something, we don't have to ask some lending institution for the money. We just go to our heavenly Father to see what He has to say about it. If His Word says we can have it, we ask Him for it. Then we do what the Bible says and believe we receive it and talk like we have it (Mark 11:21–24).

Personally, I like doing business that way because with God's accounting system there is no limit. His resources are inexhaustible!

Ken and I didn't realize that forty years ago. We didn't understand that God was giving us the answer to our seemingly unsolvable financial problems when He told us to stop borrowing money. A great many other people we knew didn't understand it, either. They thought borrowing money was a smart thing to do. They thought it was a great idea.

But God knew better. He always does.

IT'S NOT JUST WHAT YOU KNOW, IT'S WHAT YOU DO

Every time you open your Bible, remember that God's Word is His wisdom and His wisdom is higher than human wisdom. In other words, He is just plain smarter than we are. As He says in Isaiah 55:8–9: "'My thoughts are not your thoughts, nor are your ways My ways,' says the Lord. 'For as the heavens are higher than the earth, so are My ways higher than your ways, and My thoughts than your thoughts.'"

When you're reading the Bible and it says something you disagree with, don't ignore it. Don't argue with God about it. Don't try to convince Him you're right and His Word is wrong. He is always right, so agree with Him. Make the changes you need to make and live according to His wisdom rather than according to your own opinions or what the world says about things. Remember, the Bible says, "We know that we are of God, and the whole world lies under the sway of the wicked one. And we know that the Son of God has come and has given us an understanding, that we may know Him who is true; and we are in Him who is true, in His Son Jesus Christ. This is the true God and eternal life" (1 John 5:19–20). We surely can't follow the world and enjoy the goodness of God at the same time.

But if you obey the wisdom of God, you'll experience ever-increasing amounts of blessing and honor. Your children will be blessed, your bank account will be positively affected. Your life will get better in every way. I know it will because the Bible says:

- "Prize Wisdom highly and exalt her, and she will exalt and promote you; she will bring you to honor when you embrace her" (Proverbs 4:8, AMP).
- "I [Wisdom] love those who love me, and those who seek me early and diligently shall find me. Riches and honor are with me, enduring wealth and righteousness (uprightness in every area and relation, and right standing with God). My fruit is better than gold, yes, than refined gold, and my increase than choice silver. I [Wisdom] walk in the way of righteousness (moral and spiritual rectitude in every area and relation), in the midst of the paths of justice, that I may cause those who love me to inherit [true] riches and that I may fill their treasuries . . . Now therefore listen to me, O you sons; for blessed (happy, fortunate, to be envied) are those who keep my ways. Hear instruction and be wise, and do not refuse or neglect it. Blessed (happy, fortunate, to be envied) is the man who listens to me, watching daily at my gates, waiting at the posts

of my doors. For whoever finds me [Wisdom] finds life and draws forth and obtains favor from the Lord. But he who misses me or sins against me wrongs and injures himself; all who hate me love and court death. (Proverbs 8:17–21, 32–36, AMP).

- "Blessed is the man who fears the Lord, who delights greatly in His commandments. His descendants will be mighty on earth; the generation of the upright will be blessed. Wealth and riches will be in his house, and his righteousness endures forever" (Psalm 112:1–3).

- "My son, do not despise the chastening of the Lord, nor detest His correction; for whom the Lord loves He corrects, just as a father the son in whom he delights. Happy is the man who finds wisdom, and the man who gains understanding; for her proceeds are better than the profits of silver, and her gain than fine gold. She is more precious than rubies, and all the things you may desire cannot compare with her. Length of days is in her right hand, in her left hand riches and honor. Her ways are ways of pleasantness, and all her paths are peace. She is a tree of life to those who take hold of her, and happy are all who retain her" (Proverbs 3:11–18).

- "Wisdom is as good as an inheritance, yes, more excellent it is for those [the living] who see the sun. For wisdom is a defense even as money is a defense, but the excellency of knowledge is that wisdom shields and preserves the life of him who has it" (Ecclesiastes 7:11–12, AMP).

You can't just read the Word and enjoy all the benefits those verses promise without being a *doer* of the Word. You must make a lifestyle of going after the Word of God to see what He says to you about different areas of your life. Then be willing and obedient to change. It's the Word acted on that gets results.

When it comes to God's wisdom, it's not just what you know that counts, it's what you do.

If you ever stop doing what the Lord tells you to do, you'll get stuck. Even if you keep reading and studying the Bible, you'll notice you aren't hearing from God the way you did before. His Word won't speak to your heart like it used to.

When you think about it, it's easy to understand why. There's no reason for God to reveal something else to you if you haven't done the last thing He told you to do. Obey Him and He'll keep the revelation flowing.

It may be difficult at times. It may look like your obedience is going to cost you too much, but that's where faith comes in. God is always right! I can promise you, in the end, obeying God doesn't cost—it pays. So the minute you see what God wants you to do, start acting on His Word and don't stop. Keep applying God's wisdom to the affairs of your daily life and let these words from Proverbs be your guide:

> Hear, ye children, the instruction of a father, and attend to know understanding. For I give you good doctrine, forsake ye not my law. . . . Let thine heart retain my words: keep my commandments, and live. Get wisdom, get understanding: forget it not; neither decline from the words of my mouth. Forsake her not, and she shall preserve thee: love her, and she shall keep thee. Wisdom is the principal thing; therefore get wisdom: and with all thy getting get understanding. Exalt her, and she shall promote thee: she shall bring thee to

honour, when thou dost embrace her. She shall give to
thine head an ornament of grace: a crown of glory
shall she deliver to thee. Hear, O my son, and receive
my sayings; and the years of thy life shall be many. I
have taught thee in the way of wisdom; I have led thee
in right paths. When thou goest, thy steps shall not be
straitened; and when thou runnest, thou shalt not
stumble. Take fast hold of instruction; let her not go:
keep her; for she is thy life. Enter not into the path of
the wicked, and go not in the way of evil men. Avoid
it, pass not by it, turn from it, and pass away. For they
sleep not, except they have done mischief; and their
sleep is taken away, unless they cause some to fall. For
they eat the bread of wickedness, and drink the wine
of violence. But the path of the just is as the shining
light, that shineth more and more unto the perfect day
(Proverbs 4:1–18, KJV).

No matter what happens, keep seeking and obeying God. Go
down His shining path. Don't ever quit. Don't slow down. Don't
back up. Hold fast to His instructions, keep the Word of God in your
heart and in your mouth and don't let the devil talk you out of it.

He'll certainly try! He'll come along and say things like, "God
doesn't love you. His Word won't work for you. You've been acting
on it two whole weeks and you haven't seen any change in your situation yet. You might as well give up and do your own thing again."

Jesus said the devil is a liar (John 8:44). He will do everything he
can to talk you out of your confidence in God. *Confidence* is another
word for "faith." Recognize that a lack of confidence is a lack of faith.
Refuse to buy Satan's lies. Say, "No, Devil! I resist you. Shut up and
get out in the Name of Jesus!" Then reaffirm your faith. Say out loud,

"I take firm hold of the instruction of God. I trust Him with my life. I will not change. I act on the Word of God. God loves me and I believe His Word." Learn to think and talk like that. You have to tell Satan what to do or he will tell you what to do. The Bible says to submit to God, resist the devil and he will flee from you. The next verse says to draw near to God and He will draw near to you (James 4:7–8).

If you'll just keep seeking and following the wisdom of God, you'll get where you want to go because God's way is perfect. He'll get you on track, and keep you on track. He'll give you the strength to keep going, even when enemies rise against you and the going gets rough.

I like what David said about that. On the day the Lord delivered him from his enemies and from the hand of King Saul, he talked about the tough times he had faced and about how he'd sometimes felt overwhelmed. Then he declared:

> "The Lord is my rock and my fortress and my deliverer; the God of my strength, in whom I will trust; my shield and the horn of my salvation, my stronghold and my refuge; my Savior, You save me from violence. I will call upon the Lord, who is worthy to be praised; so shall I be saved from my enemies. When the waves of death surrounded me, the floods of ungodliness made me afraid. The sorrows of Sheol surrounded me; the snares of death confronted me. In my distress I called upon the Lord, and cried out to my God; He heard my voice from His temple, and my cry *entered* His ears. . . . He sent from above, He took me, He drew me out of many waters. He delivered me from my strong enemy, from those who hated me; for they were too strong for me. They confronted me in the

day of my calamity, but the Lord was my support. He also brought me out into a broad place; He delivered me because He delighted in me. The Lord rewarded me according to my righteousness; according to the cleanness of my hands He has recompensed me. For I have kept the ways of the Lord, and have not wickedly departed from my God. . . . For You are my lamp, O Lord; the Lord shall enlighten my darkness. For by You I can run against a troop; by my God I can leap over a wall. As for God, His way is perfect; the word of the Lord is proven; He is a shield to all who trust in Him. "For who *is* God, except the Lord? And who *is* a rock, except our God? God *is* my strength and power, and He makes my way perfect. He makes my feet like the feet of deer, and sets me on my high places. He teaches my hands to make war, so that my arms can bend a bow of bronze. You have also given me the shield of Your salvation; Your gentleness has made me great. You enlarged my path under me; so my feet did not slip" (2 Samuel 22:2–7, 17–22, 29–37).

Ken and I have proven over the years that if we follow David's example, and refuse to quit believing and acting on the Word, we'll receive everything God has promised. We've also learned it takes some strength to do that. We've had to be bold about it, not allowing ourselves to be moved by what the devil said or by what natural circumstances seemed to be saying.

Sometimes, receiving God's promise took longer than we wanted it to. But, the wait gave us the opportunity to develop patience and endurance, qualities the Bible says make you whole and complete, lacking nothing (James 1:4).

God's Word will do the same thing for you it did for us. If you'll expect the Holy Spirit to speak to you through it and obey what He tells you to do, God's Word will take you through to victory in every situation.

God's Word will deliver you from trouble. It will solve seemingly impossible problems . . . and it will *always* connect you to the Master Plan.

KEY FOUR

—〰—

*Make it a priority to spend time
with God in His Word.*

Five

PUT YOUR FOOT
IN THE WATER

—⁜—

Not only does the Word of God equip you with the divine wisdom and direction you need to live according to His Master Plan, it supplies you with something else you need—something positively vital to your success. It provides you with faith. As Romans 10:17 says, "Faith comes by hearing, and hearing by the word of God."

If you want to see just how essential faith is to connecting with God's Master Plan for your life, consider once again our example, the Israelites. It was lack of faith that initially stopped them from taking the Promised Land. It was lack of faith that robbed an entire generation of God's people of their divine inheritance and the glorious blessings He had in store for them.

What a tragic moment when that happened! There they were, camped on the border of two very different kinds of land. Behind them was a desert wilderness, a place so barren even their food and water had to be supernaturally supplied. It was a place so devoid of resources God had to wring water from a rock to keep them from dying of thirst.

In front of them was a land that flowed with milk and honey, so fertile it took two of the Israelite spies to carry back one cluster of the grapes that grew there. It was "a good land, a land of brooks of water, of fountains and springs, that flow out of valleys and hills; a land of wheat and barley, of vines and fig trees and pomegranates, a land of olive oil and honey; a land in which you will eat bread without scarcity, in which you will lack nothing" (Deuteronomy 8:7–9). It was a land where the Israelites could build houses, have herds, flocks, silver, and gold.

The choice looked like a no-brainer. Given those two alternatives, who in their right mind would choose the wilderness?

The Israelites did. But they aren't the only ones. We've all made choices like that at one time or another. We've all disconnected from God's Master Plan on occasion. In the past, we've all had times when receiving the fulfillment of God's promises looked impossible to us—the obstacles seemed too great, the hindrances too many. We simply couldn't believe we could receive it.

That's the situation the Israelites faced. They knew God had promised them the land of Canaan, but they didn't believe they could overcome the giants in that land. Caleb, one of the two men of faith among the spies, tried to convince them otherwise, saying, "Let us go up at once and take possession, for we are well able to overcome it" (Numbers 13:30). But the other Israelites who had spied out the Promised Land didn't believe that. They argued with Caleb, saying:

> "We are not able to go up against the people, for they
> are stronger than we." And they gave the children of

Israel a bad report of the land which they had spied out, saying, "The land through which we have gone as spies is a land that devours its inhabitants, and all the people whom we saw in it are men of great stature. There we saw the giants (the descendants of Anak came from the giants); and we were like grasshoppers in our own sight, and so we were in their sight" (Numbers 13:31–33).

STEPPING OUT IN FAITH

Hebrews 3:19 sums up the situation this way: The Israelites "could not enter in because of unbelief."

That statement could easily apply to many Christians today. Like the Israelites, they may have glimpsed God's wonderful plan for them. They may have heard His promises of abundant life, but they can't step into them because the obstacles appear overwhelming. "Oh, we could never receive those blessings. We could never achieve that kind of success," they say. "We don't have the education. We don't have enough money. We don't have the ability. That's too good to be true."

That's what Ken and I were tempted to say when the Lord directed us to pack up our little family, head to Tulsa, and enroll Ken at ORU. It looked to us like there were giants in that land who could eat us alive. The biggest one was lack of money. We didn't even know how we were going to afford Ken's tuition. Where would we get the finances for that?

If we did somehow come up with it, how would Ken make a living if he were a full-time student? In fact, how would Ken make it as a student at all? He was thirty years old, hadn't been in school for years, and hadn't liked it much when he had been. How was he going to wrap his brain around things like college algebra when he couldn't even remember the algebra he had learned in high school?

The whole thing looked impossible. Absolutely impossible!

That's often the way it is when you're living according to God's Master Plan. You frequently have to do things that seem impossible to you. You have to step out in faith, believing God will enable you to slay the giants and move the mountains threatening to keep you out of your promised land.

Ken and I didn't have much faith back then because we didn't know much about the Word. We did know, however, that the Bible promised if we'd seek God first, He'd see to it our needs would be met (Matthew 6:33). So, with that scripture and a little dab of faith, we stepped out on God's promise.

We went to Tulsa, using what little money we had to rent a place to live. Then Ken went to register for school . . . with no money. While he was standing in line wondering what he would do when the registrar asked him for payment, he decided to call his parents—*collect,* of course. His father answered and gave him the astonishing news that someone had come by his office the day before with some money for Ken. His dad had already deposited the money into our account. We never knew who it was. They wanted to remain anonymous.

After Ken finished registering, he clearly heard the Lord say, *Go to the top floor.* He knew full well students weren't allowed up there and tried to argue with God, but the Lord just said, *You do what I tell you. They work for Me.* So Ken went to the floor where the executive offices were located, walked up to the receptionist, and said, "I'm a qualified commercial pilot. If anyone needs anything like that, I sure do need work. Thank you. God bless you."

Almost before he finished the sentence, Oral Roberts stepped out of his office and walked behind Ken. For a moment, Ken wasn't sure if that was a good thing or a bad thing. After all, he'd violated student protocol to do this, and now Oral Roberts himself, whose imposing 6-foot-3-inch frame towered over Ken, was about to personally address the situation.

"My name is Oral Roberts," he said, offering Ken his hand. He had overheard Ken say he was a commercial pilot and asked if Ken could handle his ministry's airplane.

"Yes, sir, I can," Ken had answered.

Oral Roberts then told Ken, "Two weeks ago I started to hire a copilot for our evangelistic team's airplane. But the Lord said there's a student coming who's supposed to have the job. You're my man!"

It was definitely a very supernatural day.

I'll admit, at one hundred dollars for one week's work each month, that job didn't exactly qualify as a financial windfall. But along with some money from the GI Bill and some finances that came through Ken's parents, it did give us an income. And, frankly, that income matched our level of faith. We had just a little dab of faith and it brought us a little dab of provision. Since then, both our faith and our provision have increased, thank heaven.

Spiritually, however, Ken's job was invaluable because he not only helped fly Oral Roberts and his team to the healing campaigns, but once they arrived, Ken was in charge of ministry in the invalid tent. After each meeting, Ken was expected to go to the tent, give a five-minute synopsis of the sermon and get the people ready to have Oral Roberts lay hands on them for healing. Ken worked right alongside Oral Roberts, laying hands on the sick and learning directly from him how to minister to people.

Ken saw tremendous miracles during those times. He saw a woman spit a malignant stomach tumor onto the ground. He saw paralyzed people instantly healed, crippled people cast off their body braces and run, and many other signs and wonders—including thousands of people coming down the aisles to make Jesus their Lord and Savior. In one instance, a little girl who couldn't move anything except her eyes jumped up and ran, completely healed. Those things alone would have been more than Ken could have asked for . . . but that's not all he received.

In addition to working the invalid tent, Ken was assigned to drive Oral Roberts to and from the meetings. Although Ken didn't say anything on those drives, Oral Roberts sometimes talked to him about ministry, and during those talks Ken was greatly blessed by Dr. Roberts' wisdom.

It still amazes me, through that one job, God not only provided some finances for us, but He arranged for Ken to be personally trained in ministry by Oral Roberts. What are the odds of something like that happening? Naturally speaking, about zero. But we weren't walking in the natural, we were walking in the supernatural. We were walking out God's Master Plan.

"That's great," you might say, "but how do I know God would do that kind of thing for me?"

Because God is no respecter of persons. He doesn't love one of His children any more than another. So, what God did for Ken and me when we dared to step out in faith and obey Him, He will do for you if you do what He tells you. He'll prepare your way. He'll order your steps (Psalms 37:23). As Psalm 138:8 says, "The Lord will work out His plans for my life" (NLT).

But He can't lead you to victory if you won't follow Him and dare to believe He'll do the impossible for you.

God won't usually tell you in advance how He is going to work things out. It would have been far easier for Ken and me if God had said, "OK, you go to Tulsa, and I'll arrange for someone to pay Ken's school tuition. I'll give him a job as a copilot flying the best airplane he's ever flown. Plus I'll make sure Oral Roberts personally trains him to lay hands on the sick."

Had He told us all that, we would have gone in a heartbeat, without giving it a thought. It would have been an easy step to take, but wouldn't have required any faith . . . and everything in the kingdom of God requires faith. It takes faith to connect with God's Master Plan and to *stay* connected.

FAITH DOESN'T FOCUS ON THE GIANTS

Faith is the currency of the spiritual realm. It's the force that brings resources, strength, wisdom, help—whatever we need—from heaven to earth. "Faith is the substance of things hoped for, the evidence of things not seen" (Hebrews 11:1). Faith makes tangible the things God has promised us in His Word. It gives substance to those things we've been hoping to receive. Hope is good, but it takes faith to give substance. Substance is something you can see, touch, and experience in this natural world. Substance is earthly materiality.

Thank God, as believers, we've already been "blessed . . . with every spiritual blessing in the heavenly places in Christ" (Ephesians 1:3). All the resources of heaven have been made available to us. But, as long as we're here on the earth, those resources don't help us much . . . *unless* we learn how to transfer them from heaven to earth.

That's exactly what faith is designed to do. It lays hold of God's promises and makes them a reality on the earth through believing, speaking (confessing), and acting on God's Word, even in the face of contrary circumstances. When finances are scarce, faith believes the Word and says, "My God meets my needs according to His riches in glory by Christ Jesus." (See Philippians 4:19.) It brings divine provision on the scene. When sickness attacks, faith believes the Word and says, "By Jesus' stripes I was healed" (see 1 Peter 2:24), until it brings healing on the scene. When confusion attacks and you don't know what to do to connect with God's Master Plan, faith believes the Word and says, "God gives me His wisdom liberally (see James 1:5–7). I have the mind of Christ." (See 1 Corinthians 2:16.) It brings wisdom on the scene and your next step is revealed.

Romans 10 describes the operation of faith this way:

> But the righteousness of faith speaks in this way, "Do not say in your heart, 'Who will ascend into heaven?'" (that is, to bring Christ down from above) or, "'Who will descend into the abyss?'" (that is, to bring Christ up from the dead). But what does it say? "The word is near you, in your mouth and in your heart" (that is, the word of faith which we preach): that if you confess with your mouth the Lord Jesus and believe in your heart that God has raised Him from the dead, you will be saved. For with the heart one believes unto righteousness, and with the mouth confession is made unto salvation. For the Scripture says, "Whoever believes on Him will not be put to shame." So then faith comes by hearing, and hearing by the word of God (Romans 10:6–11, 17).

If you want to see just how essential faith is to the Christian life, consider the following New Testament facts:

- "Without faith it is impossible to please [God], for he who comes to God must believe that He is, and that He is a rewarder of those who diligently seek Him" (Hebrews 11:6).

- As believers, we're to "walk by faith, not by sight" (2 Corinthians 5:7).
- It's through faith and patience we inherit God's promises (Hebrews 6:12).
- The Bible declares repeatedly that "the just shall live by faith" (Habakkuk 2:4, Romans 1:17; Galatians 3:11; Hebrews 10:38).
- It's "because of our faith in [Jesus] we dare to have the boldness (courage and confidence) of free access (an unreserved approach to God with freedom and without fear)" (Ephesians 3:12, AMP).
- Faith in God's Word makes all things possible for us because with Him nothing is impossible, and "all things are possible to him who believes" (Mark 9:23).

That last point is especially important when it comes to connecting with God's Master Plan because, as we've already seen, many things in that plan will initially seem like total impossibilities. You won't be able to see how they're all going to work out. But if you're walking by faith and not by sight, you don't have to have it all figured out ahead of time. To walk by faith, all you need to see is what God's Word says, and all you need to know is the next step.

God's Word . . . and the next step. If you will act in faith on those two things, you will always connect with the Master Plan. That's what the Israelites eventually discovered—and that discovery launched them into the Promised Land. Joshua 1 tells us exactly how it happened.

After the old, unbelieving generation died out in the wilderness, a new generation of Israelites arose. They had a fresh perspective—an attitude of faith. Instead of focusing on the giants and the impossibilities involved in taking the Promised Land, this group of people was willing to follow the example of Joshua, the man of faith God raised up to lead them. Joshua continually kept his eyes on the Word of God, not on the giants of Canaan. He heeded the instructions God gave him and believed Him when He said:

> Be strong and courageous for you are the one who will lead these people to possess all the land I swore to their ancestors I would give them. Be strong and very courageous. Be careful to obey all the instructions Moses gave you. Do not deviate from them, turning either to the right or to the left. Then you will be successful in everything you do. Study this Book of Instruction continually. Meditate on it day and night so you will be sure to obey everything written in it. Only then will you prosper and succeed in all you do. This is my command—be strong and courageous! Do not be afraid or discouraged. For the Lord your God is with you wherever you go (Joshua 1:6–9, NLT).

Joshua didn't know exactly how he would defeat the heavily armed giants in the Promised Land. He didn't know how he would get past the fortified walls of cities like Jericho. God hadn't revealed that. God say, in short, "Follow Me. I've given you land."

So, Joshua kept his eyes on that Word, and told the rest of the Israelites to do the same thing: "Remember what Moses, the servant of the Lord, commanded you: 'The Lord your God is giving you rest and has given you this land.' . . . They answered Joshua, 'We will do whatever you command us, and we will go wherever you send us'" (Joshua 1:13, 16, NLT-96). What an attitude of faith!

FACING THE FLOODWATERS
OF IMPOSSIBILITY

Once the eyes of their hearts were fixed firmly on God's promise and they had received it by faith, the Israelites were raring to go. They consecrated themselves to God and spent three days gathering up their stuff and getting ready for the march into Canaan. There was just one problem. They couldn't really go anywhere because the Jordan River was in their way and they couldn't get to the Promised Land without crossing it.

There were several million of them, the river was running at flood stage . . . and there was not a boat in sight. Talk about an impossible situation! What do you do when faced with that kind of impossibility?

You do exactly what the Israelites did. You take the next step.

Sometimes that step may seem peculiar. Many times you can't see how taking it will lead to your success. But if you'll take it anyway, in faith and obedience to the leading of the Lord, God's mighty power will miraculously open the way for you and you'll find yourself doing the impossible.

That's what happened to the nation of Israel. God told them to assemble behind the priests who carried the Ark of the Covenant and begin walking toward the river, expecting to cross it:

> "And it shall come to pass, as soon as the soles of the
> feet of the priests who bear the ark of the Lord, the Lord
> of all the earth, shall rest in the waters of the Jordan,
> that the waters of the Jordan shall be cut off, the waters
> that come down from upstream, and they shall stand as
> a heap." So it was, when the people set out from their

camp to cross over the Jordan, with the priests bearing the ark of the covenant before the people, and as those who bore the ark came to the Jordan, and the feet of the priests who bore the ark dipped in the edge of the water (for the Jordan overflows all its banks during the whole time of harvest), that the waters which came down from upstream stood still, and rose in a heap very far away at Adam, the city that is beside Zaretan. So the waters that went down into the Sea of the Arabah, the Salt Sea, failed, and were cut off; and the people crossed over opposite Jericho. Then the priests who bore the ark of the covenant of the Lord stood firm on dry ground in the midst of the Jordan; and all Israel crossed over on dry ground, until all the people had crossed completely over the Jordan (Joshua 3:13–17).

What faith it must have taken for those Israelites to put their feet in that water. They had no power in themselves to push back the Jordan River, no ability of their own to get to the other side. Think how foolish they would have felt had they stepped into that water and nothing happened. But they refused to think about that. They chose instead to focus on God's Word and take the next step.

That's the secret of walking in God's Master Plan. That's the secret to releasing God's power and seeing impossible things happen in your life. *Believe God's Word and take the next step.*

Fear will try to keep you from doing that. It will try to hold you back. The devil will tell you to look at the floodwaters of impossibility instead of the promises of God. He'll tempt you to focus on your own weaknesses and inabilities. But when he does, resist him and make him flee (James 4:7). Keep God's Word before your eyes, in your ears and in your heart. Remain determined to obey what He says and act on the instructions He gives you. If you'll do that, you will be as courageous as Joshua and the Israelites. You can look at those impossibilities before you and say, "With God all things are possible and I believe God!" You can put your foot in the water by faith . . . and step miraculously into God's Master Plan.

How can I be so sure? It is the written Word of God and because that's what Ken and I and others we know have been doing for more than forty years now, and we've found it doesn't matter how impossible the challenge might seem, if we'll keep taking the next step, if we keep walking in faith and refuse to quit, God will consistently, faithfully, supernaturally do through us and for us things far beyond what we have the ability and resources to do.

A PRAYER GOD IS SURE TO ANSWER

Actually, when it comes to the things that are really important in life, like doing the works of Jesus, which all of us who believe in Him are called to do (John 14:12), God never intended that we get them done in our own strength. If we tried, we'd fail miserably. Even those things we are naturally good at, if we do them in our own might and power, they never amount to much. They don't bear any eternal fruit.

No, the good works God planned for us to walk in are primarily works we *can't* do. We don't have the ability, power, or brilliance to accomplish them. How then, does God expect them to get done? He expects to do them *through* us. He expects us to become channels for His abilities, vessels of His power. In other words, God's Master Plan is fulfilled when we allow God to do what He wants to do in and through our lives.

"But, Gloria," you might say, "I'm not called to the ministry. Does God still want to work that powerfully through me?"

Certainly, He does! You may not be called as a full-time minister, but if you're a believer, you are called to walk by faith and signs are supposed to follow you (Mark 16:17–18). You're called to be a blessing to people and to let the power of Jesus flow through you in whatever vocation God calls you to. God doesn't just need preachers. He needs doctors, lawyers, and teachers. He needs people in every walk of life, demonstrating His love and power.

What's more, no matter what your vocation, if it's God-ordained there will be times it will involve taking steps of faith. Just staying alive takes faith. No matter what God calls you to do, at some point, you'll have to put your foot in the water.

For example, God might call someone to be a doctor who has no idea how he will pay for all those years of medical school. That person may not even feel confident he is smart enough to learn everything he needs to know. If he has been out of school for a while, he may think he's too old to go back.

A person in that situation might say, "I can't go to medical school. It will take me ten years to finish and I'll be fifty years old by then!"

How old will you be in ten years if you don't go?

What should that person do? If he wants to connect with God's Master Plan, he'll ask God to show him the next step. Then, he'll take it.

Billye Brim, a good friend of mine, did that some years ago at a very difficult point in her life. Her husband had just gone home to be with the Lord and she found herself a widow in midlife. She'd been preaching and teaching in the United States for several years and planned to continue, but God had some other things in His Master Plan she hadn't counted on. He unexpectedly changed the direction of her whole life and ministry by telling her to go to Israel and study the Hebrew language.

She would have never thought of that on her own. She didn't know exactly how to do it. Where in Israel would she go? Who would pay the bills while she was gone? How long would she stay? What would happen after that?

Billye didn't know the answers to those questions, so she did what she knew to do. She took the next step. She began checking out Hebrew schools in Israel and making plans.

It took courage for Billye to step out in faith at such a tough time in her life. When she initially put her foot in that water, she couldn't imagine the things God had in store for her. But I'm sure she'll be forever glad she took those steps of faith because they launched her into the next phase of her destiny. She now has a ministry very involved with and close to Israel and the Jewish people and is planning a large facility in Israel, where Christians can come to pray and study the Bible in the Land. It is a thrilling, fulfilling part of God's Master Plan for Billye's life, in addition to her worldwide ministry. She is just like the widow Jesus talked about who also gave her all and excelled in obedience to such a degree, He spoke of her in Mark 12:42–43 and Luke 21:1–4.

As you seek God's plan for your life, keep that story in mind. Remember, when He reveals the next stage of His plan for you, you may not be able to see how, in the natural, you can get it done. You probably will not understand the whole plan the first day. But if you'll receive that Plan and take the next step of faith . . . and then another, the Lord will reveal more to you.

Don't put those steps off. Don't wait for all the hows and whys to be clear. Just start doing—and keep doing—what you can to move forward. Begin to make plans and preparations.

I've learned through the years that no matter how impossible a project might seem, if God directs us to do it, we can always take the next step. God will keep showing me what to do until it's finished. I say, "Lord, give me the wisdom I need. I'm willing to do whatever you want. So tell me how to take the next step, and I'll do it."

The Bible promises He will always give us wisdom liberally if we'll ask for it in faith. So that's a prayer God is sure to answer.

If you're eager to connect with God's Master Plan for your life, pray that prayer today. Ask Him to show you what His Word says about your life and the things He has planned for you. Then ask Him to reveal the next step you must take to get there.

When He does, start moving forward by faith. Put your foot in the water. Act on the direction God gives you and His plan will begin to unfold. The waters of impossibility that have stopped you before will begin to roll back under the powerful hand of God. Little by little, the pathway to your promised land will open before you. If you'll keep putting one foot in front of the other, taking one faith step at a time, eventually, you'll find yourself out of the wilderness and in the land of milk and honey. You'll find yourself in places you never thought you'd be, doing things you never dreamed you could do.

You'll find yourself right in the center of God's Master Plan.

Six

FOLLOWING THE FAITH
OF ABRAHAM

—ᵐ—

The power of faith will not only launch you into the promised land of God's Master Plan for your life, it will also give you the power to conquer the giants once you get there. It will move every mountain that tries to stand in your way.

Faith will bring God's power on the scene to do whatever needs to be done in your life. It will heal your marriage and straighten out your children. It will fill your bank account. Faith in God's Word will do whatever it says in your life. "And this is the victory that overcometh the world—even our faith" (1 John 5:4, KJV).

That's why, when Ken and I moved to Tulsa and began hearing the message of faith, we just couldn't get enough of it. We wanted to hear it . . . and hear it . . . and hear it. We'd drive through ice storms, slipping and sliding, to Kenneth E. Hagin's meetings just to hear him preach—morning and evening for three weeks straight. I think every meeting he would teach faith from Mark 11:22–24. We received it and WE GOT IT!

In those verses, Jesus said:

> "Have faith in God. For verily I say unto you, that whosoever shall say unto this mountain, Be thou removed, and be thou cast into the sea; and shall not doubt in his heart, but shall believe that those things which he saith shall come to pass; he shall have whatsoever he saith. Therefore I say unto you, What things soever ye desire, when ye pray, believe that ye receive them, and ye shall have them" (KJV).

When Ken and I first started studying those verses, we had more mountains in our lives than we knew how to climb. We were defeated in almost every area. We had countless questions and very few answers. So when we heard that faith would move mountains, we were eager to find out more about it—and we've been learning about it ever since. Even now, we don't know everything there is to know, but we know a lot more than we did when we started. We know not only from the Word but also from experience, that it doesn't matter what kind of problem we run into, faith in God's Word will always fix it.

Actually, I learned early on that faith would fix even *me!* That was an important discovery because I had some natural weaknesses and shortcomings that could have kept me from fulfilling God's plan. I didn't possess the natural talents and inclinations necessary to do what He had called me to do. Like everyone else who sets out to do God's will, I had what you might call an *ability gap*.

That was demonstrated quite clearly when Ken preached his first meeting. Before Ken spoke, the pastor of the church hosting the meeting asked me to stand up and say a few words to the congregation. (Traditionally, that's what preachers' wives were expected to do.)

My response was, "No!"

That's all I said. I didn't add, "I'm glad to be here" or "God bless you." Nothing else. I didn't intend to be rude, but, I felt very uncomfortable speaking in front of people and I didn't want to do it. That was the sad shape I was in when we went into the ministry.

Of course, after the service I repented. "Lord, I'm sorry about that," I said. "The next time someone calls on me, I will jump up, open my mouth by faith, and expect You to fill it." I've done exactly that ever since. Little did I know then how thoroughly the Lord would take me up on that promise.

GOD GIVES US THE ABILITY TO SEE HIS PLANS THROUGH

In the years since, I've preached to thousands of people again and again. How have I done it? With the ability God provides. When I tap in to His grace by faith, it is always sufficient for me. God's strength truly is made perfect in my weakness.

That's a fact you'll want to remember because as you step into God's Master Plan for your life, one of the first things you're sure to realize is that you don't have the ability to do all God is telling you to do. When He unfolds His plan before you, you may be tempted to say, "Lord, You've got to be kidding. Have You looked at me lately? Have You checked the balance in my checking account? Are

You aware that I have a track record of failure in that area? I don't think I'm Your best choice to carry out this plan!"

If you've ever had thoughts like that, don't be discouraged; you're in good company. Abraham, the famous Old Testament father of faith, felt the same way when God told him that he and his barren, old wife were going to have a baby. Although that was part of God's Master Plan for him and for the nation of Israel, Abraham thought the idea was so far out, he actually fell over laughing. That's right! The Bible says in Genesis 17:17, he "fell on his face and laughed, and said in his heart, 'Shall a child be born to a man who is one hundred years old? And shall Sarah, who is ninety years old, bear a child?'"

When Sarah heard God's promise, she had the same reaction. She "laughed within herself, saying, 'After I have grown old, shall I have pleasure, my lord being old also?'" (Genesis 18:12).

Why did Abraham and Sarah consider God's plan so outlandish? Because they looked at themselves and each other every day. They were old! They saw the wrinkles and gray hair. They knew their history of barrenness. Physically, they had absolutely no ability to have children. So the idea that they were about to become the father and mother of nations seemed ridiculous.

But when Abraham and Sarah realized God was serious, they stopped laughing. They got serious and did exactly what Jesus said we should do. They had faith in God. They began to speak His Word and believe His promise would come to pass in their lives. The New Testament confirms that. It says:

> Therefore it is of faith, that it might be by grace; to the
> end the promise might be sure to all the seed; not to
> that only which is of the law, but to that also which is

of the faith of Abraham; who is the father of us all (as it is written, I have made thee a father of many nations), before him whom he believed, even God, who quickeneth the dead, and calleth those things which be not as though they were. Who against hope believed in hope, that he might become the father of many nations, according to that which was spoken, So shall thy seed be. And being not weak in faith, he considered not his own body now dead, when he was about a hundred years old, neither yet the deadness of Sarah's womb: He staggered not at the promise of God through unbelief; but was strong in faith, giving glory to God; and being fully persuaded that, what he had promised, he was able also to perform (Romans 4:16–21, KJV).

Abraham looked at his old body and said, "Body, I'm not even considering you. I believe God can make me able to have a son despite your inadequacies." He looked at Sarah and said, "Honey, it doesn't matter how many years you've failed to have children, this is a new day. We don't have to consider those failures. God is going to give us the power to overcome them!"

Sarah agreed with him, too. We know she did because Hebrews 11:11–12 says: "By faith Sarah herself also received strength to conceive seed, and she bore a child when she was past the age, because she judged Him faithful who had promised. Therefore from one man, and him as good as dead, were born as many as the stars of the sky in multitude—innumerable as the sand which is by the seashore."

Sarah and Abraham proved that faith works! They demonstrated it can overcome every obstacle. It can even turn barren, wrinkled centenarians into the beaming parents of a new baby boy.

They proved the lengths God will go in order to accomplish His Master Plan. OK, so it takes a miracle. God does miracles. When you look around you with your natural eye, everything you see is a miracle. It all came from a seed—words that came out of God: "Let there be!" And there was.

When the Master has a plan, He can see it through. Miracles? Not a problem!

If faith in God's Word enabled Abraham and Sarah to birth nations, it can do anything you need it to do. It can equip you and fully enable you to successfully live out God's Master Plan. So let's take a closer look at the faith of Abraham and Sarah and find out what we must do to follow their example.

DEVELOPING THE FAITH THAT TAKES

First, as we've just seen, Abraham and Sarah believed they received God's promise, just like Mark 11:24 says to do. Exactly what does it mean to believe you receive? I can tell you what it doesn't mean. It doesn't mean we just sit back and say, "Well, I'll accept whatever happens. I'd like to have God's promises fulfilled in my life but . . . I'll just leave it all up to the Lord."

Although that may sound very spiritual, it's actually unscriptural. Some people have the idea that if God wants to give them something, He'll do it without requiring any action on their part. So when they fail to see God's promises come to pass in their lives, they assume God just didn't want to fulfill those promises in their particular situation. But they're mistaken. God always fulfills His promises when His conditions are met. He is a promise-keeper, not a promise-breaker.

Mark 11:24 clearly commands us to *believe we receive* what we ask for when we pray. We can't leave up to the Lord what He has left up to us. And He has given us the responsibility not only to believe, but to receive the things He has promised us in His Word.

The Greek word translated *receive* in Mark 11:24 is a strong, aggressive, action word. It means "to take, to get hold of,"[5] "to receive to oneself,"[6] "to take back."[7] It is an action word. I think *seize* would be an appropriate word to describe it.

If we don't seize by faith what God has offered to us in His Word, it's not His fault—it's ours. God has already done His part. He has provided every blessing, every good gift we could ever need, and has extended those gifts to us through His Word. But that by itself, does not complete the transaction. For a gift to be exchanged, there must be a giver *and* a receiver.

We all know that's true in the natural world. Imagine, for example, it was your birthday today and I walked up to you with a lovely gift. I could say, "Happy Birthday!" and offer it to you. But if you just stood there looking at it with your hands at your sides, that gift would never do you any good. Even though it belonged to you, and I had already bought and paid for it, if you didn't reach out and take it, you'd go home empty-handed.

On the other hand, if you would take hold of that gift, you'd take

---

5. *Strong's Exhaustive Concordance of the Bible,* (Nashville: Thomas Nelson Publishers, 1984).

6. *Vine's Expository Dictionary of Biblical Words* (Nashville: Thomas Nelson Publishers, 1985).

7. Robert Young, *Analytical Concordance to the Bible* (Grand Rapids: Wm. B. Eerdmans Publishing Co., 1974).

possession of it. You could open it up and enjoy it. When you did, both you and I would be greatly pleased and blessed.

We must do the same thing with God's promises. To enjoy their benefits, we must receive them. We must say, "Thank You, Father, for that promise. I believe it's mine and I take it by faith right now." *We must begin to think, speak, and act as if that promise is already ours.* That's just how faith works.

You see, faith isn't passive. It doesn't just fold its hands quietly and wait for God's will to be done. Faith is active. It is a taker and appropriator. That means when we read God's Word and see, "I can do all things through Christ which strengtheneth me" (Philippians 4:13, KJV), we say, "I believe I receive the truth in that scripture. I take it now. It's mine! I *can* do all things through Christ. He makes me able—and He does it now!"

Then, when the devil tries to talk us out of that promise, we refuse to give it up. We rebuke the devil and tell him to get his hands off our situation, in the Name of Jesus. When we do that, we'll experience victory.

"But, Gloria," you might say, "what if I believe I receive and nothing seems to happen?"

You have to believe you received the answer. Continue to act and talk like it is done. Refuse to consider contrary circumstances. Remember our example, Abraham. There was probably no visible change in his body the first day he believed God's promise, either. He probably looked just as old and wrinkled as ever. It may have taken some time for the Word of God to change the circumstances in Abraham's life, and it may take some time for it to change yours. But if you'll just keep considering God's promise and refuse to let your belief waver, that change will take place.

Ken and I have proven that in our own lives time and again.

We've received everything for which we persevered in faith. (And we've believed *big* because we needed big things to do what He called us to do. At least they seemed big to us!) Many of those things took a while to develop. We didn't get them overnight. But that's no surprise. Even the biblical heroes of faith sometimes had to wait in faith for God's promised blessings.

The Israelites who took the Promised Land, for instance, had to be patient after they crossed the Jordan River because God didn't immediately drive out all the giants and give them the whole land. Instead, He drove out their enemies "little by little" over a period of years. So, the Israelites had to exercise both faith and patience to inherit God's promises.

Ken and I have had to do that too . . . and so will you, if you want to receive all God has for you. But that's okay. Exercising faith and patience will always get the job done. In the end, you'll be glad you held fast because victory is so exciting. God's promises are always well worth the faith. Hebrews 6:12 says, "That ye be not slothful, but followers of them who through faith and patience inherit the promises" (KJV).

LET YOUR MOUNTAINS HEAR YOUR VOICE

Another important lesson about faith we can learn from Abraham and Sarah is that they imitated God's example by calling "those things which be not as though they were" (Romans 4:17, KJV). God Himself convinced them to do that by giving them new names. A year before Isaac was born, He changed Abram to *Abraham,* which means "father of many nations," and Sarai to *Sarah,* which means "mother of multitudes. " So Abraham and Sarah made a confession of faith every time they said their names.

Why is that important? Because, according to Mark 11:23, one primary characteristic of faith is that it speaks the Word of God and believes that those things it says will happen. Real, Bible faith is never silent. It continually speaks God's promise. Faith has a voice—the voice of victory!

Many Christians don't realize that. They diligently study the Word, and faith arises in their hearts, just as Romans 10:17 says it will. Faith comes to them as they hear the Word. But because they never open their mouths to speak by faith, their faith never bears fruit. It dies unborn!

Remember this: Faith *comes* by hearing, but faith *goes* into action by saying! It is applied to the situation by words of faith.

"Well, I just don't think my faith is big enough to get the job done," someone might say. "I think that's my problem."

If so, that's no problem at all because Jesus told us what to do about that. When the apostles came to Him and said, "Lord, Increase our faith," He answered:

> If you had faith (trust and confidence in God) even [so small] like a grain of mustard seed, you could say to this mulberry tree, Be pulled up by the roots, and be planted in the sea, and it would obey you. Will any man of you who has a servant plowing or tending sheep say to him when he has come in from the field, Come at once and take your place at the table? Will he not instead tell him, Get my supper ready and gird yourself and serve me while I eat and drink; then afterward you yourself shall eat and drink? (Luke 17:6–8, AMP).

According to Jesus, it doesn't matter how small our faith is, if we'll plant it by speaking out what we are believing, it will grow up and get the job done. When we release our faith with the words of our mouth, it goes to work for us like a servant and does what we send it to do.

That's one of the first principles Ken and I learned when we began to study faith. I'll never forget the day the revelation of it fully dawned on me. I had been listening to Kenneth E. Hagin's tape *You Can Have What You Say* on an old, 6-inch, reel-to-reel tape recorder. I had taken copious notes and was excited about what I was hearing. Revelation was coming to my heart and mind.

In Mark 11:22–24, Jesus clearly put a great emphasis on the words we say. As I took notes and listened to Kenneth E. Hagin preaching from this scripture about faith and the power of our words those many years ago, suddenly, the Holy Spirit spoke to my heart. He said, *In consistency lies the power.*

That's when it hit me. It's not just what we say in prayer or in church, but what we say continually, that makes the difference. What we say consistently will come to pass in our lives because that's what we really believe in our hearts. Jesus said, "For out of the abundance of the heart the mouth speaks" (Matthew 12:34). What you say continually is what is abiding in your heart. If you want to know what is in your heart, listen to your mouth. It's very revealing. Most of the time, it's too revealing for comfort.

At that moment, sitting in our shabby, little rented house back in 1967, I decided I had to take control over my words. I made up my mind to start speaking words of faith not just in church or when reading my Bible, but all the time. I saw it wouldn't work for Ken and me to speak faith words for a while, then quit when results didn't come right away and we felt discouraged. We couldn't afford to lie in bed and murmur to each other about our problems at times like that. We couldn't declare a faith *timeout* and say, "Why isn't the Word of God working for us?" "Why aren't we getting any results?" "What is going to happen to us?" "How will we make it?" "What are we going to do now?"

Those negative words would undermine the whole faith process. We literally could not afford to say them at any time. *Every word we said was important.* That was a revelation to me. I now understood how things came to pass in my life—good and bad.

That revelation turned our lives around. From that point on, we endeavored not to say anything we didn't want to have in our lives, and made a commitment to consistently speak only the things we wanted to come to pass. Changing our speech was difficult at first because it was such a dramatic change. We certainly didn't do it perfectly, but when we made a mistake, we'd repent and purposely undo the word damage we'd done. We'd say something like, "I rebuke that negative confession. It will not come to pass! I break the power of those words over my life, in Jesus' Name."

I remember one day when Ken was painting a room in our house, his negative words worked before he even had time to correct himself. He spoke words about his paintbrush, saying, "This sorry thing is coming all to pieces!" After a few more shakes, the brush totally fell apart in his hands. In the light of what we were learning about words, that experience left a lasting impression on us.

Of course, most Christians in those days thought we were crazy to take our words so seriously. The operation of faith was totally foreign to them. They just thought everything was up to God. If they were sick, they figured it was God's will. If they got healed, it was God's will. If they didn't get healed, then that was God's will too. They had no idea they had any *say* in the matter.

But that's not what Jesus taught. He said we do, quite literally, *have a say* in the matter. He said what we say makes all the difference. He didn't tell us to receive the mountains in our lives as blessings from God as His perfect will. He told us to speak to them in faith and move them out of the way.

"Well, I don't feel comfortable talking to mountains," someone might argue. "I'll just ask God to move them for me."

You can do that if you want to, but that's not what Jesus instructed us to do. He told us to speak directly to the thing that needs to be changed. Ken and I learned that included speaking to our finances. We talked to our debts and commanded them to be removed. We talked to sickness when it attacked our bodies and commanded it to be removed from us. We learned to speak to the mountains in our lives, and found they actually listened to us and moved out of our way.

YOUR FUTURE IS STORED UP IN YOUR HEART

Of course, there were plenty of naysayers along the way who looked at us and said, "They've gone off the deep end." They said we were extreme. So, I looked up the meaning of *extreme*. They were right. It is such a blessing to be extreme in the Lord. It's been wonderful. *Webster's New Twentieth Century Dictionary, Unabridged, Second Edition* defines *extreme* as "outermost, utmost point, farthest; going to great lengths; utmost in degree; excessive; immoderate, radical in opinion, drastic, ultimate."

We didn't care about those people's opinions. We cared about Jesus' opinion, and He not only said speaking words of faith changes things, He demonstrated it repeatedly when He was on earth:

- When He spoke to the fig tree and told it not to bear fruit again forever, that fig tree dried up from the roots (Mark 11:12–21).
- When He rebuked the stormy wind and sea, and said "Peace be still!" the wind ceased and there was a great calm (Mark 4:39).
- When He spoke to the deaf man's ears and said, "Be opened," the man was immediately able to hear (Mark 7:34–35).

I'm absolutely convinced that had Ken and I not followed Jesus' example and begun confessing God's Word over our lives rather than words of unbelief, we could never have connected with God's Master Plan. We would have remained stuck in our old patterns of defeat and inadequacy. Instead of stepping into the bright, new future God had planned for us, we would have continued walking around and around the paths of the past.

The same is true for you. To successfully walk out God's Master Plan for your life, you must start saying what God says about you. You must come into agreement with God. That will put you where you need to be!

Doing that one thing will literally change the course of your life. James 3 guarantees it:

> If anyone does not offend in speech [never says the wrong things], he is a fully developed character and a perfect man, able to control his whole body and to curb his entire nature. If we set bits in the horses' mouths to make them obey us, we can turn their whole bodies about. Likewise, look at the ships: though they

are so great and are driven by rough winds, they are steered by a very small rudder wherever the impulse of the helmsman determines. Even so the tongue is a little member, and it can boast of great things . . . (James 3:2–5, AMP).

Your words will steer you toward your future as surely as a bit guides a horse, or a rudder directs a ship. Even if you've been going in the wrong direction for years, you can change your course by changing what you say. You can set sail for God's Master Plan by speaking positive, faith-filled words, not just now and then when you're inspired to do it, but all the time.

Be forewarned, though. You can't do that just by human willpower alone because your natural desires will perpetually push you into talking about your problems. That's why the Bible says, "No man can tame the tongue" (James 3:8). Ken and I found out very quickly just how true that is. When we began working on our words, our biggest problem was financial, and we were sorely tempted to talk about the symptoms of lack we were experiencing. They were alarming! We felt tremendous pressure to fuss and fret out loud about our unpaid bills and the threat of a lawsuit.

Naturally speaking, that's normal. As human beings, we all feel compelled to talk about the bad things in our lives. If our biggest problem is sickness, the first thing we want to do when we wake up in the morning is find our husband or wife and talk about how bad we feel. It doesn't help anything, but for some reason, we just feel compelled to do it.

The only way to counter that compulsion and keep your tongue pointed in the right direction is to keep your heart full of the Word of God. It's an unchangeable law: *What is in your heart in abundance is what will consistently come out of your mouth.* Jesus left no doubt about that when He spoke to the Pharisees:

> "A tree is identified by its fruit. Make a tree good, and its fruit will be good. Make a tree bad, and its fruit will be bad. You brood of snakes! How could evil men like you speak what is good and right? For whatever is in your heart determines what you say. A good person produces good words from a good heart, and an evil person produces evil words from an evil heart. And I tell you this, that you must give an account on judgment day of every idle word you speak. The words you say now reflect your fate then; either you will be justified by them or you will be condemned" (Matthew 12:33–37, NLT-96).

Obviously, if you want to maintain your confession of faith you must do more than just train your tongue, you must fill your heart with the "right stuff." The Word of God is definitely the right stuff!

It will take some time to do that. If you're like most people, you've spent years filling your heart with the wrong things. You've spent untold hours thinking about how impossible your situation is, or how many shortcomings you have, or how sick, or weak or defeated you are. You may have ideas that run contrary to God's Word that were planted in your childhood as a result of what your parents believed and said.

It will take some time to replace those thoughts and images of defeat with God's Words of victory. You'll have to roll up your spiritual sleeves and go to work reading, studying and speaking the Word. You'll have to turn off the television sometimes and listen to good, anointed preaching of the Word instead. You may have to practice confessing the Word of God while you're driving to work instead of listening to talk radio. In other words, YOU WILL HAVE TO DO WHATEVER IT TAKES! Filling your heart and mouth with the Word won't be effortless and easy, but you can do it. It's the most important project of your life. It controls everything.

In fact, you *must* do it if you want a future filled with the goodness of God, because your future is stored up in your heart and brought forth with your mouth!

DON'T GET BLOWN AWAY

If, after all I've said, you're still not quite convinced that your words can make—or break—your connection with God's Master Plan for your life, consider this verse from Proverbs: "Death and life are in the power of the tongue, and those who love it will eat its fruit" (Proverbs 18:21).

You can interpret that verse any way you like, but personally I have chosen to take it quite literally. It's a good thing I have, too, because had I not, God's plan for my life could have been cut short several years ago. I would have, in the truest sense of the phrase, been *blown away*.

Do you remember when that term became popular some time ago? It seemed like a handy way to express amazement or surprise, so I added it to my vocabulary. "Oh, that story just blew me away!" I'd say. Or, "That concept just blows my mind!"

I didn't even think about it until one night in 1995, while listening to a friend of ours preach about words, he mentioned the Lord had instructed him to stop using that phrase. In my heart, immediately, I knew he was right. *Why have I been saying I'm blown away?*

I thought. *That's not really something I want to come to pass in my life!*

It didn't occur to me at the time that being blown away would ever, really be a threat to me. But I decided it was a good idea to stop saying it anyway.

Two weeks later, I was conducting Healing School in the Civic Center in Tallahassee, Florida, and a tornado hit the building. At first, I didn't realize what was happening, but I knew there was a storm outside. I'd heard the thunder and the wind, but I hadn't really paid much attention to it. Suddenly, I realized my Bible was getting wet. When I looked up to see where the water was coming from, there was a hole in the roof of the building!

Then the big, heavy door behind me broke loose and would have crushed me had it not been caught by one, stubborn hinge that just wouldn't let go.

There was no question about it, we were in danger of literally being blown away. So I did what Jesus did—I spoke to the storm. I rebuked it, in Jesus' Name, and the believers who were with me all joined in.

The next day when the newspaper came out in Tallahassee, the front page featured an article about the storm, verifying it had been a tornado. It showed the storm's path—where it started on the outskirts of town, the course it had traveled through the city, and where it had stopped—right at the Civic Center where we were holding our meeting. That tornado never went anywhere else. It was stopped in its tracks by believers taking authority over it, in the Name of Jesus.

I sometimes consider what might have happened had I ignored the Holy Spirit's promptings and just kept saying, "That blows me away!" I'm so glad I took my words seriously and made that little change. It didn't seem like much at the time—just a good idea. It was a simple step of obedience to God.

When it comes to what we say, obeying God makes an enormous difference. Death and life really are in the power of the tongue. So, with every word you speak—choose life!

KEY FIVE

*Fill your heart and mouth with the Word of God
and believe those things it says will come to pass.*

Seven

HIS STRENGTH IS MADE PERFECT IN YOUR WEAKNESS

—◊◊—

As we've already seen, taking just one step of faith—as the Israelites did when they stepped into the Jordan River on their way to the Promised Land—can connect you to God's Master Plan. That first step is vital and exciting. But if you want to *stay* connected with God's Plan, that first step must be followed by a second . . . and a third . . . and a fourth. . . . It must lead to a walk of faith that continues every day—through big things and small. Whether you realize it or not, you are constantly connecting or disconnecting from God's Master Plan.

As I've ministered to believers over the years, encouraging them to find and follow God's plan for their lives, I've noticed many people start out strong. When they first hear God's Word and begin to grasp His will for their lives, they start taking bold steps of faith. Often, God confirms His Word to them by moving supernaturally in their lives right away. He'll roll back a sea of impossibility like He did for the Israelites, or miraculously provide for an urgent need—or open a door like He did for Ken on his first day at ORU. Encouraged by the evidence of God's faithfulness, those believers take more steps of faith and, for a while, all goes well.

Then the unexpected happens. Maybe some things go wrong and they become angry or frustrated. Maybe they experience a delay and something they've believed God for takes longer to come to pass than expected. Maybe God asks them to do something they feel totally unable to do, or maybe they just don't *want* to do it.

At times like that, it's tempting to draw back and disconnect from God's plan. But the Bible directs us not to do that. In Hebrews, a letter originally written to believers who had encountered unexpected difficulties, it says:

> Do not cast away your confidence, which has great reward. For you have need of endurance, so that after you have done the will of God, you may receive the promise: "For yet a little while, and He who is coming will come and will not tarry. Now the just shall live by faith; but if anyone draws back, My soul has no pleasure in him." But we are not of those who draw back to perdition, but of those who believe to the saving of the soul (Hebrews 10:35–39).

According to those verses, God isn't pleased when we draw back from His plan. It grieves His heart because He wants us to fulfill our destiny. What's more, we ourselves suffer loss. The moment we disconnect from God's Master Plan, things begin deteriorating in our lives—inwardly and outwardly.

That's why Hebrews 10:39 connects drawing back with *perdition*. The word translated *perdition* comes from a Greek root word which speaks of "ruin" or "waste." Drawing back from God's plan causes us to waste precious hours, days, months, or even years we could be spending accomplishing God's will on the earth. That's tragic because we don't have forever to finish our earthly assignment. Jesus is coming back for us soon and we have work to do before He comes. Besides, our time on earth is limited. As someone said, "This may not be the last generation before Jesus comes, but for sure it's my last generation!" We have a limited time to fulfill His plan.

Certainly, if we live according to God's plan we'll be the most satisfied people on earth. We'll be the most blessed, productive, successful people around. But we don't connect with God's plan for that reason alone. Our motive is to obey and honor God because other people's lives and eternal destinies depend on it and because the kingdom of God itself will suffer loss if we don't fulfill His Master Plan.

People need to be saved, healed, and delivered. As Jesus' disciples, we must reveal Him to the world in every conceivable way, through every area of our lives. That's our mission as Christians, and it's an urgent one because there are people who will never see Jesus at all if they don't see Him through us.

It is of utmost importance for every child of God to get connected and stay connected to the Master Plan. We simply cannot afford to disconnect. We must become aware of the dangers and deceptions the devil uses to draw us off course, and determine to conquer them at any cost.

WANTED: THE MOST UNLIKELY CANDIDATES

As I've already mentioned, the major reason many draw back from the plan of God is that it repeatedly requires them to do what seems impossible. God's Master Plan continually challenges us to do what:

- We don't have the natural ability to do.
- We don't have the time to do.
- We don't have the money to do.
- We don't know how to do.
- We don't want to do.

In the years Ken and I have been walking with God, most of the major assignments God has directed us to do initially seemed impossible. But God makes the impossible possible. He doesn't only call the naturally gifted orator to preach His Word. He doesn't necessarily select the most spiritual to do His work. And I know He doesn't just call the richest people to build His Kingdom. Again and again, when I've spoken to ministers, I've asked for a show of hands to indicate whether any had ever had money in the bank to accomplish what God told them to do when He first spoke to them about it. I don't think I've ever seen a hand go up. Why, Ken and I had nothing but debt when we heard His call.

Many people with no money are called to do expensive things for God's kingdom. Naturally shy, quiet people like me may be chosen to stand up in front of thousands of people and preach. God has to take what He can get when He has a job to do in the earth. Sometimes, He calls the most unlikely candidates. But not to worry—He plans to do the work *through* them. He looks for a willing vessel, not a perfect one. You don't need natural ability to accomplish God's work. He just requires grace, faith, and obedience.

It shouldn't really shock us when we find we're not naturally equipped to do something God is asking us to do. From God's perspective, He can use anyone who is willing to answer His call and walk it out step by step in faith—totally dependent on Him. We might as well stop being fearful each time we face the impossible and start getting used to it! God has not given His children a spirit of fear, but of power, love, and a sound mind (2 Timothy 1:7).

God called the Israelites to do the impossible again and again. After they put their feet in the Jordan River and watched God roll back the water, they walked across on dry ground to the Promised Land. But they didn't get to relax and take a vacation. They had to continue on assignment after assignment, including conquering Jericho—something they were naturally unable and totally unequipped to do.

Jericho was completely protected by impenetrable walls. The Israelites had no way to get in. Had they been looking at their own ability, they would have thrown up their hands and said, "Forget this! It can't be done. There's just no way." As a result, they wouldn't have enjoyed the victory God wanted to give them.

Sadly, that's exactly what happens to far too many believers today. They let their own natural thinking rob them of the fullness of God's blessing. They forget that 1 John 4:4 says, "You are of God, little children, and have overcome them, because He who is in you is greater than he who is in the world." They forget the Greater One within them "is able to do exceedingly abundantly above all that we ask or think, according to the power that works in us" (Ephesians 3:20). Instead of focusing on the supernatural abilities of God, they fix their eyes on their own inabilities, disconnecting themselves from God's Master Plan.

When the Israelites went into the Promised Land, they didn't make that mistake. They dared to believe that God was mighty and able to do for them, and through them, all that needed to be done. They encouraged themselves in Him and prepared to accomplish the impossible. How did they do it?

First, they remembered their covenant with God.

Second, they waited on Him until they received His instructions.

Third, they kept marching forward by faith.

Doing those three simple things kept the Israelites connected to God's Master Plan. It turned them into the most victorious nation of overcomers the earth had ever seen. And since they are our examples, we would do well to study and follow in the footsteps of their success.

FIRST, REMEMBER YOUR COVENANT

Joshua 5 tells us the first thing the Israelites did after crossing the Jordan River and preparing to conquer the Promised Land was to circumcise all the men who, because of their wilderness birth, had not been circumcised. To new covenant believers, that might seem like just a religious ritual. But to the Jews of that day, it had a deep spiritual meaning.

Circumcision was first instituted when God made covenant with Abraham. (See Genesis 17:10–11.) It was the sign of the Jews' covenant with God. It qualified them to receive all His promised blessings and benefits, and gave them confidence that He, in all His omnipotence, would back them in every battle and empower them to take the Promised Land.

The uncircumcised condition of the wilderness-born Israelites indicated their heritage of Egyptian slavery and forty years of wandering had dimmed the memory of their divine covenant and left them feeling weak and defeated. But Joshua 5:9 says when they were circumcised on the West Bank of the Jordan River, God said, "This day have I rolled away the reproach of Egypt . . ." (AMP). By re-establishing the sign of their covenant, God severed them from the slavery mentality they'd developed during their years of bondage and reminded them that they were truly the chosen people of God. They were covenant people!

To understand what all that has to do with us as New Testament believers, consider this: The Old Testament rite of circumcision is a symbol of the New Testament reality of the new birth. The new birth does for us spiritually what circumcision did for the Israelites naturally. It puts us in blood-covenant relationship with God and gives us access to the wealth of His divine resources. It makes us part of a chosen race of people who belong to God.

Our faith in Jesus sets us apart from what we used to be and makes us new creatures in Christ—the Messiah, the Anointed One. It *spiritually* circumcises us. We are reborn in our spirits as children of the Most High God. How exciting is that? We become children of the *truly* royal family—the First Family! The New Testament itself verifies this. Speaking to us, as believers, it says:

> In Him [Jesus] you were also circumcised with the circumcision made without hands, by putting off the body of the sins of the flesh, by the circumcision of Christ, buried with Him in baptism, in which you also were raised with Him through faith in the working of God, who raised Him from the dead. And you, being dead in

your trespasses and the uncircumcision of your flesh, He has made alive together with Him, having forgiven you all trespasses, having wiped out the handwriting of requirements that was against us, which was contrary to us. And He has taken it out of the way, having nailed it to the cross. Having disarmed principalities and powers, He made a public spectacle of them, triumphing over them in it (Colossians 2:11–15).

Once you're born again, you're no longer just a weak, ordinary human being. You're a new creation in Christ Jesus with His life, His nature, and His ability. Next time you feel weak and inadequate to do what God is calling you to do, remind yourself that He is in you. Remind yourself that through the new birth, your old, inadequate, sinful self has been done away with and you've become a covenant child of Almighty God. "You are of God, little children, and have overcome them, because He who is in you is greater than he who is in the world" (1 John 4:4).

Remember that Jesus Christ Himself, who defeated every power of hell and conquered every impossibility, is living in you. Open your mouth and declare, "Greater is He who is in me than he who is in the world!" and shake the reproach of Egypt off *you*.

PERFECTLY DESIGNED FOR GOD'S PURPOSE

Once you adopt that attitude, your natural inabilities and inadequacies won't bother you anymore. You'll realize that as a new creation in Christ, you've been supernaturally equipped to do everything

God has planned for you to do. You are perfectly designed to fulfill His purpose. You are truly "God's [own] handiwork (His workmanship), recreated in Christ Jesus, [born anew] that we may do those good works which God predestined (planned beforehand) for us . . ." (Ephesians 2:10, AMP).

How could you possibly lack anything? God planned out your life before you were ever born. He designed your purpose and destiny before you ever took your first breath. And God is an awesome planner. He would never design a plan for you and then neglect to give you the ability you need to fulfill it. Even human beings know better than that. When engineers or inventors design a machine, they see to it that every part—even the hidden parts most people never know are there—is put in place so the machine can do what it was designed to do. They make sure the machine is fully equipped to carry out its purpose.

God did the same thing when He created us. He planned our days in advance. He created us carefully and wonderfully according to exact specifications so we could fulfill our God-ordained purpose. Psalm 139 says:

> You made all the delicate, inner parts of my body and knit me together in my mother's womb. Thank you for making me so wonderfully complex! Your workmanship is marvelous—how well I know it. You watched me as I was being formed in utter seclusion, as I was woven together in the dark of the womb. You saw me before I was born. Every day of my life was recorded in your book. Every moment was laid out before a single day had passed. How precious are your thoughts about me, O God. They cannot be num-

bered! I can't even count them; they outnumber the
grains of sand! And when I wake up, you are still with
me! (Psalm 139:13–18, NLT).

Obviously, if God put that much thought into creating you, He
had the foresight to include in your reborn nature everything you
need to successfully walk out His plan. He equipped you as a new
creation in Christ Jesus with all the abilities necessary to do what
you're called to do.

You might look at yourself right now and wonder how that can
possibly be true. You may be thinking, *If I do have the ability, it's certainly well hidden.* But if you'll just keep obeying the written Word,
walking by faith, believing, and confessing, "I can do all things through
Christ who strengthens me," the Holy Spirit will help you find those
hidden abilities. He'll bring out of your innermost being the capacity
to do things that no one—including you—ever thought possible.

The Holy Spirit is an expert at that. He's been doing it for thousands of years. Consider, for example, what He did with Gideon in
the Old Testament. That story should inspire all of us to believe that
God can use even seemingly ordinary people to do absolutely extraordinary things.

Judges 6–7 record the story. There, the Bible tells us about a time
in the history of Israel when its enemies, the Midianites and the Amalekites, were ruthlessly attacking. Year after year, these Canaanite marauders destroyed Israel's crops and herds and left the entire nation in
poverty. When the Israelites cried out to the Lord to raise up a leader
to deliver them from the situation, God chose Gideon for the job.

Talk about an unlikely candidate! Gideon was not some well-muscled, highly skilled warrior from a military family, just waiting
for an opportunity to fight for his country. On the contrary, Gideon
spent his days hiding from the Midianites in a winepress, trying to

thresh his wheat in secret. By his own admission, he was from the weakest family in Israel, was the least in his father's house (Judges 6:15) . . . and he was afraid.

Even so, the angel God sent to inform him of his assignment greeted him by saying, "The Lord is with you, you mighty man of valor!" (Judges 6:12).

Mighty man of valor? Clearly, God sees things in us that we ourselves cannot. *The Amplified Bible* says when given his assignment from the Lord, Gideon said, "How can I?" Does that sound familiar? God's answer is still the same today: "Surely, I will be with you."

It took a while for the angel of the Lord to convince Gideon that God was serious, and actually calling *him* to lead the Israelites into battle against the Midianites and Amalekites. But Gideon finally believed it and accepted his mission. Once he did, he was able to gather a good-sized army of thirty-two thousand men.

Naturally speaking, a big army is a good thing when you're taking on strong enemies. But, as we've already noted, God doesn't always do things in a way that makes sense to us. So God told Gideon to start sending soldiers home. Twenty-two thousand left the first day. That's a major reduction of troops, but from God's perspective there were still too many. By the time He was finished whittling Gideon's army to a satisfactory size, there were only three hundred left! Imagine—three hundred Israelites against multiplied thousands of Midianites and Amalekites. Clearly, God was asking them to do the impossible. What's more, He told them to do it without the aid of conventional weapons. They were not to take swords or shields into the fight. Instead, God gave Gideon an unusual battle plan.

> He divided the three hundred men into three companies, and he put a trumpet into every man's hand, with empty pitchers, and torches inside the pitchers.

And he said to them, "Look at me and do likewise; watch, and when I come to the edge of the [enemies'] camp you shall do as I do: When I blow the trumpet, I and all who are with me, then you also blow the trumpets on every side of the whole camp, and say, 'The sword of the Lord and of Gideon!'" So Gideon and the hundred men who were with him came to the outpost of the camp at the beginning of the middle watch, just as they had posted the watch; and they blew the trumpets and broke the pitchers that were in their hands. Then the three companies blew the trumpets and broke the pitchers—they held the torches in their left hands and the trumpets in their right hands for blowing—and they cried, "The sword of the Lord and of Gideon!" And every man stood in his place all around the camp; and the whole army ran and cried out and fled (Judges 7:16–21).

Not only did the enemy armies run, they also drew their swords and turned on one another. Gideon's three hundred defeated the Midianites and Amalekites without ever having to fight.

GOD DON'T MAKE NO JUNK

It's been thousands of years since that Old Testament event took place but God hasn't changed His ways. He is still calling ordinary people to do extraordinary things today. For example, no one would have chosen Oral Roberts to be a great preacher and healing evangelist. Not only did he stutter, but when he was in his late teens, he was bedridden and within a few days of dying of tuberculosis. It didn't look like he would live, much less preach.

Yet God chose and equipped him. He healed his body and made him an eloquent preacher and a blessing to millions of people. He has laid hands on more than 2 million people and healed the sick.

Although not everyone is called to a public ministry, we, as believers, are all called to lay hands on the sick and share the good news of the gospel. (See Mark 16:15–18.) We are to help and bless people in ways that stagger the natural mind. Each of us is a finely designed masterpiece of God, perfectly equipped to do great and mighty works.

How can I be so sure? Because that's what God says in the Bible.

Besides that, we're all His handiwork and, as someone once said, "God don't make no junk."

"Well, if I'm called to do great and wonderful things, I sure don't know it," you might say. "I don't feel like I have any particular calling in life at all."

Neither did I the first few years I was born again and baptized in the Holy Spirit. When Ken first went into ministry, I just assumed I would continue being a wife and mother, and help behind the scenes when necessary. Nothing more. Unlike Ken, who sensed the call of God to preach very early in life, I had absolutely no clue I'd ever preach. On the contrary, I intended to keep a very low profile. Since I had flatly refused to say anything the first time I was asked to greet a congregation, most people would agree that my prospects as a Bible teacher were, in the natural, very dim.

One day, however, someone wrote to me and prophesied that God had something He wanted me to do. He didn't say what it was, and I certainly didn't know. So, one morning while praying on the porch, I just said, "Lord, I don't know what You want me to do, but if You'll make it plain to me, I'll do it."

I didn't get an answer from Him right away, but I didn't worry about it. After all, I was willing to do anything He said, and I'd learned He doesn't mind making things plain to you when you have that attitude. He'll oblige you. He'll give you clear direction.

Later that morning as I was washing my hair, I heard the voice of the Spirit in my heart. It wasn't an audible voice, but inwardly, the Lord spoke to me very clearly and said, *I want you to start teaching on healing. Add a service to every meeting and share with others what you've learned over the years, as you've studied the Scriptures, prayed and believed for healing for your own family and your own children.*

Although it had never occurred to me before to teach healing, as I thought about it, I realized I had definitely learned some things in that area. From the time my children were very young, if they ever got sick, Ken and I would lay hands on them, pray the prayer of faith, and they would recover. As far as I remember, we never had to take them to the doctor for sickness. (We would have if it had been necessary. It just wasn't necessary.) The only times we took them to the doctor were to get their immunizations, and to get John checked or stitched after one of his many adventures.

As soon as Ken awoke that morning, I told him what the Lord had said. (I wanted to get myself committed quickly before I had the chance to talk myself out of it.) Ken agreed right away. "OK, let's do it!" he said.

I wasn't thrilled at the prospect. The thought of standing in front of a group of people and speaking still made me uncomfortable, and I certainly didn't feel I had the natural ability to do it. But I was determined to obey God and thought, *Well, if I make a fool of myself, that's just too bad. I'm going to do what God wants me to do.*

That's one key to staying connected with God's plan. Get yourself off your mind. When you're trying to protect yourself, worrying about how you look and what people will think if you make a mistake, you're very likely to draw back and disconnect from God's plan. But when you get your attention off yourself and fix your mind on pleasing God and being a blessing to people, you'll be able to push the fear out of the way and do whatever the Lord tells you to do.

If you make a mistake, just correct it and go on. Keep following God and His plan and you'll continue improving and developing the hidden abilities God wants to bring out in you. That's what I did. The first time I taught healing, I don't think I did a very good job of it. Someone later told me I didn't move the whole time. I just stood still behind the podium and read one healing scripture after another.

But what does it matter? I wasn't doing it to impress people. I was doing it because I wanted to obey God. So I just did the best I could, believed God to help me, and kept at it.

Even after I began teaching the healing services, I didn't realize for quite some time that teaching healing was a major part of God's Master Plan for me. I figured I'd just do it for a few months and then I could stop. But right before the last healing meeting I planned to have, Ken prophesied to me from the platform that the Lord wanted this "Healing School" (that's the first time I heard it called that) to continue until He returned. So that settled it. I knew I'd be teaching healing until I left the earth. There is no way out for me.

At the time, I didn't think I'd like teaching Healing School for the rest of my life, but I was wrong. It has turned out to be one of the greatest blessings of my life. In my own, natural strength, I could never have done it. I couldn't have taught one decent message on healing, much less laid hands on someone and they were healed. But I don't do it in my own strength. I do it with the ability God provides. Throughout the years, God has healed people from all over the world of all kinds of sickness and disease in Healing School, and I've loved watching it happen. Few things thrill me more than seeing people healed.

GOD THINKS BIGGER THAN YOU DO

If you'll stay connected to God's Master Plan, the same kind of thing will happen in your life. If you'll dare to look away from your own inability and trust God's ability in you, you'll wind up doing things you never thought you could do—and loving it. Some of those things will be bigger than anything you ever could have thought of on your own because God is a big thinker.

He can afford to be. He's not concerned about your natural weaknesses. He's not wringing His hands over the size of your bank account, wondering how you'll ever afford to do what He has called you to do. All God is concerned about is finding someone who thinks enough of Him to trust Him—someone who will dare to believe He knows what He is doing. He is looking for someone who has enough faith and determination to finish the job—even though He knows He has to work with the likes of you and me.

One person who was bold enough to believe that was the Apostle Paul. No one except Jesus, Himself, has had a greater impact on the Church or a more amazing ministry than Paul. Yet Paul declared God didn't choose him because of his strength, but because of his weakness. In his New Testament letters, he wrote:

> This is a true saying, and everyone should believe it: Christ Jesus came into the world to save sinners—and I was the worst of them all. But that is why God had mercy on me, so that Christ Jesus could use me as a prime example of his great patience with even the worst sinners. Then others will realize that they, too, can believe in him and receive eternal life. . . . Though I did nothing to deserve it, and though I am the least

deserving Christian there is, I was chosen for this special joy of telling the Gentiles about the endless treasures available to them in Christ (1 Timothy 1:15–16, NLT-96; Ephesians 3:8, NLT-96).

According to Paul, Jesus chose him to be an apostle in order to encourage the rest of us. By choosing Paul, Jesus proved He could take the worst possible candidate for ministry—a man who had persecuted the Church, entering homes, forcing men and women to be put in prison, and taking pleasure in a crowd stoning a Christian to death[8]—and turn him into a believer, who loved souls enough to live and die to get the gospel to them. That in itself is amazing, but the Bible tells us something else remarkable about Paul. Even after he received Jesus as Savior and Lord, he wasn't an especially gifted orator. (See 2 Corinthians 10:10.) Yet God anointed this man, who was naturally weak and unimpressive in his speech, to be one of the greatest revealers of truth the Church has ever known.

If God can do that with Paul, surely He can do amazing things with us too. And He will, if we will take the attitude of faith Paul took. If we'll stop worrying about our weaknesses and inabilities, start believing the Greater One is in us, and expect Him to do the work, we'll stay connected and keep living God's great plans. We'll prove in our own lives, just as Paul did, that God's strength and power truly are made perfect and show themselves most effectively, in our weakness. Like that great apostle of old, we'll be able to say:

Therefore, I will all the more gladly glory in my weaknesses and infirmities, that the strength and power of

---

8. See Acts 8:1 (KJV) *consenting:* (Strong's Exhaustive Concordance of the Bible): "assent to, feel gratified, be pleased, have pleasure," Acts 8:3.

Christ (the Messiah) may rest (yes, may pitch a tent over and dwell) upon me! . . . For when I am weak [in human strength], then am I [truly] strong (able, powerful in divine strength) (2 Corinthians 12:9–10, AMP).

Let's stop seeing ourselves in ourselves, begin to see ourselves in Him, and start seeing the Greater One in us, remembering 1 John 4:4: "You are of God, little children, and have overcome them, because He who is in you is greater than he who is in the world."

Eight

SUPERNATURAL STRATEGIES/ SUPERNATURAL SUCCESS

—⁂—

irst, remember your covenant with God.

Second, wait on Him until you receive His instructions.

Third, keep marching forward by faith and don't quit.

When Joshua led the Israelites into the Promised Land, that simple three-step strategy enabled them to do the impossible. It kept them connected to God's Master Plan in the face of seemingly insurmountable obstacles.

We've already seen how we, as New Testament believers, can follow their example by reminding ourselves of our covenant with God. We've studied the importance of looking away from our weaknesses and focusing on His strength. But we must remember that's just the first phase of Israel's three-part strategy. They couldn't do the impossible on their own. Had they tried, they surely would have gotten into trouble.

Imagine how differently things might have turned out, had the Israelites raced full speed ahead toward Jericho, full of faith in God's ability to give the victory . . . but without getting His instructions on how to fight the battle. What would have happened had they simply rushed those huge city walls and tried in their own strength to knock them down?

Nothing!

The walls would have remained standing and the Israelites would have most likely retreated, wondering why God had allowed them to suffer such humiliation and defeat.

Sometimes, that's what happens to us when we try to walk out some aspect of God's Master Plan on our own. We get a glimpse of what He has called us to do. We believe He has the ability to do it through us. And, without taking time to ask Him for His divine strategy, without receiving His wisdom through prayer and the Word, we rush ahead and try to do things our way. We make our own plans and expect God to back them. That's not a good idea. At best, it's naive and immature. At worst, it demonstrates a lack of reverence for the Lord and dependence on Him. Proverbs 16 warns us against such attitudes and teaches us to let the Lord direct our ways instead. It says:

> Roll your works upon the Lord [commit and trust them wholly to Him; He will cause your thoughts to become agreeable to His will, and] so shall your plans be established and succeed. The Lord has made everything [to accommodate itself and contribute] to its own end and His own purpose—even the wicked [are fitted for their role] for the day of calamity and evil. Everyone proud and arrogant in heart is disgusting, hateful, and exceedingly offensive to the Lord; be as-

sured [I pledge it] they will not go unpunished. By mercy and love, truth and fidelity [to God and man—not by sacrificial offerings], iniquity is purged out of the heart, and by the reverent, worshipful fear of the Lord men depart from and avoid evil. When a man's ways please the Lord, He makes even his enemies to be at peace with him. . . . A man's mind plans his way, but the Lord directs his steps and makes them sure (Proverbs 16:3–7, 9, AMP).

When we first plunge into the life of faith, most of us don't realize how vital it is for us to let the Lord direct our steps, so we sometimes make some messy mistakes. I remember one time in particular, when Ken and I could have easily done that. It was during our early days in Tulsa when we were still in financial trouble. We had just begun to realize our heavenly Father, with all His infinite riches, would truly supply all our needs and give us the things we asked Him for in faith. At that point, however, we hadn't learned to receive very much. We'd just begun to believe for basic necessities, like food and clothing. It was a stretch of faith just for the one hundred fifteen dollars we needed to pay our rent each month. But we stretched . . . and each month God provided.

So, Ken and I came up with a great idea. Instead of asking God for monthly rent on the old house we were living in, why not just believe Him for a nice, new house? God certainly could afford it, and we were confident He loved us enough to give it to us. Why not just go ahead and buy a nice house? It seemed like a good plan to us, so we went to a new neighborhood where some nice three-bedroom houses were being built, to see about buying one. We planned to make our home in Tulsa. (That's what *we* planned.)

We found one we liked and began talking to the realtor about it.

Of course, she asked how we planned to pay for it. Those houses probably didn't cost much by today's standards, but by our standards, back then, they cost a fortune. We didn't have a dime of savings in the bank, so Ken just said, "Well . . . my Father is going to pay for it."

Actually, we were on the right track by thinking that way. We were looking away from our financial inadequacies and considering instead, the resources of God. But if we had plunged ahead and signed a contract for a house on that basis alone, we would have been in trouble. Why? Because God wasn't leading us to buy a house at that time.

You see, God is not only a generous Father, but also a wise one, and He knew our faith wasn't developed enough yet to appropriate a house of that expense. We were just beginning to learn how to believe God for grocery money. Even if we had figured out a way on our own to purchase that new house, it would have landed us very quickly back in financial trouble. God also knew we would be in Tulsa only a few months.

Thank God, the Lord helped us to not jump ahead of His plan. We prayed, waited on Him, and followed the no-debt strategy He gave us instead. As we sought God and His wisdom, we were directed to move back to Fort Worth and establish Kenneth Copeland Evangelistic Association. We rented a new home in Fort Worth. God had it prepared and ready, including a great school for the children. Soon we got a better house . . . then a better one . . . until several years later, we were able to pay cash for a much nicer home than the one we had first wanted in Tulsa. Ultimately, we moved into a beautiful new home that is everything we desired. We believe we will be here until we leave the earth and will be very satisfied. You could call it "Faith House" because, of course, it was built debt free. (Remember, through faith and patience we inherit the promises!) All glory goes to our Father—the Provider.

That's just how God works. You flow with Him and He will provide the rest.

GOD'S STRATEGIES MAY NOT MAKE SENSE, BUT THEY WORK

It's always better to do things God's way. That's what the Israelites did before they marched against Jericho. Instead of figuring out their own battle plan, they got one from God instead. And as is often the case, the plan God gave them was extremely unorthodox. He said:

> "You shall march around the city, all you men of war; you shall go all around the city once. This you shall do six days. And seven priests shall bear seven trumpets of rams' horns before the ark. But the seventh day you shall march around the city seven times, and the priests shall blow the trumpets. It shall come to pass, when they make a long blast with the ram's horn, and when you hear the sound of the trumpet, that all the people shall shout with a great shout; then the wall of the city will fall down flat. And the people shall go up every man straight before him" (Joshua 6:3–5).

You know as well as I do that the Israelites would have never come up with that plan on their own. Humanly speaking, it didn't even make sense. But when the Israelites followed God's plan, everything fell into place (quite literally) and they conquered Jericho. God's plan brought them 100 percent success.

Such unorthodox strategies aren't just limited to the Old Testament. We find them in the New Testament, as well. Consider the instructions Jesus gave at the wedding of Cana, for example. Talk about a plan that didn't seem to make good sense! When Mary asked for Jesus' help with the wine for the wedding guests because the host's supply had run out, Jesus pointed to six empty water pots and said to the servants:

> "Fill the waterpots with water." And they filled them up to the brim. And He said to them, "Draw some out now, and take it to the master of the feast." And they took it. When the master of the feast had tasted the water that was made wine, and did not know where it came from (but the servants who had drawn the water knew), the master of the feast called the bridegroom. And he said to him, "Every man at the beginning sets out the good wine, and when the guests have well drunk, then the inferior. You have kept the good wine until now!" (John 2:7–10).

At first glance, you might wonder why the servants at that wedding ever followed Jesus' instructions in the first place. After all, what He told them to do was totally illogical. But something persuaded them to obey His command anyway.

What was it?

It could have been the bold faith of Jesus' mother, Mary. She said to the servants, "Whatever He says to you, do it" (John 2:5).

That's the formula for a miracle: *Whatever Jesus says to you, do it.* Of course, following that formula may require us to do things that, naturally speaking, may seem unusual. The servants at the wedding feast discovered that. They probably felt they were taking a major risk by following Jesus' plan. But they did it anyway, and in so doing, they opened the door for God to work a miracle . . . and everything turned out marvelously.

That's what I love about God's strategies. Although they sometimes don't make sense to our finite way of thinking, they always work. They bring us success every time. No wonder Proverbs 3:5–6 says: "Lean on, trust in, and be confident in the Lord with all your heart and mind and do not rely on your own insight or understanding. In all your ways know, recognize, and acknowledge Him, and He will direct and make straight and plain your paths" (AMP).

Those verses have helped Ken and me stay connected to God's Master Plan for our lives so many times. They've been our guide again and again when we've sensed God leading us to do what seemed impossible to us. Our attitude is, "Lord, we're willing to do that. We believe You're powerful enough to do it through us. Give us wisdom. Show us the next step."

We believe we receive the wisdom of God. He always gives us the plan as we continue to pray in the spirit and thank Him for wisdom. He tells us what to do and gives us the directions necessary to see the project through. It isn't always easy, but it is always doable. When God first impressed us to go on television, for instance, we had absolutely no idea how to do it. The whole process of putting together television broadcasts and getting them on the air was new to us. How to do it with no money was even more difficult. We didn't even know where to start. But we were willing and we believed God was able to help us do it.

Even so, we didn't rush into it right away. We talked and prayed about it over a period of months. Then, one day, while having breakfast at a restaurant, on a family trip from Arkansas, God just dropped in our hearts the confidence we needed to get started. We suddenly knew it was time to step out on His plan. "Why don't we just do it?"

we said. Faith was there. We believed we could do it. We believed it was the time. Nothing in the natural realm changed, but something in the spirit had changed. It was us! We were no longer looking at the giants but at God's ability to bring it to pass.

When we got home, the strategy started coming together. God showed us what steps to take, and our television ministry began. Actually, that's the way we've always done the work of the ministry. We don't look to the world for their ideas or strategies. We believe that if we will just do what God tells us to do, the way He tells us to do it, the ministry will supernaturally grow and increase. Ken and I don't have to come up with ways to make it happen. We obey directions from the top!

WISDOM WAITS WHERE THE PATHS MEET

Of course, since God is the same yesterday, today, and forever, some of the plans He has given us have been extremely peculiar by natural standards. For example, during the 1980s the ministry was struggling financially. We needed a million extra dollars to pay past-due television bills. That was a lot of money—especially in 1980.

When Ken sought God for a solution, do you know what He told us to do? Give! Ken was directed to start *sowing* the top ten percent of the gross income of the ministry to minister to the poor—people who could not return support, people like children, prisoners, and those in the mission field and other ministries that take the gospel to the poor!

That didn't make natural sense. Who gives *more* money when they're in need? No one but God has that strategy. But we followed it, and the money we needed came. The bills got paid and today we're still tithing that ten percent to the poor and absolutely love doing it. We're still increasing!

Although you may never go on television, or need to come up with an extra million dollars, you'll still face your share of challenges. You'll need God's strategies to succeed, not only in the major aspects of God's Master Plan, but also in the seemingly small, day-to-day aspects of it as well. Say, for example, God tells you to share the gospel with a particular person, or leads you to go to the hospital to anoint someone with oil and pray for them to be healed. If you've never done those things and you're relying on your own understanding, you might be tempted to ignore God's leading. You might decide it would be better to leave telling others the Good News about Jesus and praying for sick people to those more experienced than you.

But if you're confident in God's ability in you and realize you can look to Him for wisdom, you won't be afraid to acknowledge the promptings of His Spirit. You'll be bold enough to respond and say, "Lord, exactly how should I go about sharing the gospel with that person? Fill my mouth with words from heaven." Or, "How do I anoint someone with oil? What scriptures shall I use? Give me wisdom. Here I go!"

Always remember, whether we're conquering big challenges or small, the Lord never expects us to carry out His plans in our own strength. He will empower us as we obey, and show us what to do if we'll just ask Him. So, when you get an assignment from Him that is beyond what you can do, or you are uncertain about how to proceed in some area of your life, take time to wait upon Him. Find out what He has to say to you about the matter. Turn your ear to Him until you can hear Him tell you what to do. Pray about it. Listen for direction. Read His Word until you know you've received His instructions. Depend on 1 John 4:4 that says: "You are of God, little children, and have overcome them, because He who is in you is greater than he who is in the world."

Sometimes that knowing will come quickly like it did the morning the Lord spoke to me about teaching healing. I asked Him about it in prayer and, that very day, I heard His instructions in my heart. He didn't speak to me through a burning bush or write a message to me in the sky. He just gave me an inward impression, and I instantly knew what I was supposed to do.

That's just the way it is for me at times. I'll have a thought about a certain thing and know right away that thought is from the Lord. It's His answer to the situation I'm facing. You could describe it as a *knowing*. You just *know*.

At other times, however, I don't get the answer that quickly or with that kind of certainty. So I just keep seeking the Lord about it because I know, without a doubt, He will eventually give me all the wisdom I need to do His will—if I just go after it in faith and refuse to give up. Remember James 1:5–8: "If any of you lacks wisdom, let him ask of God, who gives to all liberally and without reproach, and it will be given to him. But let him ask in faith, with no doubting, for he who doubts is like a wave of the sea driven and tossed by the wind. For let not that man suppose that he will receive anything from the Lord; he is a double-minded man, unstable in all his ways."

God has promised to give wisdom to anyone who asks for it. All He requires is that we ask in faith, believing He will give it to us. That's not hard to do once you realize God isn't trying to hide His wisdom from us. On the contrary, His wisdom seeks us even before we seek it. It is actually out in the streets trying to track us down. As we've already seen in Proverbs 8:

> Does not skillful and godly Wisdom cry out, and un-
> derstanding raise her voice [in contrast to the loose
> woman]? On the top of the heights beside the way,
> where the paths meet, stands Wisdom [skillful and
> godly]; at the gates at the entrance of the town, at the
> coming in at the doors, she cries out: To you, O men,
> I call, and my voice is directed to the sons of men. O
> you simple and thoughtless ones, understand pru-
> dence; you [self-confident] fools, be of an understand-
> ing heart. Hear, for I will speak excellent and princely
> things; and the opening of my lips shall be for right
> things (Proverbs 8:1–6, AMP).

I'm especially happy that wisdom is crying out in the place "where the paths meet" because that's the place where a decision must be made. That's where we must choose to go one way or another. If we love the Lord, we earnestly want to take the path He wants us to take. We want to find the path that leads to God's Master Plan. But which one is it? This one . . . or that one?

What a relief it is to know God's wisdom is waiting for us in that place, ready to show us what to do!

Actually, it's not just waiting there. According to those verses, it's crying out. Aren't you glad wisdom isn't hiding, trying to keep us from finding it? It's trying to get our attention. The Spirit of the Lord is continually speaking to us, endeavoring to turn our hearts and minds in the direction He wants us to go.

That's why in some situations a thought will repeatedly come to you about something you should do. Even if you ignore it or shrug it off, it keeps tugging at you. After a while, you'll ask, "Is that You, Lord? Or is that just me?" Many times, you'll discover the thought was indeed the leading of the Lord. It was God's wisdom crying out to you, trying to instruct you, trying to get your attention.

So, be watching for thoughts like that. When they come, just keep thinking about them and praying about them until you know they're coming from the Lord. And when you know, act on them.

TWO FEARS TO LEAVE BEHIND

Proverbs 8 also gives us another key to discerning the direction of the Lord when it says:

> I, Wisdom [from God], make prudence my dwelling, and I find out knowledge and discretion. . . . I love those who love me, and those who seek me early and diligently shall find me. Riches and honor are with me, enduring wealth and righteousness (uprightness in every area and relation, and right standing with God). My fruit is better than gold, yes, than refined gold, and my increase than choice silver. I [Wisdom] walk in the way of righteousness (moral and spiritual rectitude in every area and relation), in the midst of the paths of justice, that I may cause those who love me to inherit [true] riches and that I may fill their treasuries. . . . Now therefore listen to me, O you sons; for blessed (happy, fortunate, to be envied) are those who keep my ways. Hear instruction and be wise, and do not refuse or neglect it. Blessed (happy, fortunate, to be envied) is the man who listens to me, watching daily at my gates, waiting at the posts of my doors. For whoever finds me [Wisdom] finds life and draws forth

and obtains favor from the Lord. But he who misses me or sins against me wrongs and injures himself; all who hate me love and court death (Proverbs 8:12, 17–21, 32–36, AMP).

Notice, in that passage, Wisdom says, "I love those who love me. . . ." As we discussed at length in Chapter 2, some people don't love God's wisdom because they're afraid of it. They think it might force them to do something that would hurt them. They're not sure following God's wisdom is always in their best interests.

Thankfully, I don't have that problem. That's one reason I've consistently been able to find the will and the wisdom of God for my life throughout the years. I simply have no fear of His will. I discovered early on in my Christian life that God is a good God. He always wants to bless me and would never do anything to harm me. I know that from the Scriptures and from personal experience. I've walked with Him for many years and everything He has ever told me to do has turned out to be for my good. Even if those things seemed difficult initially, they always brought blessing to me in the end.

I love that wisdom, because I know that acting on it will always bring good into my life. I'm looking and listening for it all the time. I constantly have my spiritual eyes and ears open so I can pick up on every instruction He gives me. It's easy for me to be diligent about seeking God's wisdom because I realize the more I find, the more of His blessings I'll enjoy.

The same will be true for you. So determine right now (if you haven't already) that you will always trust the goodness of God. Make a quality decision never to be afraid of His will. Leaving that one fear behind will take you a long way in your quest to find the wisdom of God.

There's another fear you must leave behind as well. It's the fear that you will be unable to hear the voice of the Lord or discern His leading. That fear will stop you from asking in faith for God's wisdom. It will make you like the doubting man we read about in James 1:6 who wavers back and forth like a wave in the sea. One moment you'll think you've heard from God, the next minute you'll be afraid you haven't.

"But, Gloria," you might say, "I've made mistakes in the past. I thought I heard from God . . . and it turned out I hadn't. So I have good reason to be afraid. What if I miss it again?"

So what if you do? God is merciful. He'll help you fix things and get back on track. We all miss it and make mistakes at times. But we can still boldly believe we have the ability to discern the leading of the Lord because we don't base our faith on our own experiences, but on what the Bible says. And the Bible clearly says we can do it.

- In John 10:14 and 27, Jesus said, "I am the good shepherd; and I know My sheep, and am known by My own. . . . My sheep hear My voice, and I know them, and they follow Me."

- In John 14:26, He said, "The Helper, the Holy Spirit, whom the Father will send in My name, He will teach you all things, and bring to your remembrance all things that I said to you."

- In John 16:13–14, He said, "When He, the Spirit of truth, has come, He will guide you into all truth; for He will not speak on His own authority, but whatever He hears He will speak; and He will tell you things to come. He will glorify Me, for He will take of what is Mine and declare it to you."

- Romans 8:14 says, "For as many as are led by the Spirit of God, these are sons of God."

- Hebrews 8:10–11 says, "For this is the covenant that I will make with the house of Israel after those days, says the Lord: I will put My laws in their mind and write them on their hearts; and I will be their God, and they shall be My people. None of them shall teach his neighbor, and none his brother, saying, 'Know the Lord,' for all shall know Me, from the least of them to the greatest of them."

Sure, you may have missed it a few times. No doubt, there have been occasions when you asked God a question and had difficulty hearing His answer. But that doesn't change the Word of God. It still says you have all the spiritual equipment necessary to perceive the wisdom of God and follow the leading of the Holy Spirit. You may not yet know how to use that equipment perfectly (that's OK, none of the rest of us do, either), but just keep practicing and your spiritual skills will improve. We are all in the process of growing up spiritually.

You'll learn to tune into the voice of God while tuning out the static of your own thoughts and the interference of the devil. You'll develop the ability to pick up the signals God is sending to your spirit more and more clearly. You'll learn to let peace be your umpire (Colossians 3:15, AMP). When you do, you'll see for yourself what God says is true. You'll realize even when those signals seemed vague in your heart, you were actually picking them up all along.

DIVINE DISCONNECTIONS

How do you keep from missing those signals? How do you make sure you don't unwittingly disobey the leading of the Holy Spirit simply because you were insensitive to His still, small voice?

First, you must purposely disconnect from sinful attitudes and actions that would harden your heart and make you insensitive to Him. You may even have to disconnect from old, familiar situations that, although they may not be intrinsically bad, must be left behind for you to fulfill the will of God. Friends, for example, who are headed in the opposite direction from living a Godly life. Or the old crowd you used to hang with. It could be dropping habits that used to be a way of life.

The Bible talks a lot about such divine disconnections. It is full of people who had to disconnect from something before they could even begin to step into the fullness God's Master Plan for their lives.

Abraham, for instance, was an Old Testament saint who set such a fine example of faith that the New Testament calls him the father of all of us who believe (Romans 4:16). Abraham truly connected with God's plan for his life. But before he could make that connection, he had to leave his homeland, his family, and his father's house (Genesis 12:1–2). He had to disconnect from his native land of Ur because it was a totally heathen place. The people there worshiped the moon. They knew nothing about the great God, Jehovah, who spoke to Abraham.

Abraham could have refused to leave his homeland. He could have said, "You know, Lord, I'm really attached to this place. It's my home. All my relatives are here. I'd like for You just to bless me right where I am." He could have stayed in his comfort zone. But had he done that, he never would have connected with God's Master Plan.

As I heard one minister say recently, "The blessing of God comes to you when you're in your place. If you're not in your place, you're out of God's grace. You will fall on your face. You won't finish your race."

Thankfully, Abraham got in his place. He disconnected from his old life and connected with the new life God had for him. In the short run, leaving Ur might have been difficult. But in the long run, I'm sure Abraham was glad he did it because he ended up living a long and fruitful life. The Bible describes the end of his life: "Now Abraham was old, well advanced in years, and the Lord had blessed Abraham in all things. . . . Then Abraham's spirit was released, and he died at a good (ample, full) old age, an old man, satisfied and satiated, and was gathered to his people" (Genesis 24:1, 25:8, AMP).

Abraham wasn't the only hero of faith who had to disconnect from his homeland. Moses had to do the same thing. He had to leave Egypt and the house of Pharaoh, where he was raised, before he could fulfill God's plan for him. He tried to step into his role as deliverer of the Hebrew people while he was still connected to Egypt, but it didn't work. Moses had to leave that worldly, godless, sinful environment first. He had to disconnect from his past before he could connect to his future. And he had to do it by faith. Hebrews 11:24–27 says:

> By faith Moses, when he became of age, refused to be called the son of Pharaoh's daughter, choosing rather to suffer affliction with the people of God than to enjoy the passing pleasures of sin, esteeming the reproach of Christ greater riches than the treasures in Egypt; for he looked to the reward. By faith he forsook Egypt, not fearing the wrath of the king; for he endured as seeing Him who is invisible.

Even Jesus had to leave His homeland of heaven to fulfill the plan of God. He had to leave the glory and power He originally had at the right hand of the Father to come to earth and take upon Himself flesh. He became a man, subject to the human condition, to obey His Father and fulfill His will.

The Apostle Paul had to leave his lifelong religion and his position of honor as a Pharisee, to follow Jesus and connect with God's Master Plan for his life. Writing to the Philippians about that divine disconnection, Paul gives us a sense of just how much he had to leave behind when he says:

> "[I was] circumcised the eighth day, of the stock of Israel, of the tribe of Benjamin, an Hebrew of the Hebrews; as touching the law, a Pharisee; concerning zeal, persecuting the church; touching the righteousness which is in the law, blameless. But what things were gain to me, those I counted loss for Christ. Yea doubtless, and I count all things but loss for the excellency of the knowledge of Christ Jesus my Lord: for whom I have suffered the loss of all things, and do count them but dung, that I may win Christ, and be found in him, not having mine own righteousness, which is of the law, but that which is through the faith of Christ, the righteousness which is of God by faith: That I may know him, and the power of his resurrection, and the fellowship of his sufferings, being made conformable unto his death; if by any means I might attain unto the resurrection of the dead. Not as though I had already attained, either were already perfect: but I follow after, if that I may apprehend that for which also I am apprehended of Christ Jesus. Brethren, I count not myself to have apprehended: but this one thing I do, forgetting those things which are behind, and reaching forth unto

those things which are before, I press toward the mark for the prize of the high calling of God in Christ Jesus" (Philippians 3:5–14, KJV).

If we're going to successfully connect with God's Master Plan for our lives, we must do the same thing Paul did. As we get specific direction from God, we must forget those things that are behind. We must disconnect from the devil's plan, from our own plan, and from the past if necessary, to obey the promptings of His Spirit in our spirit.

One sure place to start is to obey God's written Word. We must stop doing those things we know aren't right. We must permanently disconnect from sin. Sin (disobedience) prevents us from receiving God's blessings. It becomes a barrier that separates us from His goodness. Israel proved that again and again. They continued sinning even when the Lord spoke to them through prophets like Isaiah and Hosea, saying:

> "Behold, the Lord's hand is not shortened, that it cannot save; neither his ear heavy, that it cannot hear: But your iniquities have separated between you and your God, and your sins have hid his face from you, that he will not hear" (Isaiah 59:1–2, KJV).

> "When I would have healed Israel, then the iniquity of Ephraim was uncovered, and the wickedness of Samaria. For they have committed fraud; a thief comes in; a band of robbers takes spoil outside. They do not consider in their hearts that I remember all their wickedness; now their own deeds have surrounded them; they are before My face" (Hosea 7:1–2).

Because they refused to disconnect from sin, the Israelites failed to connect with the Master Plan. They missed out on the blessings God had for them. How do we keep from following in their footsteps? We must stop looking at, listening to, and doing the things we know aren't pleasing to God. We must put all known disobedience out of our lives and stop the sin.

"Well, I don't know if I can do that," someone might say. "After all, we live in a sinful world. It's just normal for us to have some sin in our lives."

Sin shouldn't be normal for Christians. We've been delivered from sin and darkness. We don't have any business partaking of it anymore. We shouldn't be joining in with those who are lost in their sin. As the New Testament says:

> What fellowship hath righteousness with unrighteousness? and what communion hath light with darkness? and what concord hath Christ with Belial? or what part hath he that believeth with an infidel? and what agreement hath the temple of God with idols? for ye are the temple of the living God; as God hath said, I will dwell in them, and walk in them; and I will be their God, and they shall be my people. Wherefore come out from among them, and be ye separate, saith the Lord, and touch not the unclean thing; and I will receive you, and will be a Father unto you, and ye shall be my sons and daughters, saith the Lord Almighty. Having therefore these promises, dearly beloved, let us cleanse ourselves from all filthiness of the flesh and spirit, perfecting holiness in the fear of God (2 Corinthians 6:14–18, 7:1, KJV).

The Bible makes it absolutely clear that, as believers, we are to "reverently fear and worship the Lord and turn [entirely] away from evil" (Proverbs 3:7, AMP). We're not just to turn partially away from evil. The Wisdom of God says we're to turn entirely away. Don't let your eyes look at some ungodly, lust-provoking image just because it's on network television. The fact that millions of other people are watching it doesn't make it right. When junk like that comes on, change the channel. Turn it off. Turn entirely away from it.

If you want to be spiritually sharp and able to hear the voice of the Lord, make every change you can find for good. Don't wait for God to thunder His instructions at you from heaven. Don't expect Him to grab the remote control out of your hand and change the channel for you. Ask Him to show you what pleases Him and what doesn't. Be like the psalmist who prayed, "Search me [thoroughly], O God, and know my heart! Try me and know my thoughts! And see if there is any wicked or hurtful way in me, and lead me in the way everlasting" (Psalm 139:23–24, AMP).

That's a good prayer to pray. It's wise to go to the Lord and say, "Heavenly Father, point out anything in me that offends You and lead me along Your shining path."

I assure you, if you sincerely ask Him to do that for you, He'll do it. He'll convict your heart about the things that are displeasing to Him. When He does, repent quickly and change. Don't make excuses for your behavior or try to cover over your sin. Be humble. Admit you were wrong. If you're ever tempted to do otherwise, remember Proverbs says:

> He that covereth his sins shall not prosper: but whoso confesseth and forsaketh them shall have mercy. Happy is the man that feareth always: but he that

hardeneth his heart shall fall into mischief. . . . Whoso
walketh uprightly shall be saved: but he that is per-
verse in his ways shall fall at once. . . . He, that being
often reproved hardeneth his neck, shall suddenly be
destroyed, and that without remedy (Proverbs 28:13–
14, 18, 29:1, KJV).

The second way to tune in to the leading of the Holy Spirit is to
ask God what He wants you to do. When He tells you, obey Him
every way you know how. Cultivate the habit of obedience until it
becomes the norm for you.

Of course, one thing you know God is speaking to you about is
obeying His written Word. That alone will take you a long way toward finding and fulfilling your Master Plan. Even when you aren't
hearing any specific directives about the details of your life, you can
stay busy doing the works of Jesus. Acts 10:38 tells us that He spent
His life going about "doing good and healing all who were oppressed
by the devil, for God was with Him." And since Hebrews 13:8 says
that "Jesus Christ is the same yesterday, today, and forever," we can
be sure He wants us, as His disciples, to be going about doing good,
today.

Remember that the next time you're at a loss about what to do
and don't feel you have any definite leading from God. Instead of
sitting around doing nothing, get up and act on the written Word.
Do something good for someone. Act like Jesus. Determine to spend
your day demonstrating to those around you the loving kindness of
your heavenly Father. Do what the Bible says to do:

Become useful and helpful and kind to one another,
tenderhearted (compassionate, understanding, loving-
hearted), forgiving one another [readily and freely], as

God in Christ forgave you. . . . Be imitators of God [copy Him and follow His example], as well-beloved children [imitate their father]. And walk in love, [esteeming and delighting in one another] as Christ loved us and gave Himself up for us, a slain offering and sacrifice to God [for you, so that it became] a sweet fragrance (Ephesians 4:32–5:2, AMP).

If you'll obey the written Word and do what it says, then you'll be able to hear the individual directions God has for your life. Because you'll be accustomed to listening to His written Word and obeying it, you'll easily recognize the voice of His Spirit and obey it. If you don't read the Word and you don't make the corrections and changes it tells you to make, however, you won't listen to His voice inside you telling you what to do, either. So, practice, practice, practice being attentive and obedient to God's Word.

WINNING THE INNER TUG OF WAR

Although growing in your ability to discern God's voice does take time, one thing you can do to develop that ability more quickly is to pray in other tongues—pray in the Spirit.[9] That kind of praying builds you up spiritually (Jude 20). It sharpens your inner man so you can more easily grasp what God is saying to you.

It also helps you distinguish the leading of your spirit from the pressure of your soul and your body. As a believer, you must learn to do this because you are a three-part being. You are a spirit. You have

---

9. When we pray in tongues, our spirit is in direct contact with God. Pray the Prayer for Salvation and Baptism in the Holy Spirit (see Appendix A). Confess your sin, profess your faith in Jesus Christ as Savior and Lord, and invite the Holy Spirit in.

a soul. And, you live in a body. Your spirit, or inner man, is born again. It is perfectly righteous and in total agreement with the will and plan of God. When the Holy Spirit speaks to your spirit (which is how He usually communicates with you), your spirit immediately says, "Yes!" It is always ready and willing to obey.

Your soul is made up of your mind, will, and emotions. Emotions can be up one minute . . . and down the next. They're often caught in the midst of an internal tug of war, the struggle between your soul and your spirit. "For the flesh lusts against the Spirit, and the Spirit against the flesh; and these are contrary to one another . . ." (Galatians 5:17).

When your emotions are ruled by your spirit, they can be a blessing. When they're under the influence of the love of God, for example, which flows from your inner man, your emotions become a very powerful, constructive force. They can cause you to reach out in compassion to someone who is hurting. They can motivate you to give sacrificially to meet another's need.

Joy is another powerful spiritual force that brings forth positive emotions. It can energize your own soul and body, and lift up other people's hearts as well. Doctors have found joy releases chemicals that build up our immune system. Joy is actually good for our health.

However, when our souls (mind, will, and emotions) are being ruled by natural thinking, they can wreak all kinds of havoc. If we allow it, our natural thinking will goad us into getting angry at someone and we'll start feeling emotions like bitterness, envy, and strife. They will push us into negative thinking and we'll end up with feelings of depression and anxiety—feelings that will actually destroy our health. What's more, those negative thoughts, attitudes, and emotions will cloud our ability to hear from God. They'll compete with the voice of our spirits. If we let them dominate, they will pressure us and push us right out of the will of God.

Therefore, to successfully live out God's Master Plan for our lives, we must learn to live according to our born-again spirits. We must renew our souls with God's Word and allow our spirits to become the dominant force in our lives. If we'll do that, we'll be able to walk in the spirit and not fulfill the lusts of the flesh. Galatians 5:16–18 says, "But I say, walk and live [habitually] in the [Holy] Spirit [responsive to and controlled and guided by the Spirit]; then you will certainly not gratify the cravings and desires of the flesh (of human nature without God). For the desires of the flesh are opposed to the [Holy] Spirit, and the [desires of the] Spirit are opposed to the flesh (godless human nature); for these are antagonistic to each other [continually withstanding and in conflict with each other], so that you are not free but are prevented from doing what you desire to do. But if you are guided (led) by the [Holy] Spirit, you are not subject to the Law" (AMP).

Praying in the Spirit is so important. It strengthens your spirit and stirs you up. In addition, when you pray in the Spirit, you're praying beyond what you know in the natural. You're praying out the perfect will of God for your life as the Holy Spirit gives you utterance. Even though you don't understand the words you are saying, you'll always reap great benefits from that kind of prayer. The New Testament assures us of that. It says:

> Likewise the Spirit also helps in our weaknesses. For we do not know what we should pray for as we ought, but the Spirit Himself makes intercession for us with groanings which cannot be uttered. Now He who searches the hearts knows what the mind of the Spirit

is, because He makes intercession for the saints according to the will of God (Romans 8:26–27).

> For he who speaks in a tongue does not speak to men but to God, for no one understands him; however, in the spirit he speaks mysteries. . . . He who speaks in a tongue edifies himself, but he who prophesies edifies the church (1 Corinthians 14:2, 4).

Because Satan knows the power of this kind of praying, he'll try his best to discourage you from doing it. He'll tell you you're wasting your time. "You don't even know what you're saying!" he'll argue.

When Satan sends those kinds of thoughts into your mind, resist them. It doesn't matter whether or not you know what you're saying. God knows what you're saying, and He says when you pray mysteries in tongues it edifies you—it builds you up. His Holy Spirit is giving you the words. It gives the Holy Spirit opportunity to make intercession for you beyond what you know in the natural.

Then just keep right on praying in other tongues—in the Spirit. I recommend praying that way every day. I've done it for years and it has changed my life. It has been extremely important to me.

WHEN MYSTERIES ARE REVEALED

I don't pray in the Spirit because I'm superspiritual. I pray in the Spirit and obey the promptings of the Spirit because I'm superpractical. I have discovered that it is one of the things that helps me tap in to God's strategies for my life. And when those strategies are revealed, I'm able to move miraculously, just like the Israelites did, into the promised land of God's Master Plan for my life.

Through the years, Ken and I have seen it work over and over. We wouldn't even have the ministry headquarters and property we have today had we not received God's supernatural strategy. With our natural minds, we never could have come up with the plan God gave us for acquiring that property. In fact, had we been depending on human reasoning all those years ago when the Lord first put it in our hearts to buy it, we'd have disregarded the whole idea.

As I recall, it was sometime in 1973 when the Lord first told Ken He wanted us to have the land on Eagle Mountain Lake that our ministry owns today. Ken was flying over the property when the Holy Spirit spoke clearly to his heart, telling him that property was to be ours. On the one hand, that was great news because the place had marvelous potential. It had once been a U.S. Navy base, so it already had a big runway on it. Since Ken loves anything to do with airplanes, that appealed to him. There were also a few old buildings on it that could still be used. And, there was plenty of space to work with—more than fifteen hundred acres, with two miles of it stretching around the shoreline of Eagle Mountain Lake.

On the other hand, with the ministry finances at the time, it seemed impossible. We didn't have anywhere close to the amount needed to buy that kind of real estate. But we knew if it were God's plan for us to have it, He had a way to get it to us. So we began believing for it . . . and we kept believing for ten years.

After ten years, we still didn't have the land, but the Lord began to give Ken a strategy. He led him to go talk to the man who owned it—an elderly bachelor millionaire—and tell him, "The Lord has need of that property." (That's the only time I know of when the Lord led Ken to say that to anyone.)

The first time he met with the man, Ken told him exactly what the Lord had said. The man responded, "Well, it's for sale."

Ken replied, "I don't have the money, but the Lord will get it to me." The man sat for a long time without speaking. Finally, he looked at Ken and said, "You come back and see me."

When Ken went back later, the man had a plan that enabled us to acquire the property with no money down and no debt. First, he rented the land and the buildings to us for a certain amount each month. He said, "I am dividing the property into four equal parts. When the Lord provides the money for a quarter, I will deed it to you. One hundred percent of your rent payments will go toward the purchase of the fourth quarter."

But that wasn't all. After Ken signed the contract, the owner told him about a gravel company that wanted to buy the gravel on the property. "Well, I suppose we'll have to wait until we own the property before we can sell the gravel," Ken said.

"No, you can sell it now," the man answered. "I have given you all the mineral rights."

We sold about a million dollars' worth of gravel—just about enough to pay for the first quarter. Then we began paying for the next quarter. It took a while, but there came a day when the entire property was paid for. We'd bought it a piece at a time without ever having to borrow money.

Aren't God's strategies amazing? When He first told us the property was ours, we were hard-pressed to buy anything, but we knew how to believe God, and all things are possible to him who believes. So we just kept believing God was able and we didn't quit until His plan was revealed. We stood on the Word for almost ten years, not knowing exactly how He planned to bring it to pass. It was a mystery to us. But that was okay because we knew how to pray about those mysteries. And we found that if we kept believing, praying, and obeying the promptings of the Spirit, that mystery would eventually unfold.

God has the same kind of mysteries hidden for you. He has amazing things planned for your future. Your ministry headquarters, your business ventures, your job opportunities, your personal homes—whatever you need to finish His Master Plan for you—has already been prepared. As far as heaven is concerned, it's a done deal.

So determine right now to make praying in the Spirit and with your understanding a regular part of your life. Tune your spiritual ears to the voice of the Lord and believe for His supernatural strategies. God has some mysteries He wants to reveal to *you!*

KEY SIX

—✕✕—

*Persevere in faith, knowing that God
can work beyond your natural abilities and
equip you to do the impossible.*

Nine

STAYING CONNECTED, STEP BY STEP

—⧑—

Although God will reveal mysteries to you as you pray and seek Him for direction, don't expect Him to give you a complete set of blueprints for your life all at one time. I'm not sure He ever does that. He'll usually just reveal your next step. Often, He may not even explain to you why that step is important, or what's going to happen after you take it—or what will happen if you don't.

That's why we must learn to walk by faith and not by sight. We don't know what's coming tomorrow, next month, or next year. But, God does. So we have to fully trust Him and confidently obey His instructions in big matters and small, following the leading of His Spirit, even when we don't understand it. One thing of major importance is to know that whatever He directs will always agree with the written Word. This helps so much to keep us from going in the wrong direction or from being misled.

This kind of step-by-step obedience will keep us constantly connected to the Master Plan. Failure to obey, on the other hand, will disconnect us. Sometimes what even seem to be minor acts of disobedience can result in making major, long-term differences in our lives.

If you doubt that, consider Moses. Psalm 106 says that when the Israelites angered the Lord at the waters of Meribah, "it went ill with Moses for their sakes; for they provoked [Moses'] spirit, so that he spoke unadvisedly with his lips" (verses 32–33, AMP).

One disobedient act brought great disappointment to Moses' life. He missed part of his destiny because, under tremendous pressure, he lost his temper and disobeyed the instructions of the Lord.

If you read the scriptural account of what happened, it's easy to see why he did it. At the time, he was leading the Israelites through the wilderness. They were in desperate need of water, and there was none to be found. As the people cried out, blaming Moses and Aaron, for their predicament, Moses surely must have flashed back to an earlier time when the same thing happened.

On that first occasion, Moses had cried to the Lord and said, "What shall I do with this people? They are almost ready to stone me."

> And the Lord said to Moses, Pass on before the people, and take with you some of the elders of Israel; and take in your hand the rod with which you smote the river [Nile], and go. Behold, I will stand before you there on the rock at [Mount] Horeb; and you shall strike the rock, and water shall come out of it, that the people may drink. And Moses did so in the sight of the elders of Israel (Exodus 17:5–6, AMP).

No doubt, the second time they ran out of water, Moses was remembering that initial incident. He was probably expecting God to instruct him, once again, to strike the rock. Perhaps he was even looking forward to venting some of his frustration by giving that rock a good hard whack with his rod. His anger was surely beginning to boil as the Israelites, for whom he had laid down a good portion of his life, gathered together once again and contended with him and Aaron, saying:

> "Why have you brought up the assembly of the LORD into this wilderness, that we and our animals should die here? And why have you made us come up out of Egypt, to bring us to this evil place? It *is* not a place of grain or figs or vines or pomegranates; nor *is* there any water to drink" (Numbers 20:4–5).

The last time, when Moses had struck a rock at God's command, enough water had gushed out of it to meet the need of the entire nation. This time, however, when Moses cried out for instructions, God said something a little different:

> "Take the rod; you and your brother Aaron gather the congregation together. Speak to the rock before their eyes, and it will yield its water; thus you shall bring water for them out of the rock, and give drink to the congregation and their animals" (Numbers 20:8).

Although God altered the strategy slightly in this case, His directions were still clear and simple. Moses should have had no trouble following them.

But there was one problem. Moses was angry. He probably wasn't paying close attention. He had run out of patience with this unruly bunch of people. He was tired of being blamed for everything that went wrong and tired of all their bellyaching and unbelief. So he gathered the assembly together and said,

> "Hear now, you rebels! Must we bring water for you out of this rock?" Then Moses lifted his hand and struck the rock twice with his rod; and water came out abundantly, and the congregation and their animals drank (Numbers 20:10–11).

If the story stopped there, it would appear that everything turned out all right. Even though Moses disobeyed God's instructions and struck the rock twice instead of speaking to it, water still came forth and the Israelites were satisfied. But the account doesn't end there. The next verse tells us the Lord spoke to Moses and said,

> "Because you did not believe Me, to hallow Me in the eyes of the children of Israel, therefore you shall not bring this assembly into the land which I have given them" (Numbers 20:12).

It's important for us to notice that God didn't say anything to Moses about that when He first told him what to do. He didn't say, "Now Moses, I want you to speak to the rock, and you'd better do it because if you don't, you'll miss your final destination. You'll never get to go into the Promised Land."

I don't think Moses had any idea how much of his future rested on that one simple step of obedience. He probably wasn't even thinking about what might happen if he ignored the leading of the Lord in that situation. Most likely, he was just thinking about how fed up he was with that rebellious group of people he'd been stuck with for so many years. Maybe he had the same attitude Christians sometimes have today: "I'll just yield to my flesh now and repent later. This one little sin won't make much difference in the long run."

But it did make a difference—not only to Moses but to his brother, Aaron, as well. It disconnected both of them from a part of God's Master Plan. Aaron was the first to experience the consequences. Shortly after the incident at Meribah:

> And the LORD spoke to Moses and Aaron in Mount Hor by the border of the land of Edom, saying: "Aaron shall be gathered to his people, for he shall not enter the land which I have given to the children of Israel, because you rebelled against My word at the water of Meribah. Take Aaron and Eleazar his son, and bring them up to Mount Hor; and strip Aaron of his garments and put them on Eleazar his son; for Aaron shall be gathered *to his people* and die there." So Moses did just as the LORD commanded, and they went up to Mount Hor in the sight of all the congregation. Moses stripped Aaron of his garments and put them on Eleazar his son; and Aaron died there on the top of the mountain. Then Moses and Eleazar came down from the mountain. Now when all the congregation saw that Aaron was dead, all the house of Israel mourned for Aaron thirty days. (Numbers 20:23–29).

Moses lived on a while longer, but eventually, he too experienced the cost of his own disobedience. When the Israelites' forty-year wilderness trek was over and they were about to enter the Promised

Land, Moses died. He didn't die of disease. He didn't even die of old age. The Bible clearly tells us his eyes were not dim and his natural strength was not diminished (Deuteronomy 34:7). At 120 years old, he still climbed to the top of Mount Nebo. His eyes were still sharp enough to look across the Jordan River and see the land of Canaan. But instead of letting him go into that land, the Lord said to him:

> Get up into this mountain of the Abarim, Mount Nebo, which is in the land of Moab, opposite Jericho, and look at the land of Canaan which I give to the Israelites for a possession. And die on the mountain which you ascend and be gathered to your people, as Aaron your brother died on Mount Hor and was gathered to his people, because you broke faith with Me in the midst of the Israelites at the waters of Meribah-kadesh in the Wilderness of Zin and because you did not set Me apart as holy in the midst of the Israelites. For you shall see the land opposite you at a distance, but you shall not go there, into the land which I give the Israelites. . . . So Moses the servant of the Lord died there in the land of Moab, according to the word of the Lord (Deuteronomy 32:49–52, 34:5, AMP).

There's no question about it, that's a sobering story. It demonstrates just how serious disobedience can be. There is a bright side to it, however. I realized that one day when I was feeling sorry for Moses and thinking how awful it was that he went through that whole wilderness experience, put up with all the aggravations of it year after year, and then didn't get to complete the journey into the Promised Land.

As I thought about how he died on Mount Nebo, and how God personally buried him, it dawned on me: *Since Moses was a saint of*

God, when he died he went to Paradise! He went to the real Promised Land! He bypassed all the fighting and wars that were required to take possession of Canaan, and went straight to the reward. So I never feel sorry for Moses anymore.

But the fact remains that Moses cost himself a major victory on the earth because he yielded to the wrong impulse. He yielded to the pressure of his emotions instead of the direction of God. He didn't do exactly what the Lord told him to do, and his disobedience was an expensive mistake.

This is a good opportunity to point out the great advantage of having the written Word available whenever we need it. Moses didn't have these scriptures to help him avoid the anger pitfall. I am so grateful we have written instructions such as:

> Good sense makes a man restrain his anger, and it is his glory to overlook a transgression or an offense (Proverbs 19:11, AMP).

> Let all bitterness and indignation and wrath (passion, rage, bad temper) and resentment (anger, animosity) and quarreling (brawling, clamor, contention) and slander (evil-speaking, abusive or blasphemous language) be banished from you, with all malice (spite, ill will, or baseness of any kind). And become useful and helpful and kind to one another, tenderhearted (compassionate, understanding, loving-hearted), forgiving one another [readily and freely], as God in Christ forgave you (Ephesians 4:31–32, AMP).

> But now put away and rid yourselves [completely] of all these things: anger, rage, bad feeling toward others,

curses and slander, and foulmouthed abuse and shame-
ful utterances from your lips! (Colossians 3:8, AMP).

LITTLE PROMPTINGS CAN OPEN BIG DOORS

Of course, Moses' experience was more dramatic than most of
our experiences will be. None of us carries the kind of responsibility
he did, so when we miss the mark the results aren't usually quite so
catastrophic. Our opportunities to obey or disobey, connect or disconnect with the plan of God don't normally involve honoring God
(or dishonoring Him) before an entire nation. They more often involve everyday choices that are made when very few people are
watching. But even those choices can cause us to connect or disconnect from God's Master Plan for our lives. They can unexpectedly
cost us dearly, or bring us great rewards.

That's why obedience is always best. You just never know to what
part of God's plan one simple step of obedience might connect you.

Ken and I found that out big-time some years ago when we were
facing one of the many financial challenges we've encountered since
we first stepped out into ministry. In a way, we were in a situation
similar to the one in which Moses found himself. It was not nearly as
serious, of course—just similar. We were badly in need of money to
pay past due bills for our television broadcasts. We'd faced that need
before, and God had been faithful. But this was the most onerous
deficit we had experienced. We began to think about selling our
lakefront property to bring in the extra money.

Although we hadn't been instructed by the Lord to do it, we were
assuming it was the right thing to do. We hadn't signed the papers
on the deal yet, but the plans were drawn up. We were right on the

verge of finalizing the sale when, as I was driving home one evening, I had a very clear impression from the Lord in my spirit. I sensed He was saying, *Don't do it. Don't make that deal. You'll regret it.* It was very strong. I knew it was the Lord.

When I got home, I told Ken about it. "Okay," he said, "we'll call it off."

Remember what we saw earlier in Proverbs 8:2 about wisdom crying out at the place where paths meet? That's exactly what happened to me that day. Ken and I were at a crossroads. We were about to take a particular financial path—one we thought would be a benefit. But Wisdom called out and advised us not to take that path.

We could have ignored that advice. After all, we needed the money from the sale, and didn't seem to need the land right then. What's more, the television bills needed to be paid. We wanted to do something to bring in the funds quickly. We could easily have yielded to that pressure and said, "Well, we'll just go ahead, get the money we need . . . and ask the Lord to forgive us later. After all, He's merciful. He'll understand."

Yes, God would have forgiven us had we truly repented. He would have been good to us and blessed us all He could, but we still would have missed part of His Master Plan for us because the Lord knew several things about the situation we didn't.

First, there was natural gas on that property. In the years since, we've had a number of gas wells drilled and our ministry is being blessed by the royalties from those wells. If we'd done what we originally planned to do, someone else would be getting those royalties.

Second, we were eventually able to build our dream home on part of that land. Had we ignored the leading of the Lord, the lakefront site where our home is today wouldn't have been available. It would have been part of a subdivision full of other people's homes.

Our home has been such a great blessing to us—one of the greatest blessings the Lord has given us. My, what wonderful elements of God's plan we would have missed had we decided to do things our own way in that situation. We would have traded them away for money to meet our immediate needs—needs God had already planned to meet another way.

That's just one of many examples I could give you of how disobeying the leading of the Holy Spirit could have resulted in making a major difference in our lives. I could tell you of other times when such opportunities to connect or disconnect from God's plan were even more subtle than that. Many, I don't even remember because they weren't spectacular. It could take the form of a gentle impression from the Holy Spirit to take a different road home than I usually do, for example, or call a particular person because I just couldn't seem to get them off my mind. I try to continually check my heart for leadings like that because they can be very important. Really, every leading of the Lord is important. Taking that different route home might avoid an accident. Calling that person at just the right moment can make a significant impact on their life.

So many Master Plan connections are like that. They don't seem to be a big deal at the time. Yet if we're diligent to heed those little promptings of the Spirit, they can open big doors into our promised land.

I'm not saying you'll never make mistakes. We all stumble and do things we regret at times. But when you do, repent immediately, receive God's forgiveness and cleansing and get right back on track. Pray for yourself the same prayer the author of Hebrews prayed for those believers:

> Now may the God of peace [Who is the Author and
> the Giver of peace], Who brought again from among

the dead our Lord Jesus, that great Shepherd of the sheep, by the blood [that sealed, ratified] the everlasting agreement (covenant, testament), strengthen (complete, perfect) and make you what you ought to be and equip you with everything good that you may carry out His will; [while He Himself] works in you and accomplishes that which is pleasing in His sight, through Jesus Christ (the Messiah); to Whom be the glory forever and ever (to the ages of the ages). Amen (so be it) (Hebrews 13:20–21, AMP).

Get your heart right before God and keep it right. Otherwise, your conscience will condemn you. You'll lose your confidence toward God and you won't be able to hear His voice as clearly as before. The condemnation you'll feel in your heart will hinder your ability to sense the promptings of His Spirit. You'll start missing Master Plan connections without even realizing it.

TWO SIMPLE COMMANDS

First John 3:18–23 explains it this way:

My little children, let us not love in word or in tongue, but in deed and in truth. And by this we know that we are of the truth, and shall assure our hearts before Him. For if our heart condemns us, God is greater than our heart, and knows all things. Beloved, if our heart does not condemn us, we have confidence toward God. And whatever we ask we receive from Him, because we keep His commandments and do those things that are pleasing in His sight. And this is His commandment: that we should believe on the name of His Son Jesus Christ and love one another, as He gave us commandment.

I love that passage because it boils down obedience to God to its simplest, basic components. It tells us we can please God and keep His commandments if we'll simply:

1. Believe in Jesus, and
2. Walk in love

If we'll develop the habit of obeying those two fundamental instructions God has given in His written Word, we'll have the sensitivity of heart to pick up on what He is saying to us in other areas. If we don't do those two things, we won't get anything else right, either.

If you think about it, it's easy to see why. As we've already seen, it takes faith, first and foremost, to connect with God's Master Plan. And faith is simply believing in Jesus—trusting in who He is, in what He did and in what He says. But as powerful as faith is, it will never work properly unless it is accompanied by love. The Bible leaves no doubt about that. It says plainly that "faith . . . worketh by love" (Galatians 5:6, KJV).

I've learned over the years, that if my faith isn't producing the results it should, I'd better check my love life. How have I been treating people? Nothing is going to work for me spiritually if I'm violating the commandment of love.

Of course, I didn't figure that out all by myself. I learned it from Jesus. Throughout the New Testament, He repeatedly tells us how crucial it is for us to live our lives by that command. He said:

- " 'You shall love the Lord your God with all your heart, with all your soul, with all your mind, and with all your strength.' This is the first commandment. And the second, like it, is this: 'You shall love your neighbor as yourself.' There is no other commandment greater than these" (Mark 12:30–31).
- "A new commandment I give to you, that you love one another; as I have loved you, that you also love one another. By this all will know that you are My disciples, if you have love for one another" (John 13:34–35).
- "As the Father loved Me, I also have loved you; abide in My love" (John 15:9).
- "This is My commandment, that you love one another as I have loved you" (John 15:12).

The best place to practice walking in love is at home. If we can walk in love there, we can do it anywhere because that's often where we face the greatest challenges. It's the place where we get close enough to others for them to rub us the wrong way. It's the place where we are most likely to be unkind, or irritable and harsh.

So, if you want to improve your love life, start at home. The moment you catch yourself speaking or acting in a way that's unloving, make a correction immediately. Apologize and make an adjustment. Continually aim to live according to the description of love given in 1 Corinthians 13, which says:

> Love endures long and is patient and kind; love never is envious nor boils over with jealousy, is not boastful or vainglorious, does not display itself haughtily. It is not conceited (arrogant and inflated with pride); it is not rude (unmannerly) and does not act unbecom-

ingly. Love (God's love in us) does not insist on its own rights or its own way, for it is not self-seeking; it is not touchy or fretful or resentful; it takes no account of the evil done to it [it pays no attention to a suffered wrong]. It does not rejoice at injustice and unrighteousness, but rejoices when right and truth prevail. Love bears up under anything and everything that comes, is ever ready to believe the best of every person, its hopes are fadeless under all circumstances, and it endures everything [without weakening]. Love never fails . . . (1 Corinthians 13:4–8, AMP).

The more you practice obeying God in the fundamentals like walking in love, the easier it will be to hear from Him about the details of His plan for your life. Your heart will be sensitive and ready to respond to the slightest divine leading. You'll be ready and able to discern the voice of Wisdom calling out to you at the place where the paths meet. You'll constantly stay connected to God's Master Plan.

You'll be fulfilling the love commandment and, by this, fulfilling all the commandments.

KEY SEVEN

*Be obedient to turn from sin and
disconnect from all that prevents you
from discerning God's direction.*

Ten

AVOIDING THE FIRE
AND THE SNAKES

—⚈—

I'll always be grateful for the mistakes the Israelites made on their journey to the Promised Land. Those mistakes have saved me untold trouble over the years.

The blunder Moses made when he disobeyed God by striking the rock instead of speaking to it helps remind me to resist the pressures and irritations that would encourage me to be disobedient. The painful price of his disobedience flashes like a neon sign, warning not just me, but all who want to stay connected to God's Master Plan: *Don't go this way!*

Thankfully, the Israelite wilderness is ablaze with such signs. If we pay attention to them, they will help us avoid some major disappointments. That's why the New Testament encourages us to study them as examples. That's why the Apostle Paul wrote to the Corinthian church, saying:

Moreover, brethren, I do not want you to be unaware that all our fathers were under the cloud, all passed through the sea, all were baptized into Moses in the cloud and in the sea, all ate the same spiritual food, and all drank the same spiritual drink. For they drank of that spiritual Rock that followed them, and that Rock was Christ. But with most of them God was not well pleased, for their bodies were scattered in the wilderness. Now these things became our examples, to the intent that we should not lust after evil things as they also lusted. And do not become idolaters as were some of them. As it is written, "The people sat down to eat and drink, and rose up to play." Nor let us commit sexual immorality, as some of them did, and in one day twenty-three thousand fell; nor let us tempt Christ, as some of them also tempted, and were destroyed by serpents; nor complain, as some of them also complained, and were destroyed by the destroyer. Now all these things happened to them as examples, and they were written for our admonition, upon whom the ends of the ages have come (1 Corinthians 10:1–11).

We've already discussed some of the pitfalls mentioned in that passage—pitfalls like lust, immorality, and disobedience. We've talked about the importance of disconnecting from such sinful behaviors. But there's one thing mentioned there that we haven't yet examined. It's the sin the Old Testament refers to as *murmuring*. My definition of *murmur* is to "bellyache, complain, grumble, whine, or gripe." It includes every kind of negative, unbelieving talk.

The Israelites habitually committed that sin—and it cost many their lives.

Today most believers don't even think of complaining as a sin, much less a deadly one. They just accept it as a way of life. Without giving it a second thought, they complain about the economy. They complain about the weather. They complain about the aches and pains in their bodies. They complain about their children, their jobs, or their pastors. They even gripe about God.

"Oh, no," you might say, "surely no good Christian would gripe about God."

Yes, they would. In fact, at one time or another we've all done it. We've said things like, "I just don't know why I'm in financial trouble. I've done the best I can and prayed for God to help me." (Translation: *My lack of money is God's fault. I've done everything right but He hasn't done His part.*) Or, "I know I'm called to do such and such . . . but I'm frustrated because God just hasn't opened any doors of opportunity for me!" (Translation: *God is not helping me like He should. It's not my fault!*)

That kind of talk will disconnect us from the Master Plan fast. According to the verses above, it will open the door for us to be "destroyed by the destroyer" (like the Israelites were) in some area of our lives. Because we live in the age of God's mercy and grace, that destruction isn't as immediate and drastic as it was in Old Testament times. But we want to avoid it nonetheless. So let's take a look at what happened to the Israelites when they complained. Let's see exactly what the neon sign they left in the wilderness says.

TESTING GOD'S PATIENCE

It's easy to find examples of the Israelites' wilderness complaints because there are plenty of them. It seems they grumbled at every opportunity. Even before they left Egypt, when Pharaoh's army was bearing down on them at the Red Sea, they got mad at Moses and began complaining about what a lousy deliverer he was. They said:

> "Because there were no graves in Egypt, have you taken us away to die in the wilderness? Why have you so dealt with us, to bring us up out of Egypt? Is this not the word that we told you in Egypt, saying, 'Let us alone that we may serve the Egyptians?' For it would have been better for us to serve the Egyptians than that we should die in the wilderness" (Exodus 14:11–12).

Think of it. These people had just seen God bring the most powerful nation in the world to its knees by sending ten plagues. They'd seen Moses prophesy and God move again and again in response to his words. What's more, they'd experienced God's protection through it all. When hail fell and killed all the Egyptian crops, the land of Goshen, where the Israelites lived, was protected. When thick darkness covered the land of Egypt, there was light in the land of Goshen. When the firstborn of the Egyptians died, the Israelites were protected by the blood of the Passover lamb.

No people in history had ever witnessed the power and faithfulness of God more fully than they had. Yet when things started looking bad for them at the Red Sea, they didn't call out to God for help or express their confidence in Him. They just complained about their terrible situation.

How did God respond?

With mercy. He demonstrated His faithfulness and power by dividing the sea under Moses' rod and taking the people safely to the other side. He gave them one more reason to trust Him.

But, even so, three days later the Israelites were at it again. When they found themselves in the wilderness with no water, "the people complained against Moses, saying, 'What shall we drink?'" (Exodus 15:24).

Again, God was merciful. He provided water and gave them yet another example of His faithfulness.

Still, the Israelites kept complaining. When they became hungry . . .

> The whole congregation of the children of Israel complained against Moses and Aaron in the wilderness. And the children of Israel said to them, "Oh, that we had died by the hand of the Lord in the land of Egypt, when we sat by the pots of meat and when we ate bread to the full! For you have brought us out into this wilderness to kill this whole assembly with hunger" (Exodus 16:2–3).

Again, God patiently overlooked their faithless, negative attitude and provided manna for them to eat. Day after day, He faithfully rained heavenly bread down from the sky. All was well for a while. But then they began to lust after the food they ate in Egypt and the complaints began again.

As they traveled through the wilderness, the children of Israel, like all children, kept pushing the limits of God's patience. No matter how well He took care of them or how much He blessed them, they continued to find reasons to murmur and complain.

We might be astonished at their ingratitude if it weren't for the fact that we've all had that attitude on occasion. We've all focused on the one aspect of our lives we didn't like and griped about it, rather than focusing on the myriad of blessings we enjoy and being thankful for them.

It's a good thing for us God is patient and kind and that we live in the New Testament day of grace. Otherwise, our griping might draw the same response from God the Israelites' finally did.

> Now when the people complained, it displeased the Lord; for the Lord heard it, and His anger was aroused. So the fire of the Lord burned among them, and consumed some in the outskirts of the camp. Then the people cried out to Moses, and when Moses prayed to the Lord, the fire was quenched. So he called the name of the place Taberah, because the fire of the Lord had burned among them. Now the mixed multitude who were among them yielded to intense craving; so the children of Israel also wept again and said: "Who will give us meat to eat? We remember the fish which we ate freely in Egypt, the cucumbers, the melons, the leeks, the onions, and the garlic; but now our whole being *is* dried up; there *is* nothing at all except this manna before our eyes!" (Numbers 11:1–6).

Talk about serious consequences! Some of those complaining Israelites were literally burned up. You'd think the rest of the group would have learned something from that. You'd think seeing some of their friends and neighbors scorched by the fire of God would have taught them to keep their mouths shut the next time they were tempted to complain. But not so. Just a few chapters later, despite some major, God-given victories, we find them whining again.

What sparked their dissatisfaction this time? They were weary of the whole wilderness experience. It was no fun and often difficult. It seemed to drag on forever. (Forty years is a long time to be camped out!) Numbers 21 describes the scene:

> Then they journeyed from Mount Hor by the Way of the Red Sea, to go around the land of Edom; and the soul of the people became very discouraged on the way. And the people spoke against God and against Moses: "Why have you brought us up out of Egypt to die in the wilderness? For there is no food and no water, and our soul loathes this worthless bread." So the Lord sent fiery serpents among the people, and they bit the people; and many of the people of Israel died (Numbers 21:4–6).

As shocking as it might be to see the Israelites making the same mistake again by murmuring against the Lord, we can all identify with them. We know what it's like to be "discouraged on the way." We've all encountered difficult situations and endured adverse circumstances we felt would never end. When that happens, we are often tempted to follow the Israelites' example and accuse God of letting us down.

Before we yield to that temptation, we should remember what the Israelites experienced when they complained about such things. We need to think about the neon sign they left in the wilderness which, if it literally existed, might have read: *Avoid the fire and the snakes. Keep your big mouth shut.*

Keep that sign in mind next time you're tempted to get mad at God and grumble against Him. Remind yourself that speaking against God will open the door to that old serpent, Satan. Heed the words of the Apostle Peter who wrote, "'He who would love life and see good days, let him refrain his tongue from evil, and his lips from speaking deceit'" (1 Peter 3:10).

ONE VERSE THAT WILL CHANGE YOUR LIFE

Even in the hard times, even when things aren't going the way we expected, we must always refuse to speak ill of God in any way. God is unfailingly good and righteous. He cannot be any other way. He is our answer—not our problem. Make a decision to never accuse Him and say He is not doing a good job in your life. The Old Testament book of Malachi refers to some people who got in big trouble by talking that way. They became so irritated with the circumstances in their lives that they actually said, "It's useless to serve God. We've tried to walk pleasing before Him and it hasn't profited us one bit. The wicked are more blessed than we are!" (See Malachi 3:14–15.)

God doesn't appreciate those kinds of comments. He said they were stout (or harsh) against Him. There is no faith in them and they give Him nothing to work with. We'd be wise to remember that and imprint on our minds the stern words God spoke to the Israelites when they spoke against Him in that way:

> How long will this evil congregation murmur against Me? I have heard the complaints the Israelites murmur against Me. Tell them, As I live, says the Lord,

what you have said in My hearing I will do to you: Your dead bodies shall fall in this wilderness—of all who were numbered of you, from twenty years old and upward, who have murmured against Me, surely none shall come into the land in which I swore to make you dwell, except Caleb son of Jephunneh and Joshua son of Nun. But your little ones whom you said would be a prey, them will I bring in and they shall know the land which you have despised and rejected. But as for you, your dead bodies shall fall in this wilderness. And your children shall be wanderers and shepherds in the wilderness for forty years and shall suffer for your whoredoms (your infidelity to your espoused God), until your corpses are consumed in the wilderness. After the number of the days in which you spied out the land [of Canaan], even forty days, for each day a year shall you bear and suffer for your iniquities, even for forty years, and you shall know My displeasure [the revoking of My promise and My estrangement] (Numbers 14:27–34, AMP).

This passage should serve as a sober warning to all who are tempted to murmur against God. Yet many Christians today continue to do it. Without so much as a thought, they'll say things like, "I did everything the Word said to do and God didn't come through for me. Believing Him didn't do me any good. The Word doesn't work for me." In other words, *I'm doing everything right, so everything that is wrong in my life is God's fault.*

Isn't that a foolish thing to say?

Anyone should be able to figure out it's not God's fault if something in our lives goes wrong. If anyone has messed things up, it's us—not God. He never misses it. He is always right and always faithful. He always keeps His Word. So settle that right now and always speak rightly about Him.

Notice, I said *always* speak that way. Don't say good things about God when other people are listening, then complain when you're alone with your spouse or your close friends. God is listening all the time. As the psalmist said in Psalm 139:4, "There is not a word on my tongue, but behold, O Lord, You know it altogether." God doesn't miss a word you say. He heard the Israelites even when they were complaining to each other in secret. Psalm 106 says:

> They spurned and despised the pleasant and desirable land [Canaan]; they believed not His word [neither trusting in, relying on, nor holding to it]; but they murmured in their tents and hearkened not to the voice of the Lord. Therefore He lifted up His hand [as if taking an oath] against them, that He would cause them to fall in the wilderness, cast out their descendants among the nations, and scatter them in the lands [of the earth] (Psalm 10:24–27, AMP).

It's hard not to complain when circumstances are rough. I've been there. I know how it is. When you go home, it's tempting to just let your spiritual hair down, so to speak, and feel sorry for yourself. I remember how it feels when the car is broken down, there's not enough money to pay the bills, and collectors are calling. As the pressure increases, you begin thinking things like: *I don't know why this is happening to me! I started tithing last week* (like we should get a medal for that!) *and here it is a week later and the car payment is two months past due. God just doesn't seem to care about me. He does amazing things for Pastor So-and-so, but He never does anything good for me.*

In times of trouble, we're tempted to entertain such thoughts, not only because the circumstances are pressing on us but also because the devil is working on us. He's whispering in our ears and planting thoughts of doubt in our minds. He wants us to start questioning the goodness and faithfulness of God. He's been pressuring God's people to do that ever since the Garden of Eden. Remember what he did to Eve? He suggested God had lied to her. He told her eating from the tree of good and evil wouldn't really kill her like God said it would. He went on to suggest God didn't have Adam and Eve's best interests at heart and that He was trying to rob them of real wisdom and power. He began to question God's words to them: "Can it really be that God has said, You shall not eat from every tree of the garden? . . . For God knows that in the day you eat of it your eyes will be opened, and you will be like God, knowing the difference between good and evil" (Genesis 3:1–5, AMP).

The devil is still up to those same old tricks today. When things seem to go wrong and you start to get discouraged, he'll try to convince you that you did everything perfectly. The problem, he'll suggest, is God. He's the One who didn't come through for you. He forgot about you. He didn't keep His Word to you.

Why is the devil so determined to get you in that frame of mind? Because if he can pressure you into thinking that way, he knows you'll eventually start talking that way, and he needs your words to work with. He needs you to speak ungodly words because those words are what license him to do what he wants to do in your life—steal, kill, and destroy. According to Jesus, that's always what the devil comes to do (John 10:10). He knows out of the abundance of your heart your mouth speaks. He tries to sow doubt in your heart so that he can have your words.

So stop that snake before he ever gets in the door. Refuse to entertain any thought that suggests that God is to blame for your problems. When those thoughts even try to come, remember what Proverbs 21:23 says in the *New Living Translation (96): "If you keep your mouth shut, you will stay out of trouble."* What a word of wisdom.

I'm telling you, obeying that one verse will change your life. It will keep you from speaking harsh words that grieve the Spirit of God. It will help you guard against negative words that would open the door for the devil to slip in and bite you like those fiery serpents bit the Israelites.

I'm not suggesting you should just sulk silently, however. Be sure when you do speak, you speak the right words—good words with which you and God agree. Turn your whole mind-set around and cultivate the attitude Paul described in Philippians 2 when he wrote:

> Therefore, my dear ones, as you have always obeyed [my suggestions], so now, not only [with the enthusiasm you would show] in my presence but much more because I am absent, work out (cultivate, carry out to the goal, and fully complete) your own salvation with reverence and awe and trembling (self-distrust, with serious caution, tenderness of conscience, watchfulness against temptation, timidly shrinking from whatever might offend God and discredit the name of Christ). [Not in your own strength] for it is God Who is all the while effectually at work in you [energizing and creating in you the power and desire], both to will and to work for His good pleasure and satisfaction

and delight. Do all things without grumbling and faultfinding and complaining [against God] and questioning and doubting [among yourselves], that you may show yourselves to be blameless and guileless, innocent and uncontaminated, children of God without blemish (faultless, unrebukable) in the midst of a crooked and wicked generation [spiritually perverted and perverse], among whom you are seen as bright lights (stars or beacons shining out clearly) in the [dark] world, holding out [to it] and offering [to all men] the Word of Life, so that in the day of Christ I may have something of which exultantly to rejoice and glory in that I did not run my race in vain or spend my labor to no purpose (Philippians 2:12–16, AMP).

Conquer the temptation to complain and actively cultivate a grateful attitude toward God. One way to do that is by saying positive things about Him such as, "God is good. He keeps His Word to me. He is faithful. He'll never fail me. I say what He says."

If the pressure starts getting to you and you have trouble thinking of words to say, turn back to Psalm 145, and let it be your guide. It says:

I will extol You, my God, O King; and I will bless Your name forever and ever. Every day I will bless You, and I will praise Your name forever and ever. Great is the Lord, and greatly to be praised; and His greatness is unsearchable. One generation shall praise Your works to another, and shall declare Your mighty acts (Psalm 145:1–4).

According to those verses, you should bless and praise God every day. If you have children, you shouldn't let them hear you griping and complaining about how God has let you down. Instead, gather them around you and tell them about all the ways God has blessed you. Talk about all the good things He has done. Open the Bible and talk about how He split the Red Sea for the Israelites. Talk about how He fed them with manna and never let them go hungry. Talk about the miracles of Jesus and rejoice over the fact that your God is a miracle-working God.

If you don't have family, speak to yourself and to God as you meditate on these things until you get happy and excited. Share God's Word with friends or coworkers. God will even give you opportunities to share His love with strangers, telling them how big and awesome God is. When the Word is in you in abundance, it comes out of your mouth. That's what King David was doing when he wrote the psalm quoted above. He said: "I will meditate on the glorious splendor of Your majesty, and on Your wondrous works. Men shall speak of the might of Your awesome acts, and I will declare Your greatness. They shall utter the memory of Your great goodness, and shall sing of Your righteousness" (Psalm 145:5–7).

Up to this point, you may never have seen God do wondrous things in your life, but if you'll meditate on the works He's done that are recorded in the Bible, you'll quickly see that God is King of the impossible. He is big! He is powerful! And His love is inexhaustible! Open the door of faith, and He will come in.

> The Lord is gracious and full of compassion, slow to anger and great in mercy. The Lord is good to all, and His tender mercies are over all His works. All Your works shall praise You, O Lord, and Your saints shall

bless You. They shall speak of the glory of Your kingdom, and talk of Your power, to make known to the
sons of men His mighty acts, and the glorious majesty
of His kingdom. Your kingdom is an everlasting kingdom, and Your dominion endures throughout all gen-
erations (Psalm 145:8–13).

These verses make it very clear that we, as God's people, are not
to keep silent. We're supposed to open our mouths in praise. We're
supposed to bless, speak, and make known the goodness of the
Lord—and we have plenty of reasons to do so. After all . . .

The Lord upholds all who fall, and raises up all who
are bowed down. The eyes of all look expectantly to
You, and You give them their food in due season. You
open Your hand and satisfy the desire of every living
thing. The Lord is righteous in all His ways, gracious
in all His works. The Lord is near to all who call upon
Him, to all who call upon Him in truth. He will fulfill
the desire of those who fear Him; He also will hear
their cry and save them (Psalm 145:14–19).

Start quoting verses like that in times of stress and your faith in
God will soar instead of crumble. Make a commitment to keep your
thoughts and your mouth filled with the praises of God. Settle that
right now and say, "From this day on, I will speak only good things
about God. I will never again murmur against Him. Nothing that is
wrong in my life today is His fault. He is always faithful to me. He is
perfect and good in all His ways. His desire is only and always to perfect that which concerns me, and He is always worthy of my praise."

FINDING MONEY ON THE HIGHWAY

There will be times when circumstances seem to contradict those statements. There will be seasons when things don't seem to be working out, or when answers seem long in coming. When that happens, it's sometimes a timing issue (God has very specific timelines for some things in our lives), or there are elements of the situation we simply don't understand . . . or we are just plain missing His direction.

Especially when believing God for natural things like a new home or an automobile, often the wait can be longer than expected. Many times that's because another person's obedience is involved in opening the door to that provision. Ken and I found that out very early in our faith life. For example, it seemed to us it took forever to receive the first vehicle we needed for our ministry. Waiting patiently for it was difficult because we needed it so badly. Back then, we didn't have any trucks to transport our meeting equipment. We had to carry the sound system, the kids, and all our luggage in one car. If God hadn't instructed us not to borrow money, we would have just gone to the bank, gotten a loan, and bought the car. But we refused to do that.

So we prayed, telling God exactly the kind of vehicle we needed. We released our faith and waited . . . and waited . . . and waited . . . to receive it. We didn't talk to others outside our family, of course. We just expected God to take care of it.

Months passed, and about half the money came in, but we were still short several thousand dollars.

Late one night, a man from another state called Ken and asked his forgiveness. He said the Lord had told him sometime earlier to send us an offering, but he just hadn't done it. That night, the Holy

Spirit dealt so strongly with him that he felt like he couldn't wait another minute. He called us, even at that late hour, and let us know what he was going to do. That offering was the rest of what we needed for our ministry vehicle.

That's usually the way it is with natural provision. As far as I know, God doesn't float dollar bills (or cars) down from the sky. He sends those things through other people, and sometimes people are slower to obey God than they should be. But, even so, God takes care of us in the meantime, and in the end everything turns out right.

When we first began preaching and money was especially scarce, we were driving through Oklahoma City, on our way to a meeting. The kids were little, loud, and hungry, and we needed to buy them something to eat, but we didn't have enough money.

Suddenly, Ken said, "Gloria, did you see that? Money blew across the road back there!"

I didn't recall seeing anything, but he was convinced it was there, so he turned the car around and went back to look for it. We were on a divided highway and it took some maneuvering, but when we got back to that spot, there it was—a twenty-dollar bill, blown against the fence that divided the two sides of the highway. It was just sitting there. That twenty dollars was food money. If you doubt God delivers finances to His people in such peculiar ways, think about how Peter got the money to pay the temple tax. Jesus told him to get it out of a fish's mouth. Matthew 17 tells us exactly how the conversation went. It says some Jewish leaders came to Peter and said:

"Does your Teacher not pay the temple tax?" He said, "Yes." And when he had come into the house, Jesus anticipated him, saying, "What do you think, Simon? From whom do the kings of the earth take customs or taxes, from their sons or from strangers?" Peter said to Him, "From strangers." Jesus said to him, "Then the sons are free. Nevertheless, lest we offend them, go to the sea, cast in a hook, and take the fish that comes up first. And when you have opened its mouth, you will find a piece of money; take that and give it to them for Me and you" (Matthew 17:24–27).

Miracles like that still happen today. If you're believing God to meet an urgent need, He'll meet it through a fish if necessary. He'll blow dollar bills right across your path. But for that to happen, you must be in a believing mode. You must be expecting Him to provide.

Sometimes I think back to that incident in Oklahoma City and wonder how differently it might have turned out if Ken hadn't been expecting God to send us the money we needed. He had put every dollar we had into buying gasoline to get to the meeting. He was actively looking for money all the way. Had he not been expectant, the money probably wouldn't have been there in the first place. Even if it had been, we might have missed seeing it blow across the road.

No doubt, the devil would have been on hand to make a few comments, too. He would have said, "See, God doesn't care about you. He doesn't care if your kids are hungry. He could have sent you some money, but He didn't. This is all His fault."

But, thank God, Ken was believing and expecting. So when God's provision came, he saw it. When the Holy Spirit prompted him to turn the car around to look for that money, he obeyed.

Let that story be an encouragement to you. Let it remind you in every time of trouble or need, to keep believing and keep expecting

God to show up and do what He promised to do. All things are possible with God. Stay sensitive to the leading of the Holy Spirit, and if He impresses you to go fishing and look down the throat of the first bass you pull into the boat—do it! If He shows you money beside the highway, turn the car around!

CARNAL CHRISTIANS GO NOWHERE

Remember, you cannot cultivate that kind of sensitivity and obedience to the voice of the Lord if you murmur, complain, and bellyache when things don't seem to be going your way. That kind of thinking and speaking will keep you in a carnal state. It will keep you from even hearing what the Lord is saying to you. If you do hear Him, it will hinder you from doing what He tells you to do.

Over the years, I've noticed that complaining, bellyaching Christians do nothing and go nowhere. People who complain end up stuck in the wilderness and can't seem to find their way out. Their spiritual journey can be summed up much the same way Moses summarized the journey of the wilderness-bound Israelites. Look again at what he said about them at the end of those forty years:

> "The Lord our God spoke to us in Horeb, saying: 'You have dwelt long enough at this mountain. . . . See, I have set the land before you; go in and possess the land which the Lord swore to your fathers—to Abraham, Isaac, and Jacob—to give to them and their descendants after them.' . . . 'Look, the Lord your God has set the land before you; go up and possess it, as the Lord God of your fathers has spoken to you; do not fear or be discouraged.' . . . Nevertheless you would

not go up, but rebelled against the command of the Lord your God; and you complained in your tents, and said, 'Because the Lord hates us, He has brought us out of the land of Egypt to deliver us into the hand of the Amorites, to destroy us. Where can we go up? Our brethren have discouraged our hearts, saying, "The people are greater and taller than we; the cities are great and fortified up to heaven; moreover we have seen the sons of the Anakim there."' Then I said to you, 'Do not be terrified, or afraid of them. The Lord your God, who goes before you, He will fight for you, according to all He did for you in Egypt before your eyes, and in the wilderness where you saw how the Lord your God carried you, as a man carries his son, in all the way that you went until you came to this place.' Yet, for all that, you did not believe the Lord your God . . ." (Deuteronomy 1:6, 8, 21, 26–32).

No matter how many times I read that story, it still amazes me that despite all God's promises to them, the children of Israel refused to go where He led them. They so hardened their hearts with murmuring and complaining they could not obey His voice, even when their lives depended on it.

Determine never to let that happen to you. Make a heartfelt decision right now that no matter how difficult things seem to be at times, you will remember the lesson the Israelites learned. When you're tempted to complain, think of the neon sign left flashing in the desert: *Avoid the fire and the snakes! Keep your big mouth shut!*

Then turn your attitude around by continually following the example of the psalmist who wrote: "I will bless the Lord at all times; His praise shall continually be in my mouth" (Psalm 34:1).

Don't let the sin of complaining disconnect you from God's Master Plan. Keep praising God and saying good things about Him. He will see you through.

KEY EIGHT

—⁓〰⁓—

Develop a heart of gratitude and praise God
for all the blessings He bestows upon you.

Eleven

ARE WE THERE YET?

—◊—

If you've ever taken young children on a road trip, chances are you've heard those four words again and again. When you stopped at a traffic light, when you pulled into a service station to get gasoline, when you slowed the car down for any reason, the hopeful question chanted by vacationing children everywhere repeatedly filled your ears: *"Are we there yet? Are we there yet? Are we there yet?"*

More often than not, your answer was no because the journey had just begun. You may have been on the road five minutes, but to your small, impatient passengers it had already seemed like five hours. So when you informed them the destination was still miles away, they wailed in despair, "Why does it take so long to get there?"

That's a popular question, not just among children eager to start their vacation, but also among Christians trying to stay connected to God's Master Plan. Once we get a glimpse of what God has called us to do and who He has called us to be, we often become impatient. We become weary of the growth process and the time it takes to see God's plans fully realized.

So, like children, we pester God with that familiar old question, *"Are we there yet?"*

When it becomes clear the answer is no, we can easily get cranky and irritable. We start wondering why this whole thing is taking so long. And it is at precisely this point many believers begin disconnecting from God's plan. They become discouraged and tired of waiting for their divinely inspired hopes and dreams to come true. So they start badgering God about those things, pushing Him to give them everything they want—right now!

But it takes time for God's plans to develop. Even though God has the ability to work instantly and miraculously to bring things to pass, usually, He does things by process. He brings them forth gradually—over days, weeks, months, even years. That's why, before He took the Israelites into the Promised Land, He warned them in advance that it would take time for them to overcome all the enemies there and fully occupy the land. He said:

> "But if you indeed obey His voice and do all that I speak, then I will be an enemy to your enemies and an adversary to your adversaries. For My Angel will go before you and bring you in to the Amorites and the Hittites and the Perizzites and the Canaanites and the Hivites and the Jebusites; and I will cut them off. . . . I will not drive them out from before you in one year, lest the land become desolate and the beasts of the field become too numerous for you. Little by little I will drive them out from before you, until you have

increased, and you inherit the land" (Exodus 23:22–23, 29–30).

If you listen, you'll discover God is saying the same thing to you. He is telling you in advance it will take time for all the good things He has planned for you to develop. So, if you want to stay connected, you must learn to be patient with that process. Learn to do what immature children everywhere find almost impossible—sit back and enjoy the journey.

The Israelites weren't very good at that. When they were on their journey to Canaan, their patience with God's process quickly wore thin. They didn't want to wait for God's plans regarding them to develop. So, as the days went by, they grew increasingly irritable with the tedium of the wilderness.

As we've already seen, they expressed that irritation by complaining about almost everything along the way. They griped about the dangers and fussed about the scarcity of water. They wailed about the lack of food and even after God miraculously provided food for them, they got upset because that food was too boring. They craved something spicier than the heavenly bread that continually rained on them from the sky and, most shocking of all, they doubted God's ability to provide it for them, saying: "Who will give us meat to eat? We remember the fish which we ate freely in Egypt, the cucumbers, the melons, the leeks, the onions, and the garlic; but now our whole being is dried up; there is nothing at all except this manna before our eyes!" (Numbers 11:4–6).

God doesn't respond well when His people complain and doubt His ability to care for them. They tempt Him to anger when they say, "Can God really do this for me?" Psalm 106 confirms that by giving us God's response to the Israelites' complaints. It says:

They did not earnestly wait for His plans [to develop] regarding them, but lusted exceedingly in the wilderness and tempted and tried to restrain God [with their insistent desires] in the desert. And He gave them their request, but sent leanness into their souls and [thinned their number by] disease and death (Psalm 106:13–15, AMP).

Instead of their impatient grumbling opening the door for fire and snakes to come upon them, the Israelites' request for meat resulted in something entirely different. God "sent leanness into their souls." He gave them exactly what they wanted. In fact, He gave them more than they wanted. He gave them meat to eat, but not just for a meal or two. God rained quail down for thirty days until it came out of their nostrils and became loathsome to them (Numbers 11:20). If that wasn't bad enough, "While the meat was still between their teeth, before it was chewed, the wrath of the Lord was aroused against the people." A great plague resulted. "So he called the name of that place Kibroth Hattaavah, because there they buried the people who had yielded to craving" (Numbers 11:33–34).

The moral of that story is clear: It's better to wait for God's plans concerning us to develop. If we push ahead of His timing to get what we want, we may regret it in the end. If we get impatient and try to force things to happen more quickly than God intended, the thing we thought we wanted can become a snare and a burden to us. We may get a substitute while we miss God's best. God's promised blessings, obtained too soon in a carnal way, can actually turn out to be a curse.

The Israelites proved that at least twice—once in the wilderness, and again many years after they reached the Promised Land. The second time they made that mistake, they were pushing God to give them a king. At the time, the prophet Samuel was the spiritual leader of Israel, so the people brought their demand to him. Samuel knew that the Lord had not chosen "any man to be a ruler over My people Israel" (2 Chronicles 6:5). He realized their insistence on a king displeased the Lord, but when he prayed about it, God gave him a surprising answer. He said:

> Hearken to the voice of the people in all they say to you; for they have not rejected you, but they have rejected Me, that I should not be King over them. According to all the works which they have done since I brought them up out of Egypt even to this day, forsaking Me and serving other gods, so they also do to you. So listen now to their voice; only solemnly warn them and show them the ways of the king who shall reign over them. So Samuel told all the words of the Lord to the people who asked of him a king. And he said, These will be the ways of the king who shall reign over you: he will take your sons and appoint them to his chariots and to be his horsemen and to run before his chariots. He will appoint them for himself to be commanders over thousands and over fifties, and some to plow his ground and to reap his harvest and to make his implements of war and equipment for his chariots. He will take your daughters to be perfumers, cooks, and bakers. He will take your fields, your vineyards, and your olive orchards, even the best of them, and give them to his servants. He will take a tenth of your grain and of your vineyards and give it to his officers and to his ser-

vants. He will take your men and women servants and
the best of your cattle and your donkeys and put them
to his work. He will take a tenth of your flocks, and
you yourselves shall be his slaves. In that day you will
cry out because of your king you have chosen for yourselves, but the Lord will not hear you then. Nevertheless, the people refused to listen to the voice of Samuel,
and they said, No! We will have a king over us, that we
also may be like all the nations, and that our king may
govern us and go out before us and fight our battles.
Samuel heard all the people's words and repeated them
in the Lord's ears. And the Lord said to Samuel, Hearken to their voice and appoint them a king. And Samuel said to the men of Israel, Go every man to his city
(1 Samuel 8:7–22, AMP).

You'd think after hearing God's warnings about what this king
was going to do to them, the Israelites would have reconsidered their
request and said, "On second thought . . . never mind. Maybe having a king right now isn't such a good idea after all. Maybe we should
just wait for the Lord's plans to develop."

But the Israelites wanted a king and they wanted one *right now!*
So God appointed Saul to be their king. An insightful footnote in
The Amplified Bible has this to say about the situation:

Saul was originally the people's choice, not God's
choice. The Bible nowhere teaches that "the voice of
the people is the voice of God." But it does teach that
when people make demands of God that are not in
harmony with His will, He may grant them to their

sorrow, and send "leanness into their souls" (Psalm 106:15).[10]

Why were the Israelites in such a hurry to have a king? Why did they disregard God's warning and demand He give them a ruler— even though they knew he would be hard on them? They wanted to be like all the other nations (1 Samuel 8:5, 20, AMP).

That's a tendency we, as believers, can fall prey to, as well. Sometimes as we're walking out the plan of God for our lives, we'll start envying others who are further down the road. We'll see the seasoned believer who has been tithing and giving for years, developing his faith and his confidence in God's provision. Then we'll start comparing our financial status to his. We might think, *Hey, that man has a nicer car than I do! He has a bigger house!*

Or we might look at someone who has a better job or a bigger ministry, and become dissatisfied with what God has currently given us.

Well, God loves me just as much as He loves him, we'll start thinking. *So I'm just going to step out by faith and buy that big house. I'm going to get a car just like his. I'm going to push for a higher position at work or a bigger ministry.*

There's a flaw in that kind of reasoning. Even though God loves us all equally, even though He wants to bless us all richly, He has a plan and a timetable that will bring those blessings to each of us at just the right time, in the best possible way.

---

10. See 2 Chronicles 6:5, *The Amplified Bible, Old Testament* © 1965, 1987 by The Zondervan Corporation. *The Amplified New Testament* © 1958, 1987 by The Lockman Foundation. Used by permission.

We might well get that new car and end up wrecking it the next day. We might get that new house too early and find out the utility bills, taxes, and upkeep is too much for us to handle. Or that coveted promotion at work might find us spending so many hours at the office, we don't get to see our family enough and we don't enjoy our life anymore.

We might get all the things we think we want . . . yet end up disconnected from God's Master Plan.

PATIENCE MAKES US STRONGER

How do you keep from making that mistake? Just keep trusting God and be patient. Keep believing He always has your best interests at heart. Even when things seem to move more slowly than you want them to, trust God to deliver every blessing He has promised and fulfill every righteous desire He has put in your heart. And trust Him to do it right on time.

Continually keep in mind the instructions God gave us in Hebrews 6:11–15 and see to it that:

> . . . you show the same diligence to the full assurance of hope until the end, that you do not become sluggish, but imitate those who through faith and patience inherit the promises. For when God made a promise to Abraham, because He could swear by no one greater, He swore by Himself, saying, "Surely blessing I will bless you, and multiplying I will multiply you." And so, after he had patiently endured, he obtained the promise (Hebrews 6:11–15).

When the good things you're expecting from God seem slow in coming and you begin to get anxious and in a hurry—slow down. Remind yourself of these verses and remember that the Bible says, through Jesus, you have inherited the very same blessing that Abraham received (Galatians 3:14). God has said to you, just as surely as He said to the patriarch, "Surely blessing I will bless you, and multiplying I will multiply you." He has sworn to prosper you in every area of life—spirit, soul, and body. But to fully receive those blessings, you must do the same thing Abraham did. You must patiently endure.

You can only do that if you have entered what the Bible refers to as *the rest* that belongs to those who live by faith. Sadly, the wilderness-wandering Israelites never entered that rest. That's why the New Testament repeatedly says to us, *Don't make the same mistakes they did!* Consider carefully this passage from the book of Hebrews:

> We have become fellows with Christ (the Messiah) and share in all He has for us, if only we hold our first newborn confidence and original assured expectation . . . firm and unshaken to the end. Then while it is [still] called Today, if you would hear His voice and when you hear it, do not harden your hearts as in the rebellion [in the desert, when the people provoked and irritated and embittered God against them]. For who were they who heard and yet were rebellious and provoked [Him]? Was it not all those who came out of Egypt led by Moses? And with whom was He irritated and provoked and grieved for forty years? Was it not with those who sinned, whose dismembered bodies were strewn and left in the desert? And to whom did

He swear that they should not enter His rest, but to those who disobeyed [who had not listened to His word and who refused to be compliant or be persuaded]? So we see that they were not able to enter [into His rest], because of their unwillingness to adhere to and trust in and rely on God [unbelief had shut them out]. Therefore, while the promise of entering His rest still holds and is offered [today], let us be afraid [to distrust it], lest any of you should think he has come too late and has come short of [reaching] it. For indeed we have had the glad tidings [Gospel of God] proclaimed to us just as truly as they [the Israelites of old did when the good news of deliverance from bondage came to them]; but the message they heard did not benefit them, because it was not mixed with faith (with the leaning of the entire personality on God in absolute trust and confidence in His power, wisdom, and goodness) by those who heard it; neither were they united in faith with the ones [Joshua and Caleb] who heard (did believe). For we who have believed (adhered to and trusted in and relied on God) do enter that rest, in accordance with His declaration that those [who did not believe] should not enter when He said, As I swore in My wrath, They shall not enter My rest; and this He said although [His] works had been completed and prepared [and waiting for all who would believe] from the foundation of the world (Hebrews 3:14–4:3, AMP).

Look again at the last sentence in that passage. It says God's works—all His provision for us, everything necessary to fulfill His plan for our lives—are already prepared and completed. We don't have to worry and wonder if God is going to give us what we need or be anxious and afraid that He'll run out of blessings and won't have enough for us. God has already supplied and stored up for us before the foundation of the world, everything—both natural and spiritual—that pertains to life and godliness. He made sure every blessing we could ever need would be ready and waiting for us to receive by faith.

According to the Bible, we don't have to struggle and strive to obtain those blessings. All we have to do is obey God and trust Him. All we have to do is rest in His faithfulness.

> Seeing then that the promise remains over [from past times] for some to enter that rest, and that those who formerly were given the good news about it and the opportunity, failed to appropriate it and did not enter because of disobedience, again He sets a definite day, [a new] Today, [and gives another opportunity of securing that rest] saying through David after so long a time in the words already quoted, Today, if you would hear His voice and when you hear it, do not harden your hearts . . . there is still awaiting a full and complete Sabbath-rest reserved for the [true] people of God; for he who has once entered [God's] rest also has ceased from [the weariness and pain] of human labors, just as God rested from those labors peculiarly His own. Let us therefore be zealous and exert ourselves and strive diligently to enter that rest [of God, to know and experience it for ourselves], that no one may fall or perish by the same kind of unbelief and disobedience [into which those in the wilderness fell] (Hebrews 4:6–11, AMP).

HE DWELLS IN US SO WE CAN REST IN HIM

We enter into God's rest by drawing near to Him, by dwelling, as Psalm 91 says, in the secret place of the Most High and abiding under the shadow of the Almighty. We do it by maintaining a continuous living connection with the Father and the Son through the Holy Spirit.

When we give in to impatience and anxiety, or rush ahead of God, trying to carry out His plan in our own, natural strength, that divine connection is interrupted. We get sidetracked and the power and life-flow that gives us the divine ability to do what God has called us to do begins to diminish. When that happens, no matter how much human energy we expend trying to move ourselves on down the road of God's Master Plan, nothing happens. We find ourselves revving our engines and spinning our wheels . . . going nowhere fast!

That's why Jesus so clearly told us to dwell and abide continually in Him. "Just as no branch can bear fruit of itself without abiding in (being vitally united to) the vine," He said, "neither can you bear fruit unless you abide in Me."

> I am the Vine; you are the branches. Whoever lives in Me and I in him bears much (abundant) fruit. However, apart from Me [cut off from vital union with Me] you can do nothing. If a person does not dwell in Me, he is thrown out like a [broken-off] branch, and withers; such branches are gathered up and thrown into the fire, and they are burned. If you live in Me [abide vitally united to Me] and My words remain in you and continue to live in your hearts, ask whatever you will, and it shall be done for you. When you bear (produce)

much fruit, My Father is honored and glorified, and you show and prove yourselves to be true followers of Mine. I have loved you, [just] as the Father has loved Me; abide in My love [continue in His love with Me]. If you keep My commandments [if you continue to obey My instructions], you will abide in My love and live on in it, just as I have obeyed My Father's commandments and live on in His love. I have told you these things, that My joy and delight may be in you, and that your joy and gladness may be of full measure and complete and overflowing (John 15:4–11, AMP).

I'm convinced that if we'll abide in Jesus and continually remind ourselves He is abiding in us, we can live every day in the rest of God. If we feed our hearts on His Word and meditate on the fact that we are His temple—that He not only dwells in us, He spreads Himself over us like a tent—we'll be able to patiently endure and overcome every trial and temptation the devil sends our way. We'll be able to rest quietly in faith, wait on God's perfect timing and everything He promised will come to pass in our lives.

When you think about it, what often pushes us into anxiety and impatience is our fear that God has forgotten us, or that He might be overlooking us. But such a thing would be impossible!

Read the Old Testament accounts sometime about all the attention God gave the Jewish temple. He was very particular about everything that went on there because that temple was His Old Covenant dwelling place. It was His home.

And what a magnificent home it was! Adorned with gold and precious stones, filled with beautiful vessels and immaculately dressed priests, the Old Testament temple was an absolute marvel. Yet even that temple was not adequate for our God. He said, "Heaven [is] My throne, and earth the footstool for My feet. What [kind of] house can you build for Me . . . or what is the place in which I can rest?" (Acts 7:49, AMP).

First Corinthians 3:16 answers that question. It says we, as believers, are God's house. We are His resting place. It says, "Know ye not that ye are the temple of God, and that the Spirit of God dwelleth in you?" (KJV).

If God so hovered over and cared for the details of Solomon's temple, how much more will He hover over and care for every detail in the lives of those temples who are born again in His image. We are His temple not made with hands. We can truly rest knowing that "He [God] Himself has said, I will not in any way fail you nor give you up nor leave you without support. [I will] not, [I will] not, [I will] not in any degree leave you helpless nor forsake nor let [you] down (relax My hold on you)! [Assuredly not!]" (Hebrews 13:5, AMP).

We can face every difficulty and every seeming delay in our Master Plan with the confidence of the Apostle Paul who wrote, ". . . I will all the more gladly glory in my weaknesses and infirmities, that the strength and power of Christ (the Messiah) may rest (yes, may pitch a tent over and dwell) upon me!" (2 Corinthians 12:9, AMP).

Through the years, Ken and I have spent a lot of time meditating on these truths. We've had a lot of practice patiently enduring and laboring to enter God's rest. We know more about it now than we did when we first started our walk with God. At the writing of this book, we have been in the ministry for more than forty years. Throughout that time, God has not only met our every need, He has blessed us beyond anything we could have imagined when we first began. But, many of those blessings took longer to overtake us than we planned. So we had to exercise faith and patience. We had to keep believing God when things got tough. We had to keep trusting Him through the good times and the hard times.

It wasn't always easy, but I'm so glad we did it. Every blessing has been worth the wait. Ken and I have never been more fulfilled. We've never enjoyed life more. I'd do it all again a hundred times to have the peace and satisfaction we enjoy today.

Of course, even now, we don't "have it made." We still encounter difficulties and sometimes wait longer than we'd like for certain things to happen. Things aren't always easy for us. We still have to walk by faith. But I will tell you this, they are easier—*a lot easier*—than they used to be. Why? Because through the years we've experienced for ourselves how faithful God is. Our confidence in Him has grown. Even in the hard times, it's easier to be patient because we know in advance how things are going to turn out. They're going to turn out for our good.

After seeing God come through for us again and again, it's easier now for us to do what James 1:2–4 says: "My brethren, count it all joy when you fall into various trials, knowing that the testing of your faith produces patience. But let patience have its perfect work, that you may be perfect and complete, lacking nothing."

Ken and I can wait in joy now for God's plans to develop in our lives. We've discovered that patience enables us to walk by faith until we receive full victory. It also increases our fortitude and builds our character in the process. That's why Romans 5:3–5 (AMP) says:

> Moreover [let us also be full of joy now!] let us exult and triumph in our troubles and rejoice in our sufferings, knowing that pressure and affliction and hardship produce patient and unswerving endurance. And endurance (fortitude) develops maturity of character (approved faith and tried integrity). And character [of this sort] produces [the habit of] joyful and confident hope of eternal salvation. Such hope never disappoints

or deludes or shames us, for God's love has been poured out in our hearts through the Holy Spirit Who has been given to us.

Patiently enduring the delays and hardships that come our way makes us stronger, more mature believers. It increases the blessing in our lives and prepares us for the next phase of God's plan. When we exercise faith and patience, overcoming challenges and gaining the victory, it pushes us forward into bigger and better things.

FROM SHEPHERD . . . TO GIANT-SLAYER . . . TO KING

The life of King David perfectly exemplifies that principle. He first caught sight of God's plan for him when he was just a teenager tending his father's sheep. At the time, he seemed to be the most unlikely candidate for king anyone could imagine.

So far was he from anyone's idea of royalty, that when the Lord sent the prophet Samuel to the house of David's father's in search of Israel's next king, no one even called David in from the field. Everyone automatically assumed God would choose one of his six older brothers for the honor. But, after meeting them all, Samuel said, "The Lord has not chosen these."

Then Samuel said to David's father, Jesse:

> "Are all the young men here?" Then he said, "There remains yet the youngest, and there he is, keeping the sheep." And Samuel said to Jesse, "Send and bring him. For we will not sit down till he comes here." So

he sent and brought him in. Now he was ruddy, with bright eyes, and good-looking. And the Lord said, "Arise, anoint him; for this is the one!" Then Samuel took the horn of oil and anointed him in the midst of his brothers; and the Spirit of the Lord came upon David from that day forward (1 Samuel 16:11–13).

If David were like most of us are when we first perceive God's plan for our lives, once he knew he was called to be king he probably figured he'd be ruling Israel within a few months. He probably assumed he was well-equipped for the challenge. And that was partially true. God had already been training him for what was ahead. While shepherding his father's sheep, David had already faced certain dangers and obstacles that would give him the confidence he needed to take the next step in God's plan.

Out there in the fields where David worked unseen and unappreciated, he'd had to fight a lion and a bear that came to steal lambs from the flock. Because he had spent his time meditating on God's covenant promises and because the Spirit of the Lord was upon him, David won those fights. He delivered the lambs to safety and killed the predators with his bare hands (Samuel 17:34–35).

Of course, at the time, David probably didn't fully understand the importance of those battles. He didn't know what God was preparing him to do. He didn't know he was going to be anointed king. He just knew he had to be faithful to the job God had given him at the time, which was taking care of his father's sheep.

That's often the way it is with us. There are seasons in our lives when God gives us jobs to do that seem totally unrelated to our calling. There are times when we face hardships and challenges we don't understand. As we serve God and obey Him year after year and no one seems to see or appreciate what we do, it's tough to patiently endure. But all the while, God is preparing us for promotion. He is equipping us to walk out His Master Plan.

During those seasons, we remind ourselves that somewhere down the road, this will all make sense. That's what happened in David's life. Shortly after he was anointed by Samuel, the importance of the hidden victories he'd won as a shepherd became clear. He found himself facing the giant, Goliath, who had terrified and mocked the entire Israelite army. When King Saul tried to stop young David from taking on such a fierce foe, David said, "Don't worry, King Saul . . .

> Your servant has killed both lion and bear; and this uncircumcised Philistine will be like one of them, seeing he has defied the armies of the living God." Moreover David said, "The Lord, who delivered me from the paw of the lion and from the paw of the bear, He will deliver me from the hand of this Philistine." And Saul said to David, "Go, and the Lord be with you!" (1 Samuel 17:36–37).

I love the confident attitude David demonstrated here. It's the attitude of someone who has seen God's power triumph over every attack the devil has brought against him. With every year that passes, Ken and I have developed a little more of that attitude. When the devil comes against us, the faithfulness God has repeatedly demonstrated in our lives gives us the boldness and confidence to say, like David, "Hey, we're not worried. By the grace of God, with faith in His Word and patience, we've already killed the lion and the bear . . . and we'll win this battle too. We'll come out of this trial as more than conquerors again, through Him who loves us!" (Romans 8:37).

If you're just getting connected with God's Master Plan for your life, you may feel like you could never have that kind of confidence—but you can. If you'll continually feed your faith on God's Word and keep exercising faith and patience, standing against the lions and bears that come your way, you too, will develop the boldness of a giant-slayer.

CALEB'S SPIRITUAL FITNESS PLAN

Remember, though, initially you may be enduring and overcoming those challenges in places of obscurity. Like David during his shepherding days, you may often feel unseen and unappreciated. Even though you have a kingly call of God on your life, you won't start out in the palace because God guides His people progressively to their destinies. He doesn't just drop it on them overnight. He leads and prepares them into it over time. He promotes them, as He did David, from shepherd boy to giant-killer to king.

That sounds like a simple three-step plan. But if you read the story of David's life, you'll see it was anything but simple. Even after he slew Goliath, he waited years to actually become king. What's more, those years were fraught with trouble and persecution. David may sometimes have felt like giving up on his God-given call and forgetting about being king.

That's not unusual. When the fires of testing and trial start getting hot, we all need to be reminded of the words the Apostle Paul wrote to the young pastor, Timothy: "You therefore must *endure hardship* as a good soldier of Jesus Christ" (2 Timothy 2:3).

No one said walking out on God's Master Plan would be effortless. No one said that once you connected with it you would float through life on flowery beds of ease. All you have to do is read the

Bible to see that's not true. Jesus plainly told us, "In this world you will have trouble. But take heart! I have overcome the world" (John 16:33, NIV).

Everyone who has ever done anything worthwhile in the kingdom of God has had to endure hardship. Every person in the Bible who successfully finished what God called him to do had to persevere despite trouble and disappointment, persecution and delays.

Caleb, for example, marched out of Egypt with the rest of the Israelites, full of faith and geared up to take the Promised Land. When he went into Canaan with the other eleven spies to scope out the situation, he and Joshua came back with a good report. They assured the rest of the Israelites that, despite the giants, God would enable them to take the land.

Caleb's countrymen refused to believe it. They drew back in fear. Caleb faced some serious trouble. He encountered some fierce opposition to God's plan for his life.

> And all the congregation cried out with a loud voice, and [they] wept that night. All the Israelites grumbled and deplored their situation, accusing Moses and Aaron, to whom the whole congregation said, Would that we had died in Egypt! Or that we had died in this wilderness! Why does the Lord bring us to this land to fall by the sword? Our wives and little ones will be a prey. Is it not better for us to return to Egypt? And they said one to another, Let us choose a captain and return to Egypt. Then Moses and Aaron fell on their faces before all the assembly of Israelites. And Joshua son of Nun and Caleb son of Jephunneh, who were among the scouts who had searched the land, rent

their clothes, and they said to all the company of Israelites, The land through which we passed as scouts is
an exceedingly good land. If the Lord delights in us,
then He will bring us into this land and give it to us, a
land flowing with milk and honey. Only do not rebel
against the Lord, neither fear the people of the land,
for they are bread for us. Their defense and the shadow
[of protection] is removed from over them, but the
Lord is with us. Fear them not. But all the congregation said to stone [Joshua and Caleb] with stones. But
the glory of the Lord appeared at the Tent of Meeting
before all the Israelites (Numbers 14:1–10, AMP).

Caleb actually handled that situation admirably. He refused to give
in to the unbelief of the people around him and kept saying about the
situation what God had said about it. He stayed strong on the Word.
But, even so, the Israelites clung stubbornly to their unbelief.

As a result, Caleb—through no fault of his own—had to wander
around the desert with that faithless group for forty frustrating years.
He had to endure all the hardships they experienced . . . and endure
he did. Caleb stayed with God's plan for his life year after year in the
wilderness till all the men of war except Caleb and Joshua "who came
out of Egypt perished, because they did not hearken to the voice of
the Lord; to them the Lord swore that He would not let them see the
land which the Lord swore to their fathers to give us, a land flowing
with milk and honey" (Numbers 14:30, Joshua 5:6, AMP).

Caleb refused to be deterred by disappointment or delay. Instead,
he spent those wilderness years patiently developing his God-given
dream. He spent them developing his hope, imagining what it was
going to be like to live on Mount Hebron—the place God had prom-

ised to give him. He spent the years in the wilderness getting stronger instead of weaker, so when he finally got the opportunity to take that mountain, he was ready. He went boldly to Joshua and said:

> Forty years old was I when Moses the servant of the Lord sent me from Kadesh-barnea to scout out the land. And I brought him a report as it was in my heart. But my brethren who went up with me made the hearts of the people melt; yet I wholly followed the Lord my God. And Moses swore on that day, Surely the land on which your feet have walked shall be an inheritance to you and your children always, because you have wholly followed the Lord my God. And now, behold, the Lord has kept me alive, as He said, these forty-five years since the Lord spoke this word to Moses, while the Israelites wandered in the wilderness; and now, behold, I am this day eighty-five years old. Yet I am as strong today as I was the day Moses sent me; as my strength was then, so is my strength now for war and to go out and to come in. So now give me this hill country of which the Lord spoke that day. For you heard then how the [giantlike] Anakim were there and that the cities were great and fortified; if the Lord will be with me, I shall drive them out just as the Lord said. Then Joshua blessed him and gave Hebron to Caleb son of Jephunneh for an inheritance. So Hebron became the inheritance of Caleb son of Jephunneh the Kenizzite to this day, because he wholly followed the Lord, the God of Israel (Joshua 14:7–14, AMP).

Think about that. Even at eighty-five years old, Caleb was still fighting. He was still standing against the enemies of God who were trying to steal God's blessings from him. He didn't get to sit back just because he was old, and coast into the inheritance God had promised him. It wasn't a "done deal" just because God had given him a word. He had to do battle with the enemy to take what belonged to him.

But that wasn't a problem for Caleb because he'd kept in shape—spiritually, mentally, and physically. He hadn't quit on God. He hadn't let the years of hardship wear him out. On the contrary, he was so spiritually charged he was able to go in to the Promised Land and whip the three Canaanite kings who were trespassing on his mountain. Those weren't just any old kings, either. They were sons of Anak, sons of the giants who had so frightened the Israelites forty years earlier.

But their size and strength didn't bother Caleb. He was as strong at eighty-five as he'd ever been in his life . . . so he just drove those giants off his land. I love Caleb. What an inspiration he is!

FROM JEREMIAH . . . TO JESUS

If Caleb's faith and patient endurance in the face of hardship aren't enough to inspire you, there are plenty of other people in the Bible to consider.

Think of Jeremiah, for instance. Sometimes his life seemed like little more than one hardship piled on top of another. As a young man, God called him and sent him to preach to a nation full of stiff-necked people. God told him, in advance, they wouldn't listen. (That's not the kind of word from the Lord most preachers want to hear.)

Poor Jeremiah! Instead of promising him that when he preached to the Jews, they would repent and there would be a glorious revival, God told him just the opposite would happen. He said:

Therefore thus says the Lord God: "Behold, My anger and My fury will be poured out on this place—on man and on beast, on the trees of the field and on the fruit of the ground. And it will burn and not be quenched." . . . "For I did not speak to your fathers, or command them in the day that I brought them out of the land of Egypt, concerning burnt offerings or sacrifices. But this is what I commanded them, saying, 'Obey My voice, and I will be your God, and you shall be My people. And walk in all the ways that I have commanded you, that it may be well with you.' Yet they did not obey or incline their ear, but followed the counsels and the dictates of their evil hearts, and went backward and not forward. Since the day that your fathers came out of the land of Egypt until this day, I have even sent to you all My servants the prophets, daily rising up early and sending them. Yet they did not obey Me or incline their ear, but stiffened their neck. They did worse than their fathers. Therefore you shall speak all these words to them, but they will not obey you. You shall also call to them, but they will not answer you" (Jeremiah 7:20, 22–27).

God's declarations, as always, came to pass. Jeremiah's congregation didn't appreciate him or his preaching. They were constantly getting mad at him. But still, the Bible says, he got up early in the morning and kept delivering God's messages to them. In one instance, for example, the Lord said to Jeremiah:

Stand in the court of the Lord's house [Jeremiah] and speak to all [the people of] the cities of Judah who come to worship in the Lord's house all the words that I command you to speak to them; subtract not a word. It may be that they will listen and turn every man from his evil way, that I may relent and reverse My decision concerning the evil which I purpose to do to them because of their evil doings. And you will say to them, Thus says the Lord: If you will not listen to and obey Me, to walk in My law, which I have set before you, and to hear and obey the words of My servants the prophets, whom I have sent to you urgently and persistently—though you have not listened and obeyed—then will I make this house [the temple] like Shiloh [the home of the Tent of Meeting, abandoned and later destroyed after the ark was captured by the Philistines], and I will make this city subject to the curses of all nations of the earth [so vile in their sight will it be]. And the priests and the [false] prophets and all the people heard Jeremiah speaking these words in the house of the Lord. Now when Jeremiah had finished speaking all that the Lord had commanded him to speak to all the people, the priests and the [false] prophets and all the people seized him, saying, You shall surely die! (Jeremiah 26:2–8, AMP).

Talk about a rough congregation! Jeremiah's listeners didn't just express their disapproval of his message by withholding their "amens." They didn't just frown at him and leave. They grabbed him and threatened to kill him.

Some preachers might have been tempted to placate them by saying, "Well, guys, let me go back and pray about this message some more. Maybe I missed God on this one." But not Jeremiah. He endured the hardness and stuck with God's plan.

Then Jeremiah said to all the princes and to all the people: The Lord sent me to prophesy against this house and against this city all the words that you have heard. Therefore now amend your ways and your doings and obey the voice of the Lord your God; then the Lord will relent and reverse the decision concerning the evil which He has pronounced against you. As for me, behold, I am in your hands; do with me as seems good and suitable to you. But know for certain that if you put me to death, you will bring innocent blood upon yourselves and upon this city and upon its inhabitants, for in truth the Lord has sent me to you to speak all these words in your hearing. Then said the princes and all the people to the priests and to the prophets: This man is not deserving of death, for he has spoken to us in the name of the Lord our God (Jeremiah 26:12–16, AMP).

Although Jeremiah's congregation did give up the idea of killing him, they never did warm up to his message. Eventually they got so tired of listening to him, they put him in a prison. Then, as if that weren't bad enough, they put him in the muck and mire at the bottom of a well. They did all kinds of things to Jeremiah. I don't think he ever had an easy day. But he endured and stayed connected to God's plan.

If I'm ever tempted to feel sorry for myself, I can think of Jeremiah and get inspired. I think, *If he could endure those hardships, I can certainly be patient and persevere through whatever comes my way.* Despite opposition, Jeremiah kept on preaching anyway and finally, a few people listened. As a result, a remnant of the Jews was saved from destruction.

From that remnant were four young men whose names are familiar to you—Daniel, Shadrach, Meshach, and Abednego. Those men had a major impact on the mightiest nation and one of the most powerful kings who ever lived. By patiently enduring hardships of their own (think fiery furnace and lion's den), they brought glory to God and helped preserve their nation.

Examples of men and women who patiently endured hardship and stayed connected to the plan of God are also found in the New Testament. The best one, of course, is Jesus Himself. No one has ever walked a harder road than He did. Jesus left His place in heaven at His Father's side to fulfill His Master Plan. He had to come to this sin-wracked earth, be born of a woman, endure temptations, and live out a sinless life of service to God, then pay the ultimate price of sin for us—offering Himself as the Lamb slain for us.

Jesus went through the worst experience that can be imagined—being separated from God. That was so difficult for Him that He sweat drops of blood. But He did it for the Father.

Thank God, He didn't say, "This is too hard!" Thank God, He didn't quit before He finished the plan of redemption. Had He done that, there would have been no hope for us—no way of escape from sin and death.

Once Jesus did His part, enduring the hardship, God came exploding onto the scene and did His part. He raised Jesus from the dead and restored Him to His former glory. He set Him at His own right hand, and gave Him the Name above every name—that at that Name, every knee should bow and every tongue should confess that Jesus Christ is Lord, to the glory of God the Father (Philippians 2:10–11). In the end, Jesus proved that enduring hardship and faithfully following God's plan opens the door for God to show Himself strong on our behalf. He demonstrated to all of us who would walk in His footsteps that when we patiently endure, God always sees to it that we receive our reward.

When we begin feeling overwhelmed by our little hardships and want to give up on God's Master Plan for our lives, the best thing we can do is remind ourselves that when we stay in faith and patience, we will see the victory. The best thing we can do is to get our attention off ourselves and consider what Jesus did for us. Thinking about Him will bolster our courage. That's why Hebrews 12 says:

> Let us run with patient endurance and steady and active persistence the appointed course of the race that is set before us, looking away [from all that will distract] to Jesus, Who is the Leader and the Source of our faith . . . and is also its Finisher [bringing it to maturity and perfection]. He, for the joy [of obtaining the prize] that was set before Him, endured the cross, despising and ignoring the shame, and is now seated at the right hand of the throne of God. Just think of Him Who endured from sinners such grievous opposition and bitter hostility against Himself [reckon up and consider it all in comparison with your trials], so that you may not grow weary or exhausted, losing heart and relaxing and fainting in your minds (Hebrews 12:1–3, AMP).

According to that passage, what carried Jesus through the hardships He suffered was the joy of obtaining the prize set before Him. What was that prize? The redemption of mankind. The fulfilling of the will of God. The never-ending joy of hearing His Father say, "Well done!"

When the hard times hit, that's what keeps us going: the realization that at the end of this brief time here on earth, we're going to stand before our Master and give account of what we did with the years we were given. When all the hardships and blessing of this life are over, we'll stand before the Lord Jesus Christ. Let's live our lives fully surrendered to Him and persevere to the end. We'll hear Him say, "Well done, good and faithful servant!"

I want to hear that. That is my great desire. I want to complete God's Master Plan for my life. I want to fulfill my destiny and calling and finish my assignment.

I urge you to do the same. God's plan for you and me is so much higher and better than we could think of for ourselves. And His plan is eternal. Life on earth is just the first phase of His magnificent plan.

What a plan. What a planner. What a life!

KEY NINE

—◠◡◠—

Let patience work; God has a better plan.

Twelve

THE SUPERNATURAL SYSTEM
OF SEEDTIME AND HARVEST

—⚊—

There are times when we must simply be patient and wait for our Master Plan to unfold. But there are also times when God is waiting for us. In those instances, we can make adjustments that speed the process along. We can, by more fully aligning ourselves with the Word of God, hit the spiritual accelerator and move quickly down the road.

I don't know about you, but I'm all for that. Although I've learned that good things do come to those who wait, I certainly don't want to wait any longer than necessary.

The most valuable lesson I've learned is this: the entire kingdom of God works according to one basic system. As long as I cooperate with that system, I'll keep making progress. I'll move steadily forward in the will of God, increasing in spirit, soul, and body.

What is this all-important system of operation?

The system of seedtime and harvest. It is the process God has always used to get things done in the earth—and it always will be. As Genesis 8:22 says, "While the earth remains, seedtime and harvest . . . shall not cease."

The process of seedtime and harvest isn't just a natural process. It is first a spiritual process. And the most powerful seed that exists is the seed of God's Word. It is the supernatural seed that was planted in our hearts that brought forth the new birth. It is, according to 1 Peter 1:23, incorruptible seed "which lives and abides forever."

From Genesis to Revelation, the Bible clearly teaches everything God does starts with the seed of His Word. In the beginning, when He created the earth, He did it with His Word. He said, "'Let there be light'; and there was light." He said, "'Let the earth bring forth. . . .' And the earth brought forth. . . ." (Genesis 1:3, 11, 12). The entire universe was framed and is continually upheld by the Word of God's power (Hebrews 1:3, 11:3).

That's why, several thousands of years after Creation, when God wanted to make a covenant with Abraham, He gave Abraham His Word. When God wanted to redeem mankind from sin, He did it by sending His Word—first through the prophets who foretold of Jesus' coming, and eventually through the coming of Jesus Himself. According to the New Testament, Jesus is the very embodiment of God's Word (John 1:14). In fact, the Gospel of John actually calls Him "the Word," and says:

> In the beginning was the Word, and the Word was with God, and the Word was God. He was in the beginning with God. All things were made through Him, and without Him nothing was made that was made (John 1:1–3).

There's no question about it—every plan of God that has ever been carried out in the earth has begun with the planting of His Word. Your Master Plan will be no exception. It, too, will be accomplished by the working of God's Word within you. It will come forth as God's Word is planted in your heart, cultivated, and given time to grow.

Notice, I said it *will* come forth. Not it *might* come forth. Or it *could* come forth. It *will* come forth because the supernatural seed of the Word never fails. As God says in Isaiah 55:10–11 (AMP):

> As the rain and snow come down from the heavens, and return not there again, but water the earth and make it bring forth and sprout, that it may give seed to the sower and bread to the eater, so shall My word be that goes forth out of My mouth: it shall not return to Me void [without producing any effect, useless], but it shall accomplish that which I please and purpose, and it shall prosper in the thing for which I sent it.

Unlike natural seed, which can be defective or lose its potency, God's Word is incorruptible. It remains alive and powerful forever. So when the Word is planted in good soil, it *always* produces a harvest.

Sadly, many Christians don't know that. They think of God's Word as little more than a book of rules and regulations. They're startled by the idea that the Word can be planted and bring forth fruit in their lives. They shouldn't be, because Jesus plainly taught that during His earthly ministry. He clearly referred to God's Word as spiritual seed, saying, " 'The sower sows the word' " (Mark 4:14). Later, in verses 26–29, He says:

"The kingdom of God is as if a man should scatter seed on the ground, and should sleep by night and rise by day, and the seed should sprout and grow, he himself does not know how. For the earth yields crops by itself: first the blade, then the head, after that the full grain in the head. But when the grain ripens, immediately he puts in the sickle, because the harvest has come" (Mark 4:26–29).

HOW TO AVOID SPIRITUAL CROP FAILURES

That sounds simple enough, doesn't it? Plant the Word, give it time to sprout and mature, then enjoy the harvest. It doesn't take a rocket scientist to work that system. Even a child can do it.

"If that's the case," you might say, "why does it seem there are so many spiritual crop failures? Why do so many people who hear the Word end up discouraged and disconnected from God's Master Plan for their lives?"

Jesus gave us the answer to those questions in the parable of the sower. That parable tells about a farmer who scattered seed that fell on four kinds of ground. The seed first fell on hard ground beside the road. The birds came and devoured it. Other seed fell on stony ground, where it quickly sprang up. But, because the soil was shallow there, the heat of the sun scorched the seed and it withered away.

Still other seed fell on ground with thorns in it. When the thorns grew up, they choked out the seed and ruined the crop. Finally, the seed fell on good ground where it grew up and produced a thirtyfold, sixtyfold, and even a hundredfold harvest.

Although that's an interesting parable, we might still be wondering exactly what it means, had it not been for those first disciples who heard and asked Jesus to explain it. He said:

> "Do you not discern and understand this parable? How then is it possible for you to discern and understand all the parables? The sower sows the Word. The ones along the path are those who have the Word sown [in their hearts], but when they hear, Satan comes at once and [by force] takes away the message which is sown in them. And in the same way the ones sown upon stony ground are those who, when they hear the Word, at once receive and accept and welcome it with joy; and they have no real root in themselves, and so they endure for a little while; then when trouble or persecution arises on account of the Word, they immediately are offended (become displeased, indignant, resentful) and they stumble and fall away. And the ones sown among the thorns are others who hear the Word; then the cares and anxieties of the world and distractions of the age, and the pleasure and delight and false glamour and deceitfulness of riches, and the craving and passionate desire for other things creep in and choke and suffocate the Word, and it becomes fruitless. And those sown on the good (well-adapted) soil are the ones who hear the Word and receive and accept and welcome it and bear fruit—some thirty times as much as was sown, some sixty times as much, and some [even] a hundred times as much" (Mark 4:13–20, AMP).

According to those verses, there are three reasons people experience spiritual crop failures. First, they aren't truly receptive to the Word they hear. They just let it go in one ear and out the other. Instead of receiving it by faith, they think, *Oh, that's not true. That won't work. It's just silly talk.* According to Jesus, the Word that comes to these people is like seed that falls by the wayside. Satan comes immediately and takes away the word that was sown.

The second reason people fail to benefit from the Word is because they don't hold on to it. When they first hear it, they rejoice over what they've heard, but when the devil begins to challenge them, they let it go. Jesus calls these people *stony ground* because the Word springs up for a while, but doesn't take root in their hearts. So when the circumstances get hot and the problems begin, their faith withers. They give up on the Word because living by it didn't turn out to be as easy as they expected. "Well, I tried that faith stuff and it didn't work for me," they'll say. "I tried to believe God for healing for two whole days but I still felt sick. So I quit."

If you don't want to be stony ground, you must realize, in advance, that the devil will definitely come to steal the Word that is sown in your heart. You must be determined to spend enough time in the Word to get a firm grip on it because you will have to fight for it. You will have to resist the devil when he harasses you with circumstances and tells you the Word won't work for you. You'll have to be strong enough to say, "Get behind me, Satan! You're not getting the Word out of my heart. I rebuke you in Jesus' name."

Always remember this: harvest comes from the Word you keep alive in your heart and mind—the Word you continue to hold on to and act on. So if you want to enjoy the full harvest of what God has planned for you, take hold of His Word and refuse to let go.

Throughout the years, Ken and I have developed that kind of bulldog tenacity. We've found we can have anything God promises if we'll walk by faith and not be moved by what we see. We can have a hundredfold harvest if we'll keep the Word in our hearts and in our mouths, even when things look impossible and like nothing good is happening. When we hang on to God's promises, He performs them. We always see them come to pass in our lives.

The third reason the Word doesn't produce results in people's lives is because of the thorns. They let the cares and entertainment of this world overcome and choke the Word that was sown in their hearts. They actually had the Word in their hearts, but it was overcome by an abundance of other things until it was unfruitful. They forget about the Word that they heard and fail to act on it. They stop putting the Word first place in their lives and it doesn't produce victory.

Personally, I think this is where most seasoned believers miss it. They get so busy and distracted with the natural affairs of life, they quit spending time in the Word. They start spending all their time trying to make money, or taking the kids to sporting events, or watching their favorite shows on television. Their time with the Lord is eroded by natural things.

Before long, God's Word isn't alive and active in them anymore. They may remember what it says. They may even be able to quote the same scriptures they always did. But those scriptures aren't really speaking to their hearts anymore. As a result, their faith weakens and starts to fail. They stop getting answers to their prayers. They get stuck and can't seem to move forward in God's plan.

Christians in that condition often think they're waiting for God to move on their behalf but, in reality, God is waiting for them. He is waiting for them to put more of the Word in their hearts because the Word they had before has been choked out. Although they don't realize it, they have no more seed in the ground. And without seed there can't be a harvest.

Say, for example, someone is waiting on God to meet their need for a new car. For a while they keep their heart full of God's promises of provision. Every time they turn around, they are praising Him and saying, "Thank You, Father, that You promised to supply all my needs according to Your riches in glory by Christ Jesus. Thank You, Lord, for promising me that if I'd commit my ways to You, You would give me the desires of my heart. Thank You for my new car!"

For a few months, they read scriptural promises every day. They put "provision verses" on the refrigerator. They listen to ministers who preach the Word and become convinced that God is faithful and just to fulfill these promises. That is faith. Faith is believing what God says instead of what circumstances say.

But as time goes by, they get busy. They think, *Well, I know those scriptures. I don't need to read them anymore.* So they replace the verses on the refrigerator with the phone number of the pizza delivery place. Instead of watching faith-building programs on television, they begin watching something unproductive—programs full of sin and worldliness.

Eventually, instead of rejoicing in faith and declaring the Word about the new car they need, they start getting irritated about the old clunker they're driving right now. They start saying, "This faith stuff isn't working . . . I'm going to end up driving this broken-down hunk of junk forever."

That kind of talk is a sign of heart trouble. It's an indication their hearts need a Word transfusion. They've let the cares of this world and the lies of the devil steal the Word they once had, and they aren't consuming new Word to replace it.

People who say they tried faith and it didn't work are mistaken. The truth is just the opposite. Faith tried them and *they* didn't work.

What can you do when you find yourself in that situation?

Repent . . . and start over. Ask the Lord to forgive you for yielding to unbelief, then straighten up. Start spending time in the Word again. Get your mouth back in line to agree with what God says. Do it over and do it right.

Do what I used to do when driving a car with a Global Positioning System (GPS). If I missed a turn and started going the wrong way, the system would activate and a lady's voice would say, "Make a legal U-turn at the next intersection." Since I wanted to get to the right place, I followed the instructions. I turned around and eventually arrived at my desired destination.

Thankfully, we can do the same thing when we let the Word get away from us and start missing turns on our Master Plan. We can make a legal U-turn and get back on track. We can shut off disobedience and unbelief and get our hearts and mouths full of the Word again.

What will happen if we don't make that correction? The same thing that would have happened to me had I ignored the GPS system in my car and kept going the wrong way. I would never have gotten where I wanted to go. I might have been trying to go to Dallas but went to Oklahoma City instead. I would have missed my appointed destination. I couldn't have blamed my GPS system for it because it would have been my own fault. I didn't listen and I didn't obey.

In the same way, you can't blame God or His Word if you get off track and miss some portion of His plan for your life. God's Word always works. It always produces results. If you get on the Bible road to healing and stay on it, you'll eventually be well. If you get on the Bible road to prosperity and stay on it, you will eventually prosper.

If you do happen to let the Word slip and experience needless delays, just do what it takes to get things moving again. Double your Word time. Make sure you're reading and confessing the Word every day and obeying what you learn there. Go regularly to a church where the Bible is preached and your faith is strengthened. Find one that will feed you the Word and not just motivational materials or man-made theories and ideas.

Doing these things will make you good ground for the Word. They'll help you become one of those people who "hear the word, accept it, and bear fruit: some thirtyfold, some sixty, and some a hundred" (Mark 4:20).

SAY, "MY HEART IS PROCESSING IT!"

If you're wondering what the difference is between the people who reap a thirtyfold harvest, and those who end up with sixty- or even a hundredfold harvest of God's blessings, I can tell you. It's the amount of effort they put into the Word-planting process. The more diligent we are to plant the Word in our hearts and make adjustments according to what the Word says, the better our return on it will be. Any of us can be hundredfold ground if we'll just pull out all the stops, live for God, keep our focus on His Word, obey what it says, and walk by faith, regardless of what we see or feel.

Actually, it's impossible to live like that and fail. "Therefore I say to you, whatever things you ask when you pray, believe that you receive *them,* and you will have *them*" (Mark 11:24).

What is on the inside of you is going to come out. What's hidden in your heart will eventually be revealed for everyone to see. If there's no Word in there, usually nothing supernatural is going to happen. If there's a little Word in there, you'll see a few of God's promises come to pass in your life. But if your heart is full of God's Word and you are obeying it, His whole plan is going to manifest—and no one, including the devil himself, can stop it. You'll get results in every area of life, results that the whole world can see.

Remember, in God's seedtime and harvest system there's usually a period of time when it looks like nothing is happening. There's a season when God's Word is working underground, in your heart and in the invisible realm of the spirit. During that season, people who don't understand God's basic operating system may wonder how you can be so confident that God's promise will come to pass in your life. They may make fun of you for believing when there's no natural evidence of it.

Sometimes you may even begin to question the process in your own mind, and begin to wonder why the thing you're believing for hasn't manifested yet.

The Lord showed me how to deal with that a few years ago. Ken and I had been believing for a long time for something big. We'd been standing and confessing God's Word about it for years. (Sometimes major faith projects take a while.) But we weren't discouraged. We were just as happy as can be because we knew our seed was in the ground and our harvest was on the way.

Every once in a while, I'd wonder. *Why is it taking so long? What's going on?*

The Lord taught me to answer those questions by saying, "My heart is processing that." Your heart is processing the Word of God.

That's what happens to seed when it's planted, you know. The soil begins to process it. Underground, where no one can see, the dirt goes to work on that seed, breaking down the hard, outer shell and bringing life out of it. That process takes time, but sooner or later the job gets done.

In the same way, when the Word seed is planted in the ground of our hearts, a process begins. Our hearts go to work on that Word, making faith out of it. One month might go by, two months might go by . . . even a year might go by without any visible evidence of change. But you can rest assured that as long as you keep that Word in your heart and in your mouth, the process will continue. Your heart processes the Word the way the soil processes seed. It will keep working on that spiritual seed of the Word until first the blade, then the ear, then the full corn in the ear is ready (Mark 4:28). If you don't quit, in due season, what you're believing for will come to pass.

There may be times when you believe for something for five years and because your crop hasn't come up yet, you're tempted to give up on it. You're tempted to let go of God's promise and forget the whole thing. But if you do that, you dig up your seed. There won't be anything in your heart to produce your harvest. You will have wasted those five years.

So make up your mind now that quitting is not an option. Determine in your heart that no matter how long the process takes, you're going to hang in there! Keep the Word in your heart and mouth for as long as it takes. Jesus said, "If you abide in Me, and My words abide in you, you will ask what you desire, and it shall be done for you" (John 15:7).

If you think you could be missing God somewhere but you don't know where, ask for wisdom. James 1:2–8 (AMP) says:

> Consider it wholly joyful, my brethren, whenever you are enveloped in or encounter trials of any sort or fall into various temptations. Be assured and understand that the trial and proving of your faith bring out endurance and steadfastness and patience. But let endurance and steadfastness and patience have full play and do a thorough work, so that you may be [people] perfectly and fully developed [with no defects], lacking in

nothing. If any of you is deficient in wisdom, let him ask of the giving God [Who gives] to everyone liberally and ungrudgingly, without reproaching or fault-finding, and it will be given him. Only it must be in faith that he asks with no wavering (no hesitating, no doubting). For the one who wavers (hesitates, doubts) is like the billowing surge out at sea that is blown hither and thither and tossed by the wind. For truly, let not such a person imagine that he will receive anything [he asks for] from the Lord, [for being as he is] a man of two minds (hesitating, dubious, irresolute), [he is] unstable and unreliable and uncertain about everything [he thinks, feels, decides].

Your harvest will come and when it does, it will be wonderful. You'll be so glad you didn't give up.

YOU CAN ALWAYS REJOICE

Actually, if you want to keep the faith process moving, you won't wait until harvest time comes to be glad. You'll start being joyful now. You'll obey the command the Apostle Paul gave us in Philippians 4:4: "Rejoice in the Lord always. Again I will say, rejoice!"

Notice, that verse doesn't instruct us just to rejoice when things are good. It tells us to rejoice *always*.

Why is rejoicing so important? Because the joy of the Lord is our strength (Nehemiah 8:10). Joy is a powerful fruit of the Spirit (Galatians 5:22). It helps give us the inner fortitude we need to see the process of seedtime and harvest all the way through. Joy will help keep us going when the going gets tough.

Some Christians seem to think it's impossible to rejoice always. "There are times I don't have anything to rejoice about!" they say. "How can I have joy when everything is going wrong?"

Ask the Old Testament prophet Habakkuk. He had that figured out. One time when it looked like all hell had broken loose around him, he said:

> Though the fig tree may not blossom, nor fruit be on the vines; though the labor of the olive may fail, and the fields yield no food; though the flock may be cut off from the fold, and there be no herd in the stalls— yet I will rejoice in the Lord, I will joy in the God of my salvation (Habakkuk 3:17–18).

Even in the darkest of times, Habakkuk could still rejoice because he knew God was his salvation. You can do the same thing. After all, you're a born-again child of God. Just the knowledge that you're headed for heaven instead of hell should be enough to make you glad. What's more, your almighty, heavenly Father has promised to bless you in every area of life if you'll just stand in faith and be patient. He has promised to heal and deliver you and be your salvation in the here and now, as well as in the hereafter. And He always keeps His promises.

So what if circumstances are troublesome right now? You can still rejoice in the God of your salvation! You can turn your attention away from the difficulties of the present moment and focus instead on the promises and the faithfulness of God.

If you can't stir up that joy, then you've stepped over into unbelief. You've let your faith slip. So wake yourself up. Get back in the Word. Take the verse "This is the day the Lord has made; we will rejoice and be glad in it" (Psalm 118:24).

Of course, getting glad is just half the challenge. The other half is staying that way. It's easy to be filled with joy in the morning after reading your Bible and praying . . . but by noon that joy can slip away. If you don't watch out, life will steal it from you. You'll start to fret over some difficulty, or get anxious about a dilemma you can't figure out how to solve. Before you know it, you're not rejoicing in the Lord anymore.

Through the years, I've gotten wise to that pattern. So I've learned to be vigilant and continually endeavor to follow these New Testament commands:

- "Do not fret or have any anxiety about anything, but in every circumstance and in everything, by prayer and petition (definite requests), with thanksgiving, continue to make your wants known to God" (Philippians 4:6, AMP).
- "Casting the whole of your care [all your anxieties, all your worries, all your concerns, once and for all] on Him, for He cares for you affectionately and cares about you watchfully" (1 Peter 5:7, AMP).
- "Therefore do not worry and be anxious, saying, What are we going to have to eat? or, What are we going to have to drink? or, What are we going to have to wear? For the Gentiles (heathen) wish for and crave and diligently seek all these things, and your heavenly Father knows well that you need them all. But seek (aim at and strive after) first of all His kingdom and His righteousness (His way of doing and being right), and then all these things taken together will be given you besides" (Matthew 6:31–33, AMP).

- "'Therefore do not worry about tomorrow, for tomorrow will worry about its own things. Sufficient for the day is its own trouble'" (Matthew 6:34).
- "This is the day the Lord has made; we will rejoice and be glad in it" (Psalm 118:24).

As Andrew Murray said, "I am going to do the will of God today without thinking of tomorrow."[11]

I can tell you firsthand, that's a great way to live. No worries. No dread or fear of the future. Just getting up every day and saying, "Lord, I'm going to enjoy this day. It's a gift from You and I will rejoice in it."

I've spent so many years cultivating the habit of rolling my cares over on the Lord that if you didn't know my past, you might think that I'm just a carefree kind of person by nature. I can assure you, however, that is not the case. I used to be a world-class worrier. In fact, I came from a family full of them. But I started breaking the worry habit right after I got born again. In the early years, when Ken and I couldn't pay our bills, I'd read Matthew 6 again and again. I'd remind myself that God cares about the birds and He promised to take care of me if I'd just seek Him first. Then, I'd roll all our money cares, anxieties, worries, and concerns over on the Lord. First Peter 5:7 is powerful ammunition in the worry department.

If I could do that back then—in the middle of the trouble we were in—you can do it too, no matter how trying your circumstances might be. When anxiety starts to overtake you and the devil says there's no way out for you, read and think about the above scrip-

---

11. Andrew Murray, *The Holiest of All, An Exposition of the Epistle to the Hebrews, Abridged Edition* (Fort Worth: Kenneth Copeland Ministries, abridgement of retypeset edition, 1996).

tures. Then, just roll all those cares over on the Lord and refuse to worry. Instead, verify your faith and trust in God.

"But I have to worry!" someone might say. "They're going to foreclose on my house!"

Maybe they will . . . or maybe they won't. Either way, worrying won't change the situation. If it hasn't happened yet, the Lord could still deliver you from that dilemma. Even if they do foreclose on your house, you'll live through it. And, if you just keep seeking the Lord, rolling the care of the circumstance over on Him, He'll eventually get you an even better house.

But I've realized it's not the big crises like house foreclosures that most frequently steal our joy. It's the little things—like balancing the checkbook, or cleaning house, or going to the dentist, or being hurt over something said to us or about us. Such minor events (however unpleasant they may be) don't actually amount to much in the overall scheme of things, yet most of us have developed the habit of dreading them for days in advance, so they often cast a shadow over our whole week.

Sometime ago, the Lord showed me something that helped me break that habit. He pointed out that if I have an unpleasant task to do on Monday and begin dreading it on Friday, then think about it Saturday and Sunday, several times a day, it's like doing it over and over. You build up a tremendous amount of negativity and unbelief about it. So when Monday comes, it's going to be every bit as bad as you imagined it would be, and maybe even worse, because you brooded about it for days.

Once I understood that, I started weeding dread out of my thought life. Jesus said tomorrow will have worries of its own (Matthew 6:34). I have stopped dreading unpleasant tasks. I knew if I didn't, it would keep stealing my joy, choking out the Word I'd planted in my heart and ruining a good day the Lord had made.

Eventually, it could even interfere with God's Master Plan for my life. It is a bad habit that would keep me thinking on the negative side instead of the faith side.

The same thing is true for you. Refuse to dread. Dread really is strong unbelief and a negative attitude. So get rid of dread right away.

Exactly how do you do it?

It's simple, really.

If you have to clean your house tomorrow and that's something you don't enjoy doing, just refuse to think about it today. If you have to wade into a laundry room that's five feet deep in clothes to do the wash on Thursday, determine not to give it a thought until Thursday comes. In the meantime, roll the care of it over on the Lord. Trust Him to give you the grace you'll need to clean that house, wash those clothes, and have a good time doing it. Then spend today rejoicing in the Lord.

I like the attitude a friend of mine has developed. She treats the worries of tomorrow the way Scarlett O'Hara did in *Gone With the Wind*. When trouble loomed in Scarlett's future, she just said, "Oh, fiddle-dee-dee! I'll think about that tomorrow."

I'll admit those words aren't exactly scriptural. Scarlett O'Hara definitely wasn't born again and filled with the Holy Spirit, but she did know how to deal with dread. She was determined not to let tomorrow's troubles ruin today.

I think that's a wonderful attitude! When you mix it with faith in God and His promises, saying something like *fiddle-dee-dee* by faith can become a lighthearted way to rid yourself of dread and worry—which is precisely what the Bible says we should do.

So why not try it? Do what my friend and I do. When we're talking to each other, and one of us happens to mention something we might be tempted to dread, we laugh and say, "Fiddle-dee-dee, I'll think about that tomorrow!"

Why not just say, "Fiddle-dee-dee on those clothes in the laundry room. Fiddle-dee-dee on that dentist appointment. I'm trusting God, anyway. I'll think about those things when the time comes"? If you do that, you'll have such a good day today, that when tomorrow comes, you'll have the joy and spiritual strength you need to do even your least favorite things in the power of God, with a happy attitude.

Instead of grumbling your way through the grocery shopping, you'll actually enjoy it. You might even decide to have a caffe latte and praise the Lord all the way from the produce section to the canned goods aisle! If you'll let Him, God will help you do everything from grocery shopping to laundry to balancing your budget. And He can make it all a pleasant experience.

That may sound silly to you, but it's really serious business. After all, Jesus came to give us abundant life and He wants us to enjoy that life. But He won't make us enjoy it. If we insist on being negative and living in dread each day, we'll miss out on a lot of the good life He has planned for us. If we don't learn this one, simple principle of enjoying today and not worrying about tomorrow, we'll miss out on a million wonderful moments of joy.

Not long ago, I caught myself dreading a particular ministry task I was facing. It wasn't any big deal, really—just a day's worth of work that required me to get up early in the morning, fly to another city, meet with people I didn't know, then fly home.

The day before, I began thinking, *Why did I ever agree to that? I really dislike that kind of thing!*

As I started to slip into negativity, I realized my mistake and got a grip on myself. I decided I was going to enjoy that event. "I am not going to dread it," I said. "It's the day the Lord has made and I'm changing my attitude right now. I will rejoice and be glad in it."

That day turned out to be thoroughly pleasant. The work seemed easy. My daughter, Kellie, and my granddaughters went with me, so we were able to have lunch together. I was back home by early evening. All went well because I didn't give the devil anything to work with over my day. I walked it out by faith. Instead of yielding to dread, I just kept rejoicing in the Lord, and He took care of me.

ACTING ON GOD'S WISDOM TODAY WILL SECURE YOUR TOMORROW

"But, Gloria," you might say, "isn't it irresponsible just to ignore tomorrow? Shouldn't we be concerned about our future?"

No, we shouldn't be *concerned*. We should just seek the Lord and do what He tells us to do today and stay in faith. If we do that, He'll make sure we're prepared for tomorrow. He'll give us the thoughts, plans, and wisdom we need to act wisely today, and those wise acts will positively affect our future.

Casting our cares on the Lord doesn't mean we ignore tomorrow, it just means we refuse to dread or worry about it. Worrying doesn't do any good, anyway. It doesn't help our future one bit.

What *does* help?

Doing what Proverbs 16:3 (AMP) says to do: "Roll your works upon the Lord [commit and trust them wholly to Him; He will cause your thoughts to become agreeable to His will, and] so shall your plans be established and succeed."

Make that verse your guide to tomorrow. Instead of carrying the burden of it yourself and trying in your own strength to figure out what to do about it, roll that burden over on God. Say, "Lord, I'm not going to be anxious about my future because I know You care for me. I know You are watching over me. So I believe I receive the wisdom and peace I need today. I trust You to see me through in victory tomorrow. I thank You that I am carefree."

Then refuse to worry about it anymore. Just go on your way rejoicing in the Lord and thanking Him for the answer. If it doesn't come immediately, just keep believing and rejoicing. When you're tempted to worry about your future again, resist the temptation. Refuse to be troubled about it. Reaffirm your faith by saying, "Lord, I've rolled the care of that over on You. I know You will show me what I need to know, and when You do, I'll be obedient. I'll do what You tell me and all will be well."

Once you've settled that issue, get so busy seeking God and thinking about His Word that worry doesn't stand a chance in your life. Hit the spiritual accelerator by rejoicing in the Lord always, and you'll keep moving on down the road of God's Master Plan for your life.

KEY TEN

Plant God's Word in your heart, cultivate it,
and give it time to produce.

Thirteen

LIVE LONG, STAY STRONG

—⚏—

Before we leave the subject of God's timing, there's one more thing I want to address. It's the concern believers sometimes have about growing old. That issue can begin to trouble us when the plan for our lives seems to be progressing at a particularly slow pace and we're trying to wait patiently for our divine destiny to unfold.

As you watch the days . . . and months . . . and years tick by, you can begin to wonder: *What if old age overtakes me before I can do everything I'm called to do? What if I don't live long enough to finish God's plan for me?*

If you're eighteen or twenty-five or thirty-nine, those questions may not have crossed your mind yet. But if you're in your fifties or beyond, they either have already, or soon will. When they do, don't try to ignore them. They are serious questions that need to be answered, and the Bible clearly addresses them.

Actually, whether you have asked those questions yet or not, you'd be wise to study the Scriptures and find out what God's perspective is on your latter years. Because no matter how young you are right now, you are getting older. If you want your "Golden Years" to truly be the most gloriously happy, blessedly productive years of your life, you'd better start, right now, thinking about them God's way.

God looks at aging very differently than our contemporary culture does. As you well know, the world glorifies physical youth above all. It covets the beauty of youth far more than the wisdom, maturity, and experience that can come with age. As a result, old age is more dreaded in our society than respected. People in their seventies and beyond are often written off as unimportant and unproductive.

Sadly, even many Christians have adopted that perspective. They don't rejoice in the passing years or expect to be increasingly blessed as they grow older. On the contrary, many believers expect to start declining in their latter years, and rather than pressing in to God's plan for their lives, they just lie down and let the devil run over them. They accept senility as inevitable and mentally prepare to forget things, become feeble, and die before they should. Some even base that attitude on Scripture, believing that the Bible promises we can only live seventy or eighty years.

Where do they get that idea? Usually from Psalm 90:10, which says: "The days of our lives are seventy years; and if by reason of strength they are eighty years . . . for it is soon cut off, and we fly away."

When you read the verse in context, however, you'll see this psalm isn't referring to born-again, Spirit-filled believers. It was written by Moses about the sad lives of the Israelites who lived and died in the wilderness without ever seeing the Promised Land:

> Our iniquities, our secret heart and its sins [which we
> would so like to conceal even from ourselves], You

have set in the [revealing] light of Your countenance. For all our days [out here in this wilderness, says Moses] pass away in Your wrath; we spend our years as a tale that is told [for we adults know we are doomed to die soon, without reaching Canaan]. The days of our years are threescore years and ten (seventy years)—or even, if by reason of strength, fourscore years (eighty years); yet is their pride [in additional years] only labor and sorrow, for it is soon gone, and we fly away (Psalm 90:8–10, AMP).

Clearly, God never meant for that to be our testimony. We're the redeemed of the Lord. Our sins aren't set before Him, they are washed away by the blood of Jesus. We don't pass away in God's wrath—we're saved from wrath (Romans 5:9). Therefore, as New Testament believers, we can rest assured those verses aren't talking about us. God hasn't limited our life span to merely seven or eight decades. He wants us to live a long, long time. The footnote for Psalm 90 in *The Amplified Bible* says:

This psalm is credited to Moses, who is interceding with God to remove the curse which made it necessary for every Israelite over twenty years of age (when they rebelled against God at Kadesh-barnea) to die before reaching the promised land (Numbers 14:26–35). Moses says most of them are dying at seventy years of age. This number has often been mistaken as a set span of life for all mankind. It was not intended to refer to anyone except those Israelites under the curse during that particular forty years. Seventy years never has been the average span of life for humanity. When Jacob, the father of the twelve tribes, had reached 130 years (Genesis 47:9), he complained that he had not attained to the years of his immediate ancestors. In fact, Moses himself lived to be 120 years old, Aaron 123, Miriam several years older, and Joshua 110 years of age. Note as well that in the Millennium a person dying at one hundred will still be thought a child (Isaiah 65:20).[12]

Exactly how long can we live?

Frankly, I can't say for sure. The closest numerical definition we have for long life is the one God gave Noah before the flood when He said, "My Spirit shall not strive with man forever, for he is indeed flesh; yet his days shall be one hundred and twenty years" (Genesis 6:3). To us, 120 years seems like a very long time. Most of us would really have to stretch our faith to believe for that kind of life span. Yet we shouldn't really allow even that number to limit us. After all, when God gave it, He was actually referring to the life span of the unbelieving, disobedient people who inhabited the earth just prior to the flood. He didn't say it included the righteous. In fact, it couldn't have included the righteous because Noah himself went on to live another three hundred fifty years after the flood, to the ripe, old age of nine hundred fifty (Genesis 9:28–29).

WHAT A WAY TO GO!

"Be serious, Gloria!" you might say. "Surely you don't think we should live nine hundred fifty years."

---

12. *The Amplified Bible, Old Testament* © 1965, 1987 by The Zondervan Corporation. *The Amplified New Testament* © 1958, 1987 by The Lockman Foundation. Used by permission.

I don't know any sane Christian who would even want to live that long in this time. Why should we? For us, death is not a disaster, but a departure. In fact, it's a promotion. We should go out of this earth with joy saying, like the Apostle Paul, "I ran my race. I finished my course. I'm going to heaven now to receive my crown!" (2 Timothy 4:7–8). We should leave the limitations of our natural body behind and blast into the realm of the spirit singing with joy, "I'll fly away, oh glory!"

I don't know about you, but I don't want to wait nine hundred years for that. I want to finish my work here on earth while I look forward to the next step, which will be more life than I've previously experienced. When that time comes, I'll be "well pleased rather to be absent from the body and to be present with the Lord" (2 Corinthians 5:8)!

I'm especially looking forward to the resurrected, glorified body I'm going to get. It will look far better than the one I have right now. It will be beautiful and glorious and have the ability to do marvelous things. It will be a spiritual body instead of a natural one. It's going to be great!

As wonderful as it will be, however, that day will have to wait until I've finished my assignment and life here on earth. It will have to wait until I've done everything God wants me to do. *I'm not leaving this planet until both He and I are satisfied.* I realize that's a bold statement. But I make no apologies for it because it's based on the written Word of God. It's founded on scriptures such as Psalm 91. There, the Lord promises longevity and fulfillment to every believer who sets his heart on God:

> "Because he has set his love upon Me, therefore I will deliver him; I will set him on high, because he has known My name. He shall call upon Me, and I will answer him; I will be with him in trouble; I will de-

liver him and honor him. With long life I will satisfy
him, and show him My salvation" (Psalm 91:14–16).

I intend to take God up on that promise. I plan to live a long life
and remain on this earth until I'm fully satisfied. Then, I'll follow
the example of Old Testament believers like Jacob. I like the way he
chose to depart. When he was a very old man and had lived out a full
life, he called all his family together and ministered to them. When
he finished, "he drew his feet up into the bed and breathed his last,
and was gathered to his people" (Genesis 49:33).

What a way to go! Live until you're satisfied, get everybody together and bless and instruct them, tell them good-bye, draw your
feet up into the bed . . . and take off.

"Sounds good," someone might say, "but doesn't the Bible say
we all have an appointed time to die? What if my appointed time
comes early?"

Actually, the Bible *doesn't* say you have an appointed time to die.
It says, "It is appointed unto men once to die, but after this the judgment" (Hebrews 9:27, KJV). We die once. We don't die and keep
coming back, reincarnated as a butterfly or a worm so we can learn
to be a better person. We live out our earthly lives and die just once.
We get one shot at fulfilling God's Master Plan for our lives. After
that comes the judgment and a very long time—eternity.

The Bible also teaches it's not God's will for death to come to us
early. God wants us to live righteously, according to His wisdom, so
we can enjoy—not just live, but *enjoy!*—many, many years on the
earth. Long life is, without question, part of God's Master Plan for
us. That's why He says:

My son, forget not my law or teaching, but let your
heart keep my commandments; for length of days and

years of a life [worth living] and tranquility [inward and outward and continuing through old age till death], these shall they add to you (Proverbs 3:1–2, AMP).

Notice this says, "through old age till death." When you obey the Word of God, you can expect peace and tranquillity every day you live on the earth—not just after you go to heaven. I especially like those verses because they promise more than just a long life. That's important because long life by itself isn't always a blessing. It's no fun to live long if you're sick or dependent on others to take care of you. Long life can be miserable if your days are full of turmoil and strife.

For life to be worth living, you want to live long and be strong. You want to spend your days in peace and tranquillity. You want to be walking in the Master Plan of God!

So, here is your long-life test question: According to Psalm 91:16, how long should you live? (You can pass this one—it is an open-book test!)

Answer: Till you're satisfied!

TAKE GOD'S MEDICINE DAILY AS PRESCRIBED

Some Christians struggle with the concept of living strong and healthy all the days of their lives because what they have heard others preach based on Christian traditions.

One lady wrote to us some years ago and asked, "If I keep getting healed, how will I ever die?" The answer is we don't have to be sick to die. We don't have to let our spirits be evicted from our body by sickness and disease. We can live out the full number of our days well, prosperous, and blessed. Then when we are satisfied, we've finished our work and it's time for us to go, we can just depart.

You are a spirit. You have a soul and you live in a body. When *you*, the spirit, leave your body, it dies. Dying is easy. You depart your body and go to be with the Lord and your loved ones who have gone before you. What a reunion! We live by faith in God's Word and when the time comes, we die by faith in God's Word. What a way to go! Living is the more difficult assignment.

While we are at home in this body, we live on God's health plan and take His medicine daily as prescribed in Proverbs 4:20–22 (AMP):

> My son, attend to my words; consent and submit to my sayings. Let them not depart from your sight; keep them in the center of your heart. For they are life to those who find them, healing and health [or medicine] to all their flesh.

I've taken the medicine of God's Word almost every day for years and can personally testify that it will cure whatever ails you. It will keep you strong—spirit, soul, and body—no matter how old you get. It will not only heal you of any kind of sickness or disease the devil might try to put on you, it will keep you energetic and sharp. It will renew your youth.

Of course, taking God's medicine as prescribed includes not only hearing God's Word, but acting on it. This means we let it correct our thinking and our actions. The Bible clearly assures us if we'll do that, if we'll adhere to God's principles instead of the ways of the world, we'll reap a reward of long life.

The Bible gives us examples of a number of people who proved the validity of that promise, including. . . .

- *Abraham*—He didn't even begin to walk out God's plan for his life until he was seventy-five years old. Most people would think that's too late for a new beginning, but apparently God doesn't think so. He not only called Abraham to a whole new life at that age, He also promised him a son. No doubt, Abraham figured God would have to hurry to get that promise fulfilled in time. But God didn't hurry. He waited another twenty-five years. Even then, Abraham's life wasn't over. He and Sarah lived on and raised Isaac to adulthood. When Sarah died at 127 (Genesis 23:1), Abraham married again and had even more children (Genesis 25:1–2). Talk about being productive in your old age!

- *Moses*—He was a late bloomer, too. Although he identified God's Master Plan for his life fairly early (at the tender age of forty—see Acts 7:23), four more decades passed before God spoke to him out of the burning bush and launched him into his forty-year ministry. Despite his late start, Moses finished strong. When he died at 120, "his eyes were not dim nor his natural vigor diminished" (Deuteronomy 34:7).

- *Joshua*—As Moses' successor, this Old Testament leader had a similar experience. He didn't step fully into his primary calling until he was more than eighty years old. But his age didn't slow him down. Remember what the Lord told Joshua when he got his assignment: "Moses My servant is dead. Now therefore, arise, go over this Jordan, you and all this people, to the land which I am giving to them—the children of Israel. Every place that the sole of your foot will tread upon I have given you, as I said to Moses. . . . Only be strong and very courageous, that you may observe to do according to all the law which Moses My servant commanded you; do not turn from it to the right hand or to the left, that you may prosper wherever you go. This Book of the Law shall not depart from your mouth, but you shall meditate in it day and night, that you may observe to do according to all that is written in it. For then you will make your way prosperous, and then you will have good success. Have I not commanded you? Be strong and of good courage; do not be afraid, nor be dismayed, for the Lord your God is with you wherever you go" (Joshua 1:2–3, 7–9). In his eighties and nineties, Joshua led the Israelites victoriously through some very rough-and-tumble times. Then, at the age of 110, when he was "old, advanced in age" (Joshua 23:1) and his job was done, he departed. Joshua 11:15–16 says of him: "As the Lord had commanded Moses his servant, so Moses commanded Joshua, and so Joshua did. He left nothing undone of all that the Lord had commanded Moses. Thus Joshua took all this land: the mountain country, all the South, all the land of Goshen, the lowland, and the Jordan plain— the mountains of Israel and its lowlands." This was Joshua's own testimony just before he died: "'Behold, this day I am going the way of all the earth. And you know in all your hearts and in all your souls that not one thing has failed of all the good things which the Lord your God spoke concerning you. All have come to pass for you; not one word of them has failed'" (Joshua 23:14).

- *Caleb*—He was Joshua's counterpart throughout the wilderness journey. He, too, had to wait until he was in his mideighties before his most important and challenging assignment came. He didn't slip into decline because of the delay. His eighties didn't find him sitting in a rocking chair, walking with a cane, too old and weak to take the Promised Land. On the contrary, he was still an aggressive, effective warrior at that age. He didn't have any trouble with his memory, either. He remembered quite clearly which mountain God had promised to give him. And because his youth had been renewed like the eagle's, even at eighty-five he was plenty strong enough to conquer it. He knew this and said so: "A delegation from the tribe of Judah, led by Caleb son of Jephunneh the Kenizzite, came to Joshua at Gilgal. Caleb said to Joshua, 'Remember what the Lord said to Moses, the man of God, about you and me when we were at Kadesh-barnea. I was forty years old when Moses, the servant of the Lord, sent me from Kadesh-barnea to explore the land of Canaan. I returned and gave from my heart a good report, but my brothers who went with me frightened the people and discouraged them from entering the Promised Land. For my part, I followed the Lord my God completely. So that day Moses promised me, "The land of Canaan on which you were just walking will be your special possession and that of your descendants forever, because you wholeheartedly followed the Lord my God." Now, as you can see, the Lord has kept me alive and well as he promised for all these forty-five years since Moses made this promise—even while

Israel wandered in the wilderness. Today I am eighty-five years old. I am as strong now as I was when Moses sent me on that journey, and I can still travel and fight as well as I could then. So I'm asking you to give me the hill country that the Lord promised me. You will remember that as scouts we found the Anakites living there in great, walled cities. But if the Lord is with me, I will drive them out of the land, just as the Lord said.' So Joshua blessed Caleb son of Jephunneh and gave Hebron to him as an inheritance" (Joshua 14:6–13, NLT-96). Joshua and Caleb were the only two spies who believed what God said, survived the wilderness and got their land.

PUT ON YOUR SPIRITUAL BOXING GLOVES

If you want to know how to age according to God's Master Plan, let these men of faith and others like them be an example to you. Imitate those who through faith and patience inherited God's promise of blessing, health, renewed strength, and long life. Make up your mind right now that you'll be one of the people Psalm 92 talks about when it says:

The [uncompromisingly] righteous shall flourish like the palm tree [be long-lived, stately, upright, useful, and fruitful]; they shall grow like a cedar in Lebanon [majestic, stable, durable, and incorruptible]. Planted in the house of the Lord, they shall flourish in the courts of our God. [Growing in grace] they shall still bring forth fruit in old age; they shall be full of sap [of spiritual vitality] and [rich in the] verdure [of trust, love, and contentment]. [They are living memorials] to show that the Lord is upright and faithful to His promises; He is my Rock, and there is no unrighteousness in Him (Psalm 92:12–15, AMP).

Determine today to be a living memorial to show that the Lord is upright and faithful. I've already volunteered. It's available, but we have to put active faith in God's Word to work in our lives and walk in obedience to Him.

You can't be one of those old-age fruit bearers if you passively allow the natural process of aging . . . and the devil . . . or sickness and disease, or the opinions of others . . . to dominate you. You can't give up if confusion or forgetfulness starts to plague you. You can't just say, "Well, I guess I'm getting old. Everyone says the mind is the first thing to go. I guess it's all just downhill from here. . . . Ha! Ha!"

No, this is not a joking matter. You have to put on your boxing gloves of faith and put up a fight. (A good fight is one you win.) You must rebuke those symptoms of senility. Confess the Word over them. Say, "I have the mind of Christ. My mind is sharp. My mind is alert. My memory is great. I refuse to receive confusion and forgetfulness. In Jesus' Name, my youth is renewed like the eagles!" I like to say it like this: *"I refuse to be confused."*

Don't panic just because you occasionally draw a mental blank. Just think how much more information we process every day than our ancestors had to think about. Isn't this called the Information Age? Everyone forgets things now and then and gets mixed up sometimes. The devil will try to blow those things out of proportion and convince you they're going to get worse. But don't let him do it. Instead, cultivate a mental image of yourself at ninety or one hundred years old, with your mind and body still fresh and flourishing.

That's the image the Bible tells us we should have. It doesn't paint a picture of the righteous man hobbling his way through old age, crippled up with arthritis and other kinds of age-related ailments, unable to be a blessing to people. It tells us we'll still be productive in our latter years. We'll still be declaring the Word and proclaiming the faithfulness of God. We'll be enjoying a strong life for many years to come if we'll just make the right choices, speak the right words, and obey God.

We can't have that kind of strength and longevity, however, if we choose to ignore God. We can't live half the time like the world lives and half the time like God says and enjoy God's best. We can't be wishy-washy about the Word of God, believing it one minute and doubting it the next. We must do what Psalm 92 says and make the Lord our Rock, building our lives on the bedrock of His Word. As Jesus said:

> So everyone who hears these words of Mine and acts upon them [obeying them] will be like a sensible (prudent, practical, wise) man who built his house upon the rock. And the rain fell and the floods came and the winds blew and beat against that house; yet it did not fall, because it had been founded on the rock. And everyone who hears these words of Mine and does not do them will be like a stupid (foolish) man who built his house upon the sand. And the rain fell and the floods came and the winds blew and beat against that house, and it fell—and great and complete was the fall of it (Matthew 7:24–27, AMP).

According to these verses, there are two keys to living long and strong. First, we must hear the Word. Second, we must act on the Word we hear. Hear and do. That's the one-two power punch of the Christian life.

We can live healthy and strong, free from sickness and disease, all the days of our lives by obeying God's instructions. We can follow in the footsteps of people like Abraham, Moses, Joshua, and Caleb, by applying our hearts to what the Word says about healing and health, and meditating on what God has to say about aging instead of what the world, or our physical symptoms, or the devil has to say about it.

Remember though, for optimum results, you must partake of God's medicine every day (Proverbs 4:20–26). That's the way you get well and stay well. It's the only way to keep your faith strong. Even if you have the best preacher in the world ministering to you every Sunday at church, you can't stay free of sickness if you try to live on just a couple of hours of church each week. Don't get me wrong. I appreciate good pastors. There's nothing like a good pastor to help stir you up, and keep you that way, but he just has a few hours a week with you. The devil is on duty twenty-four hours a day. Time in God's Word daily is the most important element in a believer's life.

As I write this book, I am sixty-five years old and Ken is seventy, and we both have this testimony. Over the years, every time some sickness or infirmity has attacked our bodies, the Lord has healed us. He has delivered us from things medical science said there was no remedy for. But that didn't happen while we were sitting around watching television all day. It happened because we spent time in the Word of God.

Here is some very potent medicine to take every day. Take it by eyes, ears, and mouth!

- "If you diligently heed the voice of the Lord your God and do what is right in His sight, give ear to His commandments and keep all His statutes, I will put none of the diseases on you which I have brought on the Egyptians. For I am the Lord who heals you" (Exodus 15:26).

- "So you shall serve the Lord your God, and He will bless your bread and your water. And I will take sickness away from the midst of you" (Exodus 23:25).

- "Bless the Lord, O my soul, and forget not all His benefits: Who forgives all your iniquities, Who heals all your diseases" (Psalm 103:2–3).

- "They cried out to the Lord in their trouble, and He saved them out of their distresses. He sent His word and healed them, and delivered them from their destructions" (Psalm 107:19–20).

- "Surely He has borne our griefs (sicknesses, weaknesses, and distresses) and carried our sorrows and pains [of punishment], yet we [ignorantly] considered Him stricken, smitten, and afflicted by God [as if with leprosy]. But He was wounded for our transgressions, He was bruised for our guilt and iniquities; the chastisement [needful to obtain] peace and well-being for us was upon Him, and with the stripes [that wounded] Him we are healed and made whole" (Isaiah 53:4–5, AMP).

- "When evening had come, they brought to Him [Jesus] many who were demon-possessed. And He cast out the spirits with a word, and healed all who were sick, that it might be fulfilled which was spoken by Isaiah the prophet, saying: 'He Himself took our infirmities and bore our sicknesses'" (Matthew 8:16–17).

When you're battling the devil in a specific area of life, focus on what God has to say about that particular area. That just makes sense! If you were to take natural medicine, you wouldn't just pick up any prescription bottle that was handy. You wouldn't take the medicine you used for cold symptoms to relieve a stomachache. You'd use medicine designed to treat the specific sickness you were dealing with at the time.

Although all of the Word brings healing and health as you obey it, when you are standing in faith for your healing, it's good to double up on God's Word about healing. Let the Word of God make you whole. Put these Scriptures in front of your eyes and let them go into your ears to get them in the midst of your heart. The Word of God in your heart will talk to you and manifest faith when you receive it (Proverbs 4:20–23).

LIVE UNTIL YOU'RE SATISFIED

Just hearing the Word will not drive sickness, lack, or disobedience out of your life. You have to obey it. You have to begin to talk and behave like you are what the Bible says you are and you have what the Bible says you have. And it says by Jesus' stripes you *were* [already] healed (Isaiah 53:4–5, 1 Peter 2:24).

If the Bible says you *were* healed, that means you *are* healed. Right now. Today. Regardless of any natural evidence to the contrary. That is the scriptural truth. So when sickness starts to come on your body, don't think of yourself as the sick trying to get healed. *You are the healed* and the devil is trying to steal your health.

For some time after Ken and I were saved, we didn't understand that. So when we started feeling bad, we'd just say, "Hey, I'm sick!" Then we'd put on our pajamas and go to bed. We didn't even put up a fight.

But once we realized Jesus had already borne our sicknesses and diseases, that He purchased our healing on the cross, we adopted an entirely different attitude. We started resisting sickness and disease. We'd say, "No you don't, sickness. You're not coming in to my house. You're not coming on my body. I resist you, in Jesus' Name."

Then we'd start acting like we were healed. We also learned not to whine to each other about how much our bodies hurt and how bad we felt. Instead, if I started feeling sick, I'd say, "Ken, symptoms are trying to come on my body. I want you to pray with me and let's get into agreement about my healing." Once we prayed, we continued to encourage ourselves with what God's Word says concerning our healing.

Usually, the symptoms went away fairly quickly once we began to resist them and declare the Word. On rare occasions, they lingered for a while. But in the end, we always got the victory.

Maybe you're not sure you can live in that kind of health for some reason. Maybe there's a history of heart disease or some other kind of illness in your family and your parents and grandparents died sick at an early age. When you go to the doctor and he asks for your family medical history, he might tell you that you're likely to follow the same pattern. Medically, that's an accurate report.

But remember, you have another report that's even more accurate. You have the report of the infallible Word of God. It says when you were born again, you became part of the family of God. One woman wrote me a letter and said it this way: "My family history is that Jesus bore my sicknesses and carried my diseases." (See Isaiah 53:4–5; 1 Peter 2:24.)

That lady had it right. She knew the truth!

Why worry about your natural family history? Your family members who got sick and died young probably didn't know what you know about the Word. They may not have realized that God's Master Plan for them was to live long and stay strong. They may not have chosen to hear and obey the Lord the way you do. So don't let their lives set the pattern for yours. Take your family history from the pages of the Bible. Remind yourself that you come from sturdy stock now. Your spiritual ancestry includes people who were still going strong at one hundred . . . and way beyond. You are born of *God!*

Keep that spiritual heritage in mind so when you're well advanced in age and the doctor treats you like you're too old to live much longer, his opinion won't influence you. We appreciate good doctors, but they don't have the last word. Go by the Word of God, instead. Go ahead and live until you've finished God's Master Plan for your life and you're satisfied.

Sometimes elderly people do face difficult situations. If you decide to live long and stay strong, you may well outlast some of your friends and family. You might be tempted to slip into self-pity and say, "I'm lonely. I don't have any friends or family left. I don't have much to live for anymore."

If you ever find yourself in that situation, go minister to other people. If you're alone, you may have a lot of free time. So go to the hospital or the nursing home and find people who need you. Then, be a blessing. Read the Scriptures to them. If you have a nice voice, sing for them. Pray for them. We can all do that.

This world is full of people who need help, people who need to hear about Jesus—people who need love. So don't check out early. Don't take an early spiritual retirement and put yourself out to pasture. There are people who need you to be the light of the world for them. There are folks who just need you to be cheerful and love them with the love of the Lord. Many are lonely. They need you to share yourself.

Every believer has the capacity to do these things. We can all offer our bodies as a living sacrifice to Jesus—no matter how old we are. We can all say, "Lord, I want to give myself to You and to others. Show me what to do."

It's never too late to pray that prayer. You can do it even if you're very near to your own homegoing.

Don't allow Satan to talk you into dying before you're through living. There's more you're called to do for the Lord. Don't go to heaven until you and the Lord are ready. If sickness tries to take you early, stand on the Word, release your faith, get well, and live out the full number of your days.

I know of one man who decided to do that when he was dying of a heart attack in his early fifties. He is the father of Keith Moore, who pastors Faith Life Church in Branson, Missouri. Mr. Moore knew the Lord. He also knew enough about the Word to realize he could resist death if he didn't believe it was time for him to go yet.

He waited until the very last minute to make up his mind about whether he would live or die. He was already seeing the light of God's heavenly glory when he said, "Lord, it's not time for me to go, is it?"

No, it's not, the Lord answered.

When he heard that, he began to resist death. He refused to yield to death. As a result, he ended up living in good health many more years. During that time, he had the joy of seeing his son pastor a wonderful church. One day, while sitting in that church looking at the beautiful auditorium and all the precious people gathered there, he said, "I'm so glad I didn't go before now. I'm so happy I lived to see this!"

That story should be a lesson to all of us. It should teach us not to check out on life just because death tries to take us. If we're not ready to go, we should say, "Spirit of death, I resist you in Jesus' Name. I'm staying right here until Jesus and I are satisfied."

DELIVERED FROM DESTRUCTION

Especially in this time, if we want to live out the full number of our days, there's one more thing we must know: Jesus has not only redeemed us from sickness and disease, He has also promised us protection from calamity and disaster. All we have to do is watch the evening news to see how important that is.

We're clearly living in what the Bible calls "the last days." (See 2 Peter 3:3, 1 John 2:18, and Jude 1:18.) We're living in times when wicked people are becoming worse and worse (2 Timothy 3:13). These are times of terrorism and high crime, when danger and destruction are on the increase. Even the forces of nature are becoming more violent and natural disasters more frequent.

Jesus warned us such times would come. He described the last days, just before His return to the earth:

> As Jesus was leaving the Temple grounds, his disciples pointed out to him the various Temple buildings. But he told them, "Do you see all these buildings? I assure you, they will be so completely demolished that not one stone will be left on top of another!" Later, Jesus sat on slopes of the Mount of Olives. His disciples came to him privately and asked, "When will this take place? And will there be any sign ahead of time to signal your return and the end of the world?" Jesus told them, "Don't let anyone mislead you. For many will come in my name, saying, 'I am the Messiah.' They will lead many astray. And wars will break out near and far, but don't panic. Yes, these things must come, but the end won't follow immediately. The nations

and kingdoms will proclaim war against one another, and there will be famines and earthquakes in many parts of the world. But all this will be the beginning of the horrors to come. Then you will be arrested, persecuted, and killed. You will be hated all over the world because of your allegiance to me. And many will turn away from me and betray and hate each other. And many false prophets will appear and will lead many people astray. Sin will be rampant everywhere, and the love of many will grow cold. But those who endure to the end will be saved. And the Good News about the Kingdom will be preached throughout the whole world, so that all nations will hear it; and then, finally, the end will come" (Matthew 24:1–14, NLT-96).

And when you hear of wars and insurrections (disturbances, disorder, and confusion), do not become alarmed and panic-stricken and terrified; for all this must take place first, but the end will not [come] immediately. Then He told them, Nation will rise against nation, and kingdom against kingdom [2 Chronicles 15:6; Isaiah 19:2]. There will be mighty and violent earthquakes, and in various places famines and pestilences (plagues: malignant and contagious or infectious epidemic diseases which are deadly and devastating); and there will be sights of terror and great signs from heaven . . . and there will be signs in the sun and moon and stars; and upon the earth [there will be] distress (trouble and anguish) of nations in bewilderment and perplexity [without resources, left wanting, embarrassed, in doubt, not knowing which way to turn] at

the roaring (the echo) of the tossing of the sea, men
swooning away or expiring with fear and dread and
apprehension and expectation of the things that are
coming on the world; for the [very] powers of the
heavens will be shaken and caused to totter (Luke
21:9–11, 25–26, AMP).

We see many things happening already, even as we await the
catching away of the Church to meet Jesus in the air before the Great
Tribulation. The Apostle Paul wrote in his letter to the church at
Thessalonica:

And now, brothers and sisters, I want you to know
what will happen to the Christians who have died so
you will not be full of sorrow like people who have no
hope. For since we believe that Jesus died and was
raised to life again, we also believe that when Jesus
comes, God will bring back with Jesus all the Christians who have died. I can tell you this directly from
the Lord: We who are still living when the Lord re-
turns will not rise to meet him ahead of those who are
in their graves. For the Lord himself will come down
from heaven with a commanding shout, with the call
of the archangel, and with the trumpet call of God.
First, all the Christians who have died will rise from
their graves. Then, together with them, we who are
still alive and remain on the earth will be caught up in
the clouds to meet the Lord in the air and remain with
him forever. So comfort and encourage each other
with these words (1 Thessalonians 4:13–18, NLT).

What a way to go!

How can we live long lives filled with peace and tranquillity in the midst of such times? By standing in faith on God's promises of protection. We can do it by reminding ourselves that our heavenly Father has pledged to deliver us from destruction if we'll just trust and abide in Him. Many scriptures confirm God's commitment to protect us from danger, but none settles the issue more completely than Psalm 91. It assures us we don't have to be afraid of destruction, and declares:

> A thousand may fall at your side, and ten thousand at your right hand; but it shall not come near you. Only with your eyes shall you look, and see the reward of the wicked. Because you have made the Lord, who is my refuge, even the Most High, your dwelling place, no evil shall befall you, nor shall any plague come near your dwelling; for He shall give His angels charge over you, to keep you in all your ways. In their hands they shall bear you up, lest you dash your foot against a stone (Psalm 91:7–12).

People send us reports frequently about how God has fulfilled these promises in their lives and miraculously delivered them from destruction. I could tell you many such testimonies.

One amazing example of divine protection came out of the tsunami disaster of December 2004.

We received a letter from the pastor of a church in Sri Lanka, one of the countries where more than twenty thousand were killed. He told us that when the waves began to come into their church building, located close to the ocean, they acted by faith in God's Word and commanded the water to stop rising, shouting, "Peace, be still!" It did. The waters receded immediately from their property, but engulfed the neighbors' houses. Those around them lost everything, but the water never got any higher than the floor in the church and pastor's home, which were still standing when the water receded. They were able to provide shelter for many in the surrounding area.

Another amazing example of divine protection came from the September 11, 2001, terrorist attack on the World Trade Center in New York City. Dan and Ann Stratton, pastors of Faith Exchange Fellowship, a church located in an office building across the street from the World Trade Center, had for seventeen years confessed Psalm 91 daily and taught their congregation about the power of confessing this psalm. The congregation knew the power of God's Name and how to believe in and dwell in the secret place of the Most High.

On the morning of the attack, from the church office, a Faith Exchange Fellowship member could see and hear the second plane hit and feel the concussion of the impact as the Towers exploded into flames. People on fire were falling or jumping from the building. As he left the church office and went out into the street, the building which housed the church was being hit with debris and large building parts from the Twin Towers. Its whole front was torn off by the explosion. The air was so hot, he felt as if he would burn up. People were screaming.

When he realized he was walking on body parts in the street, the man was tempted to panic, but the Lord told him not to look to the right or to the left, but straight ahead to Him. When he did what the Lord told him, he said God lifted him up above the street. He felt like he was in a bubble. Though debris was flying through the air, and choking clouds of dust, ash, and smoke swirled around him, he was totally protected. Somehow, the next thing he knew, he was across the river and in New Jersey, unharmed. When he got home, his wife said his shirt was cleaner and whiter than when he had left for work that morning. Not even the smell of smoke was on him.

Psalm 27:5–6 (AMP) says: "For in the day of trouble He will hide me in His shelter; in the secret place of His tent [His presence or His covering] will He hide me; He will set me high upon a rock. And now shall my head be lifted up above my enemies round about me; in His tent I will offer sacrifices and shouting of joy; I will sing, yes, I will sing praises to the Lord."

Another member of Faith Exchange Fellowship, despite seeing both planes crash into the Twin Towers, told God he had to get to work because he was never late. He heard the Lord tell him three times to turn around and not to cross the street toward the burning buildings or go in. But he wanted to go in and help people.

Then the Lord told him to turn and run into the entrance of the subway tunnel. He did not want to be a coward and tried to reason with the Lord. Suddenly, he realized the Lord knew better than he did. He obeyed, turned, and ran into the subway entrance. As he did, one of the towers exploded and fell. The fire went down the elevator shaft and blasted out the front door in a ball of flame that incinerated all the people standing on the street where he had been just moments before. Others tried to run into the subway entrance but were burned up or on fire.

It became so hot inside the subway tunnel he could hardly breathe. It felt as if the fire were burning there, though it was forty to fifty feet below ground level. According to heat maps made later, Port Authority Police estimated the temperature in the tunnels to have reached between 1,600 to 1,800 degrees Fahrenheit! But he was protected, sheltered in the secret place of the Most High, and escaped without harm.

These believers were hidden. If you're hidden, what does that mean? It means you can't be seen. You're surrounded. You're in His tent, in that secret place—the place of the Most High God—worshiping the Lord and giving Him praise. Hallelujah! We've got awesome protection.

No matter where you live, if you dwell in the secret place of the Most High, the same promises that protected these believers from destruction apply to you. So stand on these promises. Believe them!

Live long, stay strong, and live in supernatural safety all the days of your life. Keep your feet firmly planted on the earth until you've successfully completed God's Master Plan for your life. Then, when you and the Lord decide it's time for your departure, you will be able to confidently stand before the Master and hear those glorious words, *Well done, good and faithful servant . . . well done!*

Appendix

PRAYER FOR SALVATION AND

BAPTISM IN THE HOLY SPIRIT

———⟋⟍———

Heavenly Father, I come to You in the Name of Jesus. Your Word says, "Whosoever shall call on the name of the Lord shall be saved" (Acts 2:21). I am calling on You. I pray and ask Jesus to come into my heart and be Lord over my life according to Romans 10:9–10: "If thou shalt confess with thy mouth the Lord Jesus, and shalt believe in thine heart that God hath raised him from the dead, thou shalt be saved. For with the heart man believeth unto righteousness; and with the mouth confession is made unto salvation." I do that now. I confess that Jesus is Lord, and I believe in my heart that God raised Him from the dead.

I am now reborn! I am a Christian—a child of Almighty God! I am saved! You also said in Your Word, "If ye then, being evil, know how to give good gifts unto your children: HOW MUCH MORE shall your heavenly Father give the Holy Spirit to them that ask him?" (Luke 11:13). I'm also asking You to fill me with the Holy Spirit. Holy Spirit, rise up within me as I praise God. I fully expect to speak with other tongues as You give me the utterance (Acts 2:4). In Jesus' Name. Amen!

Begin to praise God for filling you with the Holy Spirit. Speak those words and syllables you receive—not in your own language, but the language given to you by the Holy Spirit. You have to use your own voice. God will not force you to speak. Don't be concerned with how it sounds. It is a heavenly language!

Continue with the blessing God has given you and pray in the spirit every day.

You are a born-again, Spirit-filled believer. You'll never be the same!

Find a good church that boldly preaches God's Word and obeys it. Become part of a church family who will love and care for you as you love and care for them.

We need to be connected to each other. It increases our strength in God. It's God's plan for us.

Make it a habit to watch the *Believer's Voice of Victory* television broadcast and become a doer of the Word, who is blessed in his doing (James 1:22–25).

Gloria Copeland is an author, teacher, and ordained minister. She and her husband, Kenneth (founder of Kenneth Copeland Ministries headquartered in Fort Worth), minister daily through television, the Internet, the printed page, teaching audio and video, meetings, and conventions worldwide.

Gloria presents her messages on victorious Christian living in an honest, straightforward style that is both enjoyable and easy to understand. She is perhaps best known for her "Healing Schools," where she adds practical application to scriptural instruction by personally praying for the sick.

Gloria's love of people has stirred her to share with thousands, both lost and saved, how the Word of God, as revealed in Jesus Christ, has taken her from a life of failure and defeat to a life of thrilling victory. She is eager to share the truth and freedom she has found in Him with all who are in need of help.